THE SELF IN TRANSFORMATION

THE SELF

Psychoanalysis, Philosophy,

IN TRANSFORMATION

& the Life of the Spirit

by **HERBERT FINGARETTE**

Basic Books, INC., PUBLISHERS

NEW YORK

LONDON

© 1963 BY BASIC BOOKS, INC., PUBLISHERS

LIBRARY OF CONGRESS CATALOG CARD NUMBER: 63–12846

PRINTED IN THE UNITED STATES OF AMERICA

Designed by Guy Fleming

This book is dedicated to

LESLIE

Preface

BRIEF AND ENIGMATIC THOUGH IT BE TO ALL BUT THOSE CON-
cerned, a prefatory acknowledgment is an earned and special
pleasure for an author.

My wife, Leslie, has devoted many long and weary hours
to typing all the many versions of each of these chapters in
every stage of their development. Her complete secretarial
efficiency—and stern editorial eye—has been invaluable. In
an important sense, however, the substance of the book also
is hers as much as it is mine. This book is the intellectual
manifestation of a series of spiritual quests and ordeals
which we have thought through and lived through together.
If this book *says* anything, then she, too, speaks; though I
fear her own clear voice is muffled by the scholarly apparatus and the specific formulations, for all of which I bear full
responsibility.

Over many years, I have been deeply influenced by the
persistent and penetrating questions and probings of Professor Paul Wienpahl, my friend and colleague. He has
brought me to wrestle, in the *right* way, with points of view
I either had dismissed as plainly wrong or else had too

quickly taken for granted with only a surface appreciation. He has forced me to see freshly.

Professor Donald A. Piatt showed me years ago how and why philosophy is a human enterprise as well as a demanding professional task. Later, I went through a period of intellectual shadowboxing. When, at last, I was girding myself to break free of this, the philosophical perspective he had provided me came to my rescue, and the specific philosophical views he had taught me turned out to be genuinely liberating.

And I must surely mention that, although they did not participate directly in my "professional" philosophising, the long-time informal discussion group, The Little Men, provided an atmosphere and a world within which my work was uniquely nourished and protected.

It was owing to the enthusiasm and encouragement of Professor Benjamin Nelson that I finally took courage to bring these ideas into book form. He has given his time and energies in support of the project out of a disinterested commitment to the problems and the task. He has my deepest thanks.

I would like to express my thanks to Professor Chung-Hwan Chen for the calligraphic rendering of the quotation from Book XI of Chuang-tse which appears on page xi.

I am grateful to the editor of *Philosophy and Phenomenological Research,* who has given permission to publish here Chapter 4, a slightly modified version of a paper which first appeared in that journal. Many thanks are due to the editors of *Psychoanalysis and the Psychoanalytic Review* for their kind permission to publish here Chapters 3 and 7, slightly modified versions of papers which appeared first in their journal.

HERBERT FINGARETTE

Contents

無為而
物自化
陳康書

CEASE STRIVING;

Then there will be self-transformation.

CHUANG-TSE, BOOK XI

Introduction

*In practicing and cherishing the old,
he attains the new;
Attaining the new, he reanimates
the old;
He is indeed a teacher.*

THIS BOOK ARISES OUT OF A JOURNEY OF SELF-EXPLORATION
and self-teaching. Has this journey been a professional one
or a personal one? Indeed, the distinction between the two
seems to dissolve.

In making the journey, I have had no aims. These
studies are outcomes rather than realized objectives. They
are intellectual footprints, not blueprints. The reader will
eventually identify their shape and dimensions to his own
satisfaction; he will find their place on the intellectual map
and the existential direction in which they point. Still, each
study has the form of an autonomous essay, and the reader
is therefore entitled to some general and preliminary orientation. Such informal orientation, perhaps slightly polemical, can be further justified (or excused) in view of the fact

1

that the studies themselves systematically avoid program-
matic flourishes and polemics. (I spent much of my early
philosophic training in reading and writing fundamental
"programs" and prolegomena. One day, in a way which
counted, I saw that the job was not to write the program
but to execute it. This book, with its almost totally unpredicted content, presents the intellectual aspect of the results
of the years which followed.)

The present volume is not a "collection" of papers which
I happen to have written over a period of some years. The
chapters, in spite of their internally self-sufficient structure,
have serial continuity and close, over-all unity. The unity
lies in their being intensive studies in critical phases of self-
transformation. They are studies *in* transformation and not
about transformation. That is, they were part of the process;
they were not written afterward, beforehand, or "about" it.
Nevertheless, they are not "personal" or autobiographical.
In spite of our modern romantic tendency to think otherwise, there is an objective and intellectually cogent aspect
to the life of the spirit.

Let us look at the book, then, as an objective document
rather than at the special circumstances of its writing. What
does it present to the reader? I see it as embodying three
major interests, and I shall comment on each briefly.

These studies are characterized by extensive discussion
and theoretical analysis of various problems in the area of
contemporary psychoanalysis. Specialists and others interested in these problems will find them, I hope, of substantial
and intrinsic interest independent of their context and application. For example, there are systematic analyses of
such major psychoanalytic concepts as anxiety, the ego,
identification, regression, and sublimation.

The psychoanalytic material is developed, however, in
order to be "applied." That is, it is introduced systematically
in the context of studies of the spiritual life and of classical

2

spiritual texts. I use the term "spiritual" broadly, and I mean thereby only to distinguish ethics, esthetics, religion, intuitive wisdom, and systematic philosophy on one side from psychology and science on the other.

We face a paradox. On the one hand, we note the rapid growth of psychoanalytic institutes, the substantial and still-expanding role of psychoanalysts in medical faculties, the ever-increasing demand by psychiatrists for psychoanalytic training, a demand which is so great that the institutes cannot satisfy it. All of this testifies to the great and still-growing influence on medical psychology and psychiatry of professionally organized psychoanalysis, not to speak of the ubiquitous informal influence of psychoanalytic ideas. Yet, on the other hand, as we read the literature written by humanists and other scholars outside the area of psychology, we often gain quite a different impression. In this humanistic literature, psychoanalysis appears merely as a dying, turn-of-the-century intellectual influence. At most it is something to be toyed with in a speculative, intuitive way, a kind of "philosophical" outlook.

The resolution of the paradox is not too difficult to find. Humanists have absorbed mainly the early ideas of psychoanalysis, and to read them is almost always to return to the atmosphere of those first decades. The early "classics" of Freud have been handled in the manner in which one studies the completed body of imaginative literature produced by an author now dead. Even where there is use of the concepts which properly belong with the fundamentally new developments in psychoanalysis, these concepts are usually used by humanists as if they were part and parcel of the early theoretical and therapeutic outlook. For example, important new works by contemporary humanists build elaborate "psychoanalytic" arguments on the assumption that repression and defense are inherently evil and anti-human. This is a generalization which was easily suggested, though never actually implied, by early psychoanalytic formulations. Later developments have shown clearly how antipathetic to the whole psychoanalytic conception of man this perspective is, how it fails to take into account the complexity and the creativity inherent in human development. It is an irony: a fixed core of early psychoanalytic ideas has frequently been used by humanists as a point of departure for ideology and for armchair speculation—and then this same static and ideological conception of psychoanalysis has in turn been a favorite target of humanistic criticism. Meanwhile, psychoanalysis itself has long been moving toward more amplified and sensitive conceptions of the human being.

Matters have been further complicated. Many attempts to use psychoanalytic insights in connection with matters of the spirit have run into trouble because the conceptions which were appropriate existed only in embryonic form. Freud's early discoveries and theories were clearly relevant, and compelled one to make the effort to analyze the life of the spirit; but those conceptions were also, as it turned out, clearly inadequate. The usual response—or at any rate the one best known to the lay public and to the humanistic world—was not to try to build upon these embryonic conceptions but simply to omit major segments of psychoanalytic theory and to propose quite different sorts of theories.

Jung, Fromm, Horney, and their disciples and colleagues have written much that is new and illuminating about the problems of the spirit. They do not need defense on that score. Nor is this the place to argue the merits of their variations on psychoanalysis. What is to the point is the fact that only a small proportion of psychiatrists rely principally upon the theories of these writers. Where, then, can one discover the direction and perspective which the mainstreams of contemporary psychoanalysis offer regarding the problems and the literature of the spirit?

Articles and books about religion, ethics, art, or philosophy often introduce sound psychoanalytic ideas in an occasional way. And there are individual articles on quite special topics by psychoanalysts of varying degrees of humanistic and philosophic sophistication. There are a number of biographical studies done from a psychoanalytic standpoint, but these inevitably focus on the details of the individual's special history. There are, it is true, a number of psychoanalytic works directly relevant to the main psychoanalytic or spiritual orientations of this book. One thinks of Anna Freud, Hartmann, Kris, Erikson, and some others in addition to the writings of Sigmund Freud himself. But these are either handled almost entirely within the strictly psychoanalytic language or, in the case of Erikson and Kris, are elaborated with little reference to the great variety of spiritual and philosophical languages and issues which are relevant. The present work, I believe, helps to fill the gap described. The book was not written *in order* to do this; but this is its outcome in fact. The outcome is no accident: I happen to be a philosopher, and also, in carrying out my exploration, I already had the conviction that modern psychoanalysis is viable, sensitive, and profound. My faith in it was not that it contained the revealed Truth, but simply that it was a responsible tool of inquiry, a method responsive to the integrity of humanistic values and human experience. This book is a result of my confident reliance on this conviction, and, at least in my own personal history, the writing of the book has been an important confirmation of that conviction.

There is a second major interest embodied in these studies, an interest already suggested. I have tried to clarify a cluster of notions centering around the process of spiritual self-transformation. I found myself deeply involved with these notions—often much to my surprise—in the movement of my own journey inward.

I have not been alone, of course, in sensing the force of psychoanalytic studies bearing upon the life of the spirit. But, as has many a philosophically minded person, I have also been struck by the awkwardness and philosophical naïveté which so often seem to lead such psychoanalytic studies down the road to ruin. I have in mind here two special evils. One consists in psychologizing the spiritual life ("reducing" it to psychology with nothing left over). The other evil consists in mistaking widespread, popular perversions of the spiritual life for the real thing, thus often providing incisive analyses of something which is familiar though incorrectly labeled. This mistake has lent support to the reductionist error, for the mislabeled phenomena thus studied are indeed adequately accounted for in psychological or in psychosocial terms.

The paradigms of the latter evil are Freud's incisive analyses of what he calls religion. In truth, as he himself shows, what he is analyzing is the popular sentiment and illusion which goes under the name of religion. It is as if a psychologist were to study the layman's notions and attitudes in relation to science. These are statistically the most common attitudes and beliefs, and our quite hypothetical psychologist might well argue that therefore they are *the* characteristic scientific attitudes and beliefs. In this hypothetical case, we see the error clearly. Though we might get a penetrating and valuable study of the popular attitudes and beliefs, we would not expect from our psychologist a correct perspective on the psychology of genuine scientific inquiry and creativity. Yet, if he were to study the tiny minority of men who (as we know) are the creative scientists, might not those who are naïve about science charge him with overemphasizing esoteric groups and doctrines and introducing unrepresentative population samples?

I have made similar distinctions in the present studies: I have used as a touchstone for collecting and identifying my data the very acts of the spirit rather than the majority's opinions and interpretations of those acts.

There is a set of evils complementary to those I have been discussing. The strictures I have presented against psychologizing or misidentifying the spiritual life are easily put to self-serving uses. We teeter here on the brink of mere antiscientific rhetoric, mystification, and politically expedient "dividing up of the pie" of knowledge. The recognition that there are different dimensions of life is often the occasion for shutting off inquiry into the interrelations of those dimensions. The strenuous and reactionary attempts to keep physics out of biology, biology out of psychology, and psychology out of the realm of the spirit are all too familiar in the intellectual history of the West. In truth it is just the discovery of such different dimensions of life that obligates us to study their interrelationships and the import thereof.

The problems connected with the autonomy and interdependence of the many dimensions of experience are central in this book. This concern emerges out of logical and philosophical analysis, not institutional sentiment. It is nourished by a concern with *accounting* for our experience rather than "explaining it away" by reducing it all to one "level" or by fragmenting it into absolutely independent realms of being. I have ranged through the literatures of both East and West, freely using both ancient and modern philosophy and religion. Does this suggest an intellectual *smörgåsbord*? As Lao-tse said, "My words have an ancestry, my deeds have a lord." The variety of languages and of orders of experience introduced does not arise out of my ambitions to show myself a scholar in all these areas, for of course I am not. What appears here was not sought in order to tickle the cultured palate but forced itself into the arena. The work was like a hidden magnet, attracting to itself the specific ideas and techniques which would then take on shape and reveal an underlying pattern.

So I come to the third major dimension of this book, the circumstances of its writing. And yet, even here it is important to see that there is no necessity to become "personal." Nothing need be added to what I have already said to indicate that the topics, problems, and approach grew out of what was happening in me and not what was happening in professional controversies. Nevertheless, one does not live a life independent of the forces of one's time and, more particularly, of one's professional training and interests. The reader will have noticed that, although he is being addressed by a professional philosopher, there has been as yet no mention of standard names and slogans endemic in the philosophical regions of American academia. Nor will the reader find more than an occasional explicit reference of this kind. This is not due to scorn or to lack of interest.

As a philosopher, I have seen my role as analogous to that of the artist who interprets a musical work. I have purposefully thrust the professional paraphernalia into the background. Instead of forcing the material which is to be interpreted into a pre-existent technical framework or methodology, I have tried to let the material speak for itself and make its own demands. My aim has been to use whatever seemed necessary to illuminate the subject and to modify techniques or invent new ones where needed. To submit to the music rather than to dominate it, to let its special character and unity be expressed through the medium of one's skills rather than to use it as a forum for illustrating and confirming those skills, to provide those nuances which the material calls for and not those which happen to be the glories of a particular technique—these have been guiding principles throughout.

The reader may or may not notice hovering in the background from time to time such figures as Dewey, Russell, the later Wittgenstein, or G. E. Moore. Sometimes the specific views or techniques of these men emerge, sometimes only the spirit of their philosophical work. When these do emerge, it will often enough be in unusual contexts and leading toward untypical results. Those who are most struck by the general subject matter and outcomes of this book may be surprised to discover its philosophical roots, and this brief word is intended as fair warning.

Those who have some familiarity with the works of these men and their many disciples may be taken aback at the company they keep in this book. The matter is not as strange as it seems. Much has happened in the last decade or two, and I offer this book as an example, not unique, of the unsuspected turnings into which the work of these men has led us in recent years.

The crust which was forming in the dogmatic 1930's and '40's has begun to break up. The old battle lines and war cries are history. The formulations of empirical philosophy in the first half of the century were penetrating and fertile, and they were as understandably and enthusiastically one-sided as the early formulations of Freud. In each case, it has been necessary to amplify and refine, yet without denying the substance or the spirit of the original insights.

If Master K'ung was right, we must indeed all be teachers; we must practice and cherish the old in order to discover the new; and in attaining the new, we indeed reanimate the old.

Such was the American intellectual background and atmosphere in which this work set out, and such, I hope, is its Confucian outcome. But neither the motive nor the purpose of writing is to be found here. The studies have their origin and their unity in the process of self-knowledge and self-transformation, not in the tools which happened to be available for the job. The studies were, for me, elements in an existential gesture. And, in a somewhat different way, these studies are primarily offered as such to the reader, not as a scholarly treatise. But a gesture must have a form, and this is the intellectual dimension of the form which emerged.

Part I, which immediately follows this introduction, consists of two chapters that deal, respectively, with two central notions in psychoanalysis: dynamic insight and anxiety. In these chapters, the aim is to present, by means of rigorous conceptual analysis, certain contributions to psychoanalytic "metapsychology." But Part I does not do only this. The theses presented provide suggestions and insights which link up psychoanalysis with recent thought in the biological and psychological sciences, in religion, and in philosophy. The whole, in addition to throwing light on certain specific problems of current interest, places psychoanalysis in what I believe to be a fresh and promising perspective. For the primary need is not for abandoning the mainstream of Freudian thought but for seeing fully where it really takes us.

If Part I is viewed as an attempt to place psychoanalysis within a freshly revealing perspective, then Part II may be viewed as an extended essay in the application of modern psychoanalysis. Here, instead of talking *about* what psychoanalysis *can* do, I *use* psychoanalysis and show what it in fact *does* do. It is used in connection with a central psychospiritual task: self-transformation. Whether we think of the latter as the movement from immaturity to maturity, from ignorance to insight, from bondage to liberation, from sin to salvation, or in any of a number of other ways, the challenge presented is clearly a fair one for the psychoanalytic perspective and one which is in any case profoundly important in its own right.

Although there are a number of further contributions to psychoanalytic theory in Part II, my central aim is not to add to psychoanalytic theory. It is, rather, to use contemporary psychoanalytic theory and data as a major organizing framework. Within that framework, we shall explore the self in transformation in its many dimensions. Here I hope to show, in depth, that psychoanalysis can be sensitive, catholic, and illuminating. That is, I hope to show that it positively invites us to notice the subtler features of our world rather than requiring that we lump everything into a few formula-istic categories. It brings us to welcome and to use the variety of spiritual languages, to acknowledge the various dimensions of experience without "reducing" them all or "translating" them into psychological terms. Finally, this examination of self-transformation should illuminate not only self-transformation but also the interrelations of the languages used in the course of inquiry. And it should clarify a number of important specific problems in psychology, ethics, metaphysics, art, religion, and the philosophy of science.

Part II, the study of self-transformation, can stand on its own—and may have to do so for those who can abide nothing unless its very look is psychoanalytically "orthodox." But it may appear to others, as it has to me, that the theoretical discussions in Part I locate psychoanalysis within a broader framework, one which allows lights and depths to emerge, one which is neither patronizing nor rejecting but hospitable, revealing freshly the sources of the seminal character of Freud's discoveries.

Part I

THE SEMINAL AMBIGUITY

OF PSYCHOANALYSIS

CHAPTER 1

INSIGHT AND INTEGRATION:

Meaning and Being

I

IN THIS CHAPTER IT IS MY AIM TO PROVIDE A FRESH PERSPEC-
tive on psychoanalysis and thereby to reveal a fundamental
reason for the explosive and creative impact of psychoanalysis on twentieth-century civilization. Attention will center
upon the concept of insight.

A simple but basic distinction governs the following
analysis of Freud's language. It is the distinction between
analyzing what a theory means and arguing about its truth.
This distinction needs mentioning and brief comment just
because it is so often lost from view in the polemics engendered by attempts to view Freud's theories critically or to
attain fresh perspectives on those theories.

A trivial illustration will help recall the distinction in
question. A reporter writes: "The Government rejected the
proposal out of hand." His idiomatic statement may be true,
and we who know English understand it. But the sentence
does not itself carry the instructions for correct and precise
interpretation. We have learned that, in certain contexts,
"out of hand" is not a reference to an object which is not in
someone's hand. "The Government rejects," an idiom which

is grammatically parallel to "he rejects," is nevertheless semantically more complex than the latter. The fact that the grammatical subject, "the government," is grammatically singular does not normally lead us to expect that the sentence refers to the act of a single person. Yet it should be clear that in pointing out that "the government rejects" refers to a plurality of persons rather than one, and that "out of hand" does not refer to something out of a hand, we are in no way challenging the truth of the original statement. Nor do we challenge its appropriateness; indeed the awkwardness and length of any careful analysis will confirm our sense of the economy, appropriateness, and force of the original form of the statement for use in its usual context. And, what is more, though we may have difficulties *stating how* we use such phrases, we ordinarily have no difficulty *using* the phrase correctly. (We have no difficulty walking but find it very difficult to *state* how we walk.)

The problems of analyzing the meaning of words like "know," "reasonable," "exist," "past," "cause," and a host of others have occupied philosophers through the ages. But the many problems of analysis that yet remain do not prevent us, in the meantime, from knowing things, being reasonable, existing, remembering the past, discovering genuine causes—and, what is more, *saying* so and being understood by others. Nevertheless, the puzzles over stating the analysis have led some persons to question whether it is true that we do really know anything; skeptics have questioned whether there really are causes, whether anything "really" exists. It is this mistaken skeptical cul-de-sac that I am concerned to avoid here. Specifically: there are difficulties in stating precisely and explicitly how to interpret statements about the unconscious, but this should hardly lead us to the *non sequitur* of denying that such statements can be meaningful, true, or important—and known to be so.

Since disagreements about interpretation so often slide illegitimately into denials of the truth or importance of what is to be interpreted, it may be well to restate here the moving force behind this entire book. I assume the general soundness and vital importance of psychoanalysis as a growing body of knowledge and practice; I am concerned, therefore, to see what follows from this body of knowledge and practice; I systematically use psychoanalytic ideas as a source and touchstone for evaluating consequences drawn, insights achieved; I do not reformulate psychoanalytic ideas in order to make them conform to criteria derived from extrapsychoanalytic sources. It should not be necessary to add the qualification that I do not hold psychoanalysis to be God-given gospel. It is just that it is valid enough and important enough to move me to want to see where it leads, not to try here to lead it.

With this preliminary, we can begin the present inquiry by presenting some of Freud's typical language about the key concepts of insight, repression, and the unconscious. I shall be selective in this presentation to the extent of choosing language which, by virtue of idiom and metaphors, *suggests* (but does not require) a particular ontological interpretation. My object in the first major phase of the inquiry is to show how a specific ontological interpretation of the psychoanalytic language is suggested by the psychoanalytic idiom used to *report* the facts. This interpretation suggested by the psychoanalytic metaphors is usually accepted as the correct ontological interpretation; I suggest, indeed, that this ontological interpretation is hardly ever effectively distinguished as being an *interpretation,* i.e., as being something which can be discussed critically without ever raising a question as to the truth of the original formulations.

An alternative ontological interpretation of psychoanalytic language will subsequently be presented. Furthermore, by presenting other formulations of Freud's, I hope to make clear that Freud already saw the problems which I raise and that he, too, challenged the usual ontological interpretation of his concepts without thereby questioning the truth of his formulations. Indeed I shall show that Freud adumbrated the specific alternative interpretation to be offered here. Later in the chapter we shall turn to exploring the broader implications of this alternative interpretation.

Thus, in general, this chapter deals with different ontological interpretations of psychoanalysis and their implications, not with the question as to whether psychoanalysis is valid—a point which is here assumed.

II

FREUD SAID, TYPICALLY, THAT *"the essence of repression lies simply in the function of rejecting and keeping something out of consciousness."* [1] Freud later compares the repressed mental wish to a guest who is either allowed into the drawing room, or is forced out once he is in, or is never allowed in at all. At the door is the ever-present guardian censor, for the guest is impetuous and might force his way in if the door is unguarded. [2]

Closely related to this spatial way of putting the matter is the terminology of "mental qualities" used by Freud. According to him, an idea has or has not the "quality" of consciousness. [3] There is here a suppressed analogy with vision. An object which was visible may now be hidden. This may be due to changes in the conditions of observation, and it may lead to a change in our response; but the *object* has remained essentially unchanged. The "quality" of consciousness is taken as analogous to the "quality" of visibility. The language of spatial location (the "guest in the drawing room") easily meshes with that of visibility, since visibility is ordinarily closely related to spatial location.

What does the therapist do, then, when he communicates with the patient? The answer from this standpoint is simple: the therapist uncovers for the patient what had been present but invisible; he does this in such a way and at such a time as will facilitate the patient's seeing it at last for himself. The door hiding the hidden past is opened; or the veil is ripped from the disguised present. What was in the shadow is now itself unchanged in essence, but it is illuminated. This way of thinking about the processes in question I shall call the "hidden reality" view. Put in onto-logical terms, the repressed is a continuously existent, po-tent, but hidden reality.

Now the previous discussion has purposely emphasized a blatantly metaphorical way of talking about certain kinds of events which are quite familiar to every psychoanalyst. Having used this language, one naturally wants to say—as Freud and many a psychoanalyst since have said—that we must distinguish metaphor from "literal" or "strict" mean-ing. This is easier to say than to do. Nevertheless, it is some-thing of this sort which I aim to do in the course of this discussion. I think it can be shown that the necessity not to take metaphor "literally," although often acknowledged in words, is not always clearly noted in the theoretical work of many a psychoanalyst and psychologist. Let us make a test.

Consider the statements I shall shortly present in quota-tion marks; they are about unconscious ideas, repression, and insight. They are made in language which is about as metaphorical in degree as is Freud's, but the metaphors are quite different in nature. Indeed they seem to "contradict" Freud's metaphors. Nevertheless, I suggest that they are entirely consistent with the essential content of psychoana-lytic psychology. If the reader feels a sense of dramatic op-position between the following statements and his own con-ception of psychoanalysis, then, I suggest, he has been more a victim of metaphor than he has been willing to admit even to himself. I am not proposing that the kind of language which follows be used generally in place of Freud's, though there are uses for it. I specifically use it here in order to raise the issue of ontological interpretation, or, very loosely, of "literal" interpretation.

Consider these formulations then: "The therapeutic insight does not show the patient what he is or was; it *changes* him into someone *new*." "The therapist does not present information; he presents options." "Insight in its main function does not reveal unknown events of the past but helps us to see known past events in a new way." "The phrase 'unconscious process' does not refer directly to a spatio-temporal process." "Insight into an unconscious wish is like noticing suddenly a well-formed 'ship' in the cloud instead of a poorly formed 'rabbit.' On the other hand, insight is not like discovering an animal which has been hiding in the bushes." "Insight does not reveal a hidden, past reality; it is a reorganization of the meaning of present experience, a present reorientation toward both future *and* past." Let us, for the sake of convenient tags, refer to the ontology suggested by the previous as the "meaning-reorganization" view in contrast to the "hidden reality" view.

It is appropriate now to spell out in some detail the viewpoint suggested by the metaphors I have used as alternatives to Freud's. When this has been done, we shall turn to Freud's own struggles with his own metaphors and see how he moved in the same direction as we do.

Let us think first in terms of a crude analogy to an insightful interpretation, an analogy already suggested in the previous discussion. A person sees a rabbit in a cloud. But it is not a very good "fit." Some of the visible shapes don't "belong." A friend remarks: "Why, it's really a ship!" *This* way of looking at it does fit; there are no significant shapes unaccounted for.

Let us move, without comment, to a more complex analogy. A man reads a poem. He reads the poem through, every word of it, and memorizes it. Although the words and phrases are familiar to him and understood in ordinary contexts, he feels his "understanding" of the poem, as a poem, is inadequate; his enjoyment of it is meager. He fails in his attempts at a conception of the poem which will "work" by tying together all the elements. Now a friend, a trained and sensitive critic of poetry, suggests to him an over-all organization or unifying meaning-scheme which had not occurred to him. Suddenly, it "clicks."

We can illustrate this familiar experience and also add one complication. I once had the kind of experience just mentioned, and in this case the poet himself gave me the key meaning-scheme after I had failed to find it. Then, everything fit; I was impressed and delighted. The scheme was based on the very rational philosophic speculations of the great philosopher Berkeley. Some time later I suddenly saw the poem in the light of a meaning-scheme quite alien to that which the poet mentioned, in fact a mystical meaning. The poem "clicked" again—and the impact and delight were much more than were provided by what the poet himself had consciously had in mind.

The words, without some unifying scheme of meanings, are not a poem. A poem is an experience which is generated only as there is also brought to bear some unifying scheme by the one who interprets.

Now I propose that the patient in insight therapy plays a role analogous to that of the reader of the poem: what the patient "reads" are the bits and pieces of his life. He brings these fragments of his life to the therapist who then suggests a meaning-scheme in terms of which to reorganize and unify the patient's experience. The poet had merely to mention the name Berkeley to me as a cue to the whole very familiar pattern of meanings, the philosophy of Berkeley. So the therapist has merely to make a brief comment, offer a key phrase, in order to suggest to the patient a familiar but, in this context, a hitherto unused pattern of meanings in terms of which to view the situation.

Such meaning-schemes have conceptual, conative, and affective aspects, although it is the conceptual aspect which is distinctive. They are woven into the fabric of human response—indeed they are the constitutive structure of that response insofar as it is typically human and not merely animal. This is to re-enunciate the familiar principle that man is the animal whose responses are characteristically mediated by signs, symbols, and concepts. It is true that we often think of concepts being used to reflect or to report about our experience; and for many purposes this way of speaking is just right. But concepts do not only "reflect" and report our experience; as meanings, not merely as verbalistic structures, they are *constitutive* of experience. Human experience is further distinguished from all other biological behavior in that meaning-structure is not only constitutive of the experience-content, it is efficacious with regard to the course of that content's transformations. "Meaning-scheme," as this phrase is used here, points to patterns for behavior and experience, never just patterns of words, although words and concepts are the distinctive marks and peculiarly essential elements of meaning-schemes.

It will help to turn to the analogy between the meaning-systems which give structure to experience and the rules, strategies, and piece-names in a game. When we shift from poker to bridge, we do not say we are playing the same game with different rules, principles, and piece-names. They are different games. They are different games because *the rules, principles, and piece-names establish the game.* Analogously, human experience is brought into being by language and its syntax. As Kant said in introducing his "transcendental logic," "Percepts without concepts are blind." We might add that if no concepts make us blind, an inadequate meaning-scheme makes us shortsighted. Inadequate meaning-schemes institute fragmented, erratic experience. We are faced with patches of the meaningless. From this standpoint, it is easy to see that the therapist's effective introduction of a different meaning-scheme from that formerly used by the patient is a way of *directly* acting upon, a way of reorganizing the current experience rather than a way of revealing the truth about a hidden past. Let us at once balance things by paraphrasing the rest of Kant's famous dictum. Meaning-schemes divorced from the experience in which they function are psychotherapeutically empty, are merely verbal schemes; they are, in Wittgenstein's happy image, like an engine idling. In psychoanalytic informal jargon, they are merely "intellectual" insights.

In psychotherapy, we must assume the patient's former meaning-scheme did not work; it did not tie together enough of experience. The therapist's interventions aim at suggesting schemes which do work; everything "fits" and takes on a new value when cast into this mold. Is this "relativism" or "subjectivism"? Is therapy, after all, a matter of "suggestion"? We shall return to these crucial questions later, and we shall see that polemical pros and cons, as usual, fail to do justice to a complex and potentially illuminating problem.

Let us pursue our game analogy. It is true that games are defined by meaning-schemes which are more restricted, more "artificial," and more a matter of voluntary application than the kind of "real-life" schemes which concern the patient and therapist. Nevertheless, the notion of a meaning-scheme is easily elaborated in game terms.

In bridge, the establishing of a four spade bid implies that spades are trump, that losing three tricks is possible and consistent with making the contract, while losing four tricks is consistent with the rules but implies a failure of strategy. You *must* lead if you took the last trick. You are *forbidden* to open the play if you are the successful bidder. There are many points at which the player has a range of options, others where he does not.

These typical sorts of regulations have their counterparts in real-life meaning-schemes, e.g., "buyer-seller," "parent-child," "plaintiff-defendant," "lover-beloved." Even for violations of the rules there are established penalties. Thus even "violations" are part of the game. And, in "real life," there are established penalties for law violations, insults, etc. Refusing to pay the prescribed penalty for a violation is a "meaningless" gesture, however. It has no role at all in the game. Unlike payment of the penalty for a recognized violation, a move which allows the game to go on, the refusal to pay the penalty disrupts, disintegrates the game. In "real" life, the analogous conditions of social disorder and psychic anxiety come at once to mind.

In bridge, as in life, certain gestures are "pathological" intrusions from other games. Checkmating one's opponent's ace is neither allowed nor forbidden; it is a meaningless gesture in the game of bridge. There is no penalty, reward, or other meaningful response to it. If we can identify the behavior as a segment of an action locatable in some other meaning-scheme ("checkmate" in chess), the gesture is analogous to a meaningful psychopathological symptom. Thus we identify hand-washing as a meaningful action in a context of the need for cleanliness. However, hand-washing appears as an isolated but identifiable segment of a meaningful action when performed by the compulsive.

Therapeutic interventions are analogous to temporary digressions in a game where we turn our attention to the rules, strategy, or data instead of to the making of moves in the game. But even here we "learn by doing," as it were, for the transference is a kind of real-life practice game. We can "clarify" [4] and "confront," [5] i.e., we can focus on the meaning-scheme (the rules of the game) presently being used, clarifying the patient's actual use of it and its proper use. At the opposite end of the spectrum, we may give "interpretations" and develop "constructions," [6] i.e., we can construct a new meaning-scheme (or set of rules) and thereafter play the game of life in a basically new way. In therapy, typical and complex meaning-schemes in life can be suggested by such simple "cue-phrases" as: "being the employee of," "being afraid," "being irresponsible," "being the enemy of," "being married to," "aiming to hurt," "being sad."

A therapeutic interpretation given to the patient is, as has been said, a suggestion that a new conception of one's life may be worth trying, a new "game" played. But it is more than a suggestion about a "conception": it is the dynamic (existential) offering of the conception at the appropriate moment of dramatic involvement. It is more than the suggestion of a new way of talking about one's life descriptively; it is the proposal to *experience* genuinely and *see* one's life in terms of the meaning-scheme suggested by the words. It involves the hint that the structure of experience will be more unified, i.e., that there will be fewer meaningless gaps if this new scheme can become the very frame of one's being.

Of course, life consists of a tremendous variety of patterns of meaning which interlock, overlap, and, at times, conflict. True games furnish us the delightful contrast of action structured by a consistent, unambiguous, and autonomous meaning-scheme. They produce controlled conflict and, within their framework, they *guarantee* the possibility of a meaningful resolution of conflict, win, lose, or draw. Thus, aside from any deeper involvements, they evoke and inevitably overcome a kind of artificial anxiety.

The complexity of the patterns of meaning in "real" life and of the total responses these meaning-patterns organize is vast. Each pattern may be thought of as a great web of electrical circuits which may be switched on or off if only we can find the single, conceptual switch to flick. This switch is the therapist's intervention aimed at insight; it is the carefully timed and aptly worded phrase which enables the switch-over from one pattern of responses to another overlapping pattern. The therapeutic ideal is to interconnect all functioning systems and yet not to produce an overload or a confusion of circuits; in psychoanalytic language, this is to undo repressive isolation of psychic energies while avoiding traumatic anxiety discharge by binding and neutralizing those energies in ego-syntonic patterns of discharge.

Underlying this view are certain rather obvious, broad assumptions. I have already mentioned the assumption that meaning-structure is constitutive in experience. It is also assumed that the disposition to increase the meaningfulness of life is fundamental to the human being. Where this fails, the distinctively human is gone. Freud spoke of it as "the irresistible advance toward a unification of mental life." [7] This specific drive toward meaning may be viewed in relation to the total biologic drive, the drive from organismic stress toward organismic homeostasis: a variant on the theme "where id was, there shall ego be." [8] However, we must not lose sight of the distinctively human aspect of this process—the symbol structure, the aspect of "meaning"— which is the proper focus of insight therapy. On this symbol level the drive toward integration is a drive toward that state where, according to Freud, "all the enigmatic products of life (have been) elucidated." [9] It is, that is to say, a drive toward meaning.

There is also a drive toward what may broadly be called, in a rather special sense, gratification. This is the pleasure principle. Meaning may be used to maximize pleasure and may itself provide gratification (as is especially clear in the arts). Yet the drive toward meaning is autonomous and distinct from the pleasure-aim. It remains a fact that sometimes we can purchase meaning only at the expense of pleasure. This assumption of a drive toward meaning corresponds to the assumption in psychoanalytic theory of the primary autonomy of ego functions, especially of the synthesizing ego functions. For "ego" is the name for this unifying drive toward meaning and the specific forms and outcomes of that drive. The ego's unity, ego-integration as such, is a unity of meaning. Its primary energies are its being.

This drive toward meaning per se is reflected in the clientele of the psychotherapist. The person whose life is gratifying although not very meaningful is not likely to come for therapy. Nor does the person whose life is meaningful but ungratifying come. The latter may suffer intensely and unendingly—as did Freud himself in his later years. But suffering in itself is no automatic cue to apply psychotherapy. The world was, after all, not created to please us, nor does successful psychoanalysis guarantee the banishment of suffering. Psychoanalysis can *transform* the quality of suffering through understanding, through the sublimative magic of meaning, but it cannot guarantee the elimination of suffering. There are times, said Freud, when psychoanalysis can only succeed in "transforming your hysterical misery into common unhappiness." [10]

The person who comes voluntarily to the therapist is generally the one who is unhappy and who finds his unhappiness *without meaning*. Although his suffering may be amenable to chemical, surgical, or miscellaneous psychological influences, the classical therapeutic aim of psychoanalysis is to transmute his feelings, desires, and actions through understanding. That this may, in turn, alleviate physical suffering obscures the point at issue, though it does help justify and also complicate psychotherapy as a healing art. Although the psychoanalyst, as physician, cannot help putting great practical weight upon the issue of his patient's gratifications in life, to make this the primary criterion of therapeutic success would indeed mean that the goal is "mere" adjustment rather than personal human integration. Chemical and surgical therapies may one day be the treatments of choice for maximizing gratifications but never for maximizing the meaning in life.

As a simple illustration to serve as the basis of later discussion, I shall paraphrase, from a psychiatric textbook, a verbatim transcript of a therapeutic session.[11]

During the course of therapy, a woman patient comes to the therapeutic session suffering from a headache. The headache had developed after the patient had been offered an extra week's vacation by her employer. After some preliminary discussion, the therapist suggests that she feels that the gratitude due her boss puts her in his debt. He suggests that she resents this. It threatens her typical and intense efforts to maintain her independence. This view of the matter is accepted by her. After some further discussion, the therapist proposes that her desire to be independent is in turn really a way of overreacting to a severe temptation, the temptation to give in to strong but unacceptable (unconscious) dependency needs. At this point the headache has begun to disappear.

Has the therapist revealed past but "hidden realities," feelings or thought processes of a hidden kind which were actually operating at the time of the boss's offer? The "hidden reality" interpretation of psychoanalysis implies an affirmative answer. The "meaning-reorganization" view implies the contrary. The latter view implies that there were no temporal occurrences of feelings of anger or resentment, nor did there occur any unobservable space-time event which we could call a "wish to be dependent." The therapist does indeed help point out certain past events, but these events were observable and observed. His object is to provide new descriptions, new meanings *now* for the events which were described or conceived differently *then*.

The therapist, in catalyzing psychoanalytic insight, is helping to generate a kind of imaginative reliving of the situation. In this relived situation, the former key, organizing meaning-scheme is *now* replaced with another. Originally, the patient had seen the offer of a vacation, the past event, as an act falling within the more comprehensive web of meanings centering around the concepts of generosity and friendliness. Feelings of discomfort and headaches make no sense in that context. Such responses are not a part of the "game" of being befriended. Hence they are symptoms. Now, in therapy, it is suggested that she experience the event in terms of a new meaning-scheme, one having such key organizing concepts as "frustration," "dependency," "temptation," and "fear." Both schemes, the "generosity" meaning-scheme and the "temptation" meaning-scheme, though complex, are, in general, quite familiar to her. But the "temptation" scheme never before presented itself as a "live" option in terms of which to construe the events.

We need here note only one result: since frustration, fearful temptation, and resentment are meaning-structures in experience which "imply" or meaningfully lead to the possibility of unpleasant affect, the formerly incomprehensible headache begins to loom over the horizon of the meaningful. Thus a meaning-pattern hitherto not entertained by the patient turns out to be more comprehensive and consistent in relation to the stuff of experience than her former interpretative schemes. (Just why she should be able to make the shift now and just why the headache, now meaningful, should thereupon disappear are questions we shall consider later in elaborating the meaning-reorganization viewpoint.)

We will not have made a novel comment (though the *point* of our making it is novel) when we stress that as a matter of historical fact the patient never was aware of any such feelings of fear or wishes for dependent status at the time when they are supposed to have unconsciously occurred. This was precisely what Freud saw. His inspired and classical justification for using the concept of the unconscious, though familiar, needs to be studied again.

> All these conscious acts [said Freud] remain disconnected and unintelligible if we insist upon claiming that every mental act that occurs in us must also necessarily be experienced by us through consciousness; on the other hand, they fall into a demonstrable connection if we interpolate between them the unconscious acts which we have inferred. *A gain in meaning is a perfectly justifiable ground for going beyond the limits of direct experience.* When, in addition, it turns out that the assumption of there being an unconscious enables us to construct a successful procedure by which we can exert an effective influence upon the course of conscious processes, this success will have given us an incontrovertible proof of the existence of what we have assumed.[12] [Italics added]

But what, precisely, has been provided with an "incontrovertible proof"? Have we proved the assumption that all these processes actually occurred in secret at the former time? Or is it that the patient's acceptance and use of the language of hidden wishes makes it possible for her to see herself in a different light now and, as a result, to act differently hereafter? Have we not, as Freud's own language suggests, *now provided* a new meaning for the past?

I am under no illusions as to the innumerable questions and objections which press upon us here. We shall take them up again. But it may help to turn first to Freud's own struggles along this path. This will also help us to see how the meaning-reorganization view flows naturally out of psychoanalytic theory itself.

IT WILL BE RECALLED THAT FREUD HIMSELF REPEATEDLY EX-
pressed his discontent with the spatial metaphor as the basis
for arriving at an ontological interpretation of the processes
he was studying.

> Let us replace these metaphors [said Freud] by some-
> thing that seeks to correspond better to the real state of
> affairs, and let us say instead that some particular men-
> tal grouping has had a cathexis of energy attached to it
> or withdrawn from it. . . . What we regard as mobile
> is not the psychical structure itself but its innervation.[13]

For our purposes, I would like to reformulate the point
this way: insight involves a change in the pattern of energy-
innervation and discharge. Thus repression, instead of being, as suggested by the spatial metaphors, a question of
the *location* in which an idea exists, becomes instead a question of "innervation," or even, as Freud says, of a possible
"change in the state of the idea." [14] What, precisely, is this
"change in state"?

Freud repeatedly asserts that the single identifiable characteristic of an idea which has become preconscious, other
than its accessibility to consciousness, is the association of
that unconscious idea with concepts, what he calls "verbal
images." [15] Whatever more there may be to its nature, Freud
says, is a mystery to him.[16]

The preconscious is, in effect, the accessible context
within which conscious attention ranges. And we now see
that this accessible context of experience is, as far as Freud
can see, a context whose structure is at least largely and
probably inherently verbal, conceptual. The preconscious is
a *web of meanings*. Now that we know this much about the
preconscious, we still have to pinpoint what the state of the
idea is when it is dynamically unconscious, that is, repressed.

In this connection, Freud asks the question: Why couldn't unconscious ideas become conscious directly? Why must this process be mediated by words? But what sort of thing could the "idea" minus its verbal aspect be? He answers by stating what I feel is central to the entire discussion, and I should like to quote him rather fully:

> Probably, however, thought proceeds [unconsciously] in systems so far remote from the original perceptual residues that they have no longer retained anything of the qualities of those residues, and, in order to become conscious, need to be reinforced by new qualities. Moreover, by being linked with words, cathexes can be provided with quality even when they represent only *relations* between presentations of objects and are thus unable to derive any quality from perceptions. Such relations, which become comprehensible only through words, form a major part of our thought-processes. As we can see, being linked with word presentations is not yet the same thing as becoming conscious, but only makes it possible to become so; it is therefore characteristic of the system Pcs, and of that system alone.[17] [Italics in original]

Here Freud indicates clearly why the unconscious is "so far remote" from anything in our experience: language provides the relationships; the latter do not have any perceptual qualities at all. They cannot be represented in the unconscious derivatives of perception or in the relations among these derivatives. These linguistic relationships, "one of the most important parts of our thought-processes," involve the whole complicated syntax of language, a vast and relatively autonomous patchwork web of meaning-relations. Yet the *system* of meaning-relations, as we know, is not isolated from causality. Indeed, causality is but one special kind of meaning-relation, one meaning-scheme in terms of which to integrate and, at times, to analyze our experience. Remove the meaning-relationships from any experience and it is like peeling the layers of an onion: nothing is left but the smell. Indeed, Freud warns us in effect that even the "smell," which is nonrelational, "no longer retains anything of the qualities" of a percept!

There is, then, a radical difference in nature or "quality" between what is denoted by "unconscious idea" and what is denoted by "conscious idea" (or "preconscious idea"). The simple change of adjective is a misleading simplicity. The dichotomy "unconscious idea–conscious idea" suggests a change in a single property, but Freud's phrase "they no longer retained *anything* of the qualities" suggests a complete change of ontological status. Freud's discussion shows that a therapeutically crucial and highly complex relationship had been pinpointed by an inspired idiom of linguistically simple parallelism. But the idiom has its limitations, for there are theoretical contexts in which we need to recall that we are in fact dealing with two radically different sorts of "entities." From this standpoint we are struck with the gross inappropriateness of the analogy of the man who merely leaves the corridor and steps into the drawing room. We easily picture the man, his nature unchanged, waiting in the dark. But, after his careful inquiry into the issue, Freud states repeatedly that, in the last analysis, the "real" nature of the unconscious processes is a "shrouded secret," [18] "unknowable"; [19] it is—and I stress this—"*something . . . of which we are totally unable to form a conception.*" [20] This position was arrived at by Freud and held to after intensively exploring, over many years, a variety of different possible formulations. We can see, with hindsight, that he was unable to go further because his fundamental philosophical assumption that unconscious wishes are hidden events forced him to a blind alley, and he was honest enough to say that it was a philosophical dead end, however valid as psychology. He unwittingly sketched the alternative conception of "meaning" as central. Yet, because of his implicit commitment to a "hidden reality" ontology, he could not make the new ontological move explicitly. And he was entirely justified, of course, in putting the problem aside and moving on. The fact is that the philosophical tools for making the shift were not generally available until much later, in the twentieth century.

Let us imagine that there is a wedding which we did not see or know about; and then, the next day, we see the newspaper pictures. Such a situation is not to be taken as analogous to the unconscious wish and the later conscious insight. On the contrary, it would be more appropriate to use as an analogy a judge's pronouncement in court that two persons are now adjudged to have been common-law mates as of a certain date in the past. The news pictures, in the first analogy, *reproduce* what we did not see. The judge's pronouncement in court *does not reproduce anything;* it is neither a replica nor a making public of what was secret. (For none of the events in the life of the common-law mates need have been secret.) The judge's pronouncement is a novel act, a *present* act; it is an *authoritative reconstrual* of the past, a reconstrual which is oriented toward influencing the future. The judge does not reveal a secret ceremony in the past; he *now establishes a new context for our present and future response* to the *known* events of the past. It is true that in the course of the judicial proceedings some forgotten events may be recalled or unknown past events uncovered—just as the analytic patient may recall or discover events in his past. But this is not the essential. This only helps strengthen one or another construction put upon the situation. What is essential is the reconstrual of the meaning of the events. Let all the facts be known; the judge still *must* pronounce (and he should be—but may in fact not be—guided by the facts).

A civil or religious wedding is a relatively well-defined

and local act in space and time. A common-law marriage is not an *act* at all. The phrase "common-law marriage" has a misleading verbal parallelism to "civil marriage," "religious marriage." But in truth this phrase refers to the *absence* of a ceremony and to a complex set of events, all directly knowable in principle, all subjected to a retrospective review and to an authoritative reclassification with attendant reshuffling of individual events among the new categories. Similar considerations apply to nouns qualified by "conscious" and "unconscious."

Since the point is crucial, let us particularize further, using illustrations rather than analogies. Suppose that I remember preventing my little brother from getting on his tricycle and telling him that he would hurt himself. I remember getting on it myself and saying that I would show him how to ride. I remember feelings of satisfaction when doing this and feelings of annoyance when he cried. The annoyance is accompanied by verbalized thoughts to the effect that "he does not realize that I'm trying to help him; he is a crybaby." Now these are the kinds of things that I *remember*. Nowhere do I remember feeling hatred and jealousy of him. (I could not truly *recall* such feelings, for I *felt* no such feelings at the time.) I may have forgotten but now suddenly remember that I also used to drag him off my mother's lap while crying out fearfully that he might fall. Suddenly (because of the analytic setting and work, therapeutic interventions, the fact that I am now an adult, etc.) everything hangs together in a new way—and a much more unified, meaningful way. These very events are perceived and re-experienced in terms of the meaning-scheme "jealous aggression toward brother" rather than the scheme "well-meaning help of brother." I do not discover unfelt feelings; I reinterpret the feelings I felt (and this may lead me to have new feelings and responses now). I reinterpret the known events, reinterpret them not intellectually and as an observer but existentially, as experiencing subject and responsible agent. For in therapy we vividly and imaginatively re-evoke the experience as a concomitant of evoking its real-life parallel in the transference.

Freud's insight was keen, but for *some* purposes his language was misleading: to speak of "interpolating" another "link" in the chain of events is to imply that the link is of the same sort as the other known events. More "literally," however, I substitute a new context of interpretation for these known events. There are metaphors which help us to see this point: I move from one lookout point to another, although I look at the very same landscape. I travel from east to west in a land where I had always traveled north and south. How strange and new! How familiar!

Are we here denying the truth of the proposition "unconscious motives really existed in the past and function in the present"? Not at all. We have consistently accepted the truth of the fundamental psychoanalytic propositions in our analyses. But we are now asking, "What do these statements mean?" Under what conditions are they legitimately used? We consider whether "an unconscious wish existed in the past" means that an "invisible" duplicate of a "visible" something has been discovered to have secretly coexisted with other events in the past. Or we consider an alternative: Does it not mean that the relevant events were not secret but that we could not, would not see part of their meaning? Does it not mean that the known or rememberable events of the past, along with their feelings and thoughts, can now be construed within a pattern of meanings which makes more of a unity than the meaning patterns we had formerly used?

The notion that the structure of all processes in nature must reflect directly the grammar and imagery of our true statements about nature is by now an outdated dogma. Theories within which we interpret our true statements are in no sense challenges to the truth of those statements. A simple example from physics illustrates this. Objects released near the surface of the earth ordinarily fall to the earth. This statement remains true whether we interpret it in a Ptolemaic, Newtonian, or Einsteinian framework. Indeed, knowing that the Einsteinian framework is more general, we do not infer that it is always and necessarily more useful than the Newtonian. Nor does the fact that the Ptolemaic view is suggested by the grammar and imagery of the original proposition mean that this view is more true than the Einsteinian. Likewise, the "hidden reality" and the "meaning-reorganization" interpretations of psychoanalysis are of different utilities in different contexts, though the latter is more general and both are interpretations of, not alternatives to, the body of psychoanalytic theory and practice. Yet the "hidden reality" interpretation, because it is simply an ontological elaboration of psychoanalytic language and metaphor, is often identified with psychoanalysis. Existentialist and Phenomenological psychiatrists in particular have confused these questions, and we shall return to them later and discuss them in more detail.

Although our discussion has been until now largely in terms of the conscious-unconscious dichotomy, the results can be applied directly to the later psychoanalytic theories of psychic structure and dynamics. I shall summarize the matter and show briefly its relation to the distinction between voluntary and involuntary responses.

In terms of the meaning-reorganization view, the later structural-dynamic perspective may be put schematically as follows. The ego, especially the organizing or synthetic function, represents an autonomous drive toward meaning. When the ego fails and the trend is toward disorganization, there is anxiety, meaninglessness. (This thesis will form the theme of the next chapter.) What we call a chronic symptom is to be understood as energy discharge organized in the framework of an isolated, quasi-autonomous system of meanings, one which is not itself meaningfully linked to the main fabric of meanings. It is not easily subject to influence by other meanings, and thus it tends to be repetitive, stereotyped. It is "alien," alien to the main body of integrated patterns of meaning. As we know, however, a symptom is a defense. That is, a symptom is a gesture toward meaning, however isolated or eccentric, in the face of an inability to instate a meaning-scheme which could be better integrated into the rest of the ego.

Insight therapy may now be viewed as the attempt to provide integrating meanings where before we had the "disconnected and unintelligible." [21] It is the attempt to re-weave instead of putting what Freud called a "patch on the spot where there was a rent." [22] Insight therapy is the attempt to elucidate "all the enigmatic products of life." The therapist and patient seek schemes which not only make sense of the symptom-behavior but also tie it into the main, integrated body of meanings constituting the ego. There is achieved thus the first of the two chief justifications for speaking of the unconscious: "a gain in meaning." As a result, energy discharges which were isolated are integrated within the core of the psychic system. This means that we achieve the other chief ground for speaking of the unconscious: it "enables us to construct a successful procedure by which we can exert an effective influence upon the course of conscious processes."

The psychological condition of what we call voluntary action lies here, in the ego's integration of meanings. This is the psychological source of our capacity to will with responsibility and deliberateness. For to bring behavior within the scope of certain meaning-schemes, especially motives, is precisely to bring them within the realm of those behaviors we properly call voluntary. We deal here with the difference between "I wanted to do it" and "It just happened."

In the case of the woman with the headache, the therapist introduces the meaning-scheme cued by "threat due to fear of becoming dependent." This *meaningfully* relates her felt distress to other major, genuinely adult segments of the patient's life. The internal lines of communication are re-established, and this is what we mean by rational control being restored. What she does and feels now is, by the hypothesis, sensibly motivated, integrally related to the mature ego; hitherto it "happened" as something "alien," involuntary, uncontrolled.

Had she been able to relate the headache only to neuro-physiological schemes of interpretation and not motivational ones, the headache would have become meaningful but not voluntary. Dynamic psychological techniques would then be irrelevant. The psychoanalyst aims at establishing rational, voluntary self-control through dynamic meaning-schemes. The neurologist and physiologist use other meaning-schemes to guide them in restoring "health." Which approach or combination is "best"? This must be determined in each case on the basis of prior evidence and results achieved. It also depends upon the aims of therapy. In general we can ask: Where and how, and in what combinations of the physical and chemical, the learned automatisms and the rational, can we exert the most effective leverage, and to what end?

IV

DOES THE MEANING-REORGANIZATION VIEW SUPPORT THE charge that the various insight therapies depend, in the last analysis, on various forms of "suggestion" and "influence"? Does it imply that the therapist imposes his will, his values, his interpretation of things upon the patient? Is it a disguised form of retraining or reconditioning rather than a discovery of objective truth? Is the claim of objectivity in psychoanalysis a smoke screen?

This complex of questions, when analyzed, raises the two issues we must next examine: the nature of objectivity and the nature of individual autonomy and freedom. (1) Objectivity: Are therapeutic interpretations valid merely because they are accepted and used by the patient, or must they in some sense be true, objectively grounded, in accord with a reality independent of what the patient may find useful to believe at any moment? (2) Personal autonomy: Does the therapist "implant," willfully or unknowingly, values and beliefs, valid or not, in the patient? Is the apparent autonomy of the patient in fact a spurious autonomy, a pseudo-independence of judgment and choice? Or is there some sense in which the acceptance of a new meaning-pattern in therapy is genuinely rational and voluntary, the free and responsible response of an autonomous agent?

We shall deal with the problem of truth and then in turn with the problem of value-bias and the nature of free choice.

Let us assume the thesis proposed earlier: the acceptance of a therapeutic interpretation consists in reconstructing present experience (including memories and expectations) in a more coherent manner; it is not a discovery of secret occurrences of the past. What then becomes of the truth-value, the objectivity of psychoanalytic therapeutic insights? It is easy to jump to the conclusion that, except in a crudely pragmatic sense, objectivity is impossible and that therapy is only a form of "suggestion." If, somehow or other, the patient can be enticed to accept a proffered therapeutic interpretation, then all is as well as can be, for there is no "real" meaning or event which was the historical basis for the therapeutic interpretation.

Let us raise a question familiar to us from the discussions of scientific methodology in recent decades: How do we verify a psychotherapeutic interpretation? More to the point, what difference in method of verification would be involved in shifting from a "hidden reality" conception of psychoanalytic propositions to a "meaning-reorganization" conception? This question, so dear to the early logical positivists, need no longer be thought of as a panacea for all our theoretical ills, but it will throw a helpful light on the nature of the difference in the two views under discussion. (Let us note, as a safeguard against confusion, the simple ambiguity in the word "interpretation." I speak of a "therapeutic interpretation" when referring to the therapeutic intervention, the therapist's comment to the patient about the latter's personal life. This is to be distinguished from our ontological interpretations of psychoanalytic theory and practice. This distinction is ordinarily clear in context.)

We take the "hidden reality" view first. What sort of evidence, according to this view, can be found which will confirm or disconfirm a therapeutic interpretation? Broadly speaking, a correct therapeutic interpretation is recognized as such because it awakens forgotten memories, makes sense of dreams, produces current changes in behavior which—if not actually predicted—at least are seen as meaningful.[23] According to the "hidden reality" view, we do not identify or confirm a genuine therapeutic insight because it miraculously and literally brings back the past. Nor do we identify it because it presents us with the unconscious wish itself, for "it is of course only as something conscious that we know it, after it has undergone transformation or translation into something conscious."[24] According to the "hidden reality" view, valid therapeutic insight can be identified only because it consistently makes sense of what *is* conscious and *was* senseless. Valid insight has a dynamism of its own: it generates meaning in ways unpredicted, various, and lasting. When the patient uses the interpretation sensitively, independently, with due regard to the realities of his situation, and spontaneously, we suppose that the insight is not merely an intellectualistic supposition but genuine insight.

Let us suppose, for example, that the therapist has suggested the presence of an unconscious aggressive wish. According to the "hidden reality" view, he has not *directly perceived* any single event which is that *unconscious* wish. Rather he notices, intuitively or explicitly: the patient's voice is louder and harsher than usual; his movements are more rigid; he has "accidentally" caused physical pain to his boss as a result of a quite untypical carelessness; he was, previously, criticized in a subtle but profound way by his boss; he reports a dream in which there is much fighting and destruction; until his teens, when his father died in a violent accident, he used to fly into furious rages when criticized by his father; he now uses the language of a person who is calm, and upon being questioned, he says that he is indeed calm and is not bothered by "pinpricks" any more; upon hearing the comment that he is unconsciously angry at his boss, he doggedly and repetitiously argues and denies it, and he ascribes the "charge" to character defects in the therapist which are peculiarly reminiscent of those he finds in both his father and his boss.

It should be evident that, according to the "meaning-reorganization" view, *precisely the same sort of evidence* would be essential to confirm a therapeutic insight. For, on that view, what validates a therapeutic insight is that the latter, more than any other meaning-scheme, meaningfully interrelates the previously isolated, erratic, uncomprehended behavior, feelings, dreams, symptoms, and general history of the patient; furthermore, it continues to make sensible certain new and otherwise relatively meaningless phenomena observed after the insight took hold. Past, present, and future behaviors, unnoticed as well as noticed, the "trivial" and isolated as well as the portentous, all are tied together in a meaningful pattern. This tying together is done in the course of thoughtful living in the therapeutic transference, not by means of verbalistic ingenuities. It requires careful and time-consuming exploration, "working through," before a therapeutic interpretation may be said with confidence to be confirmed. According to the "meaning-reorganization" view, it is precisely because the neurotic is not objective, cannot freely explore, test, and check his isolated meaning-schemes against the data and other meanings of his experience that he is called neurotic. It is the neurotic who, *as* neurotic, organizes his life in terms of meaning-schemes which are arbitrary, partisan, fragmented. It is the neurotic, in short, who is "subjective." It is the therapist who attempts to get the patient to found his construals of life upon as broad and deep and honest an examination of his experience as possible. The "meaning-reorganization" view implies that the point of therapy is to establish the capacity for objectivity and to be objective. The *essence* of insight psychotherapy is the rejection of partial-ity in relating of facts one to another in meaningful ways.

There is one matter which still suggests an "operational" difference between the two ontological views. What shall we say about analytic "constructions" [25] which have actually led to the discovery of real but unremembered events in the patient's early years? [26] Are not these realities of the past which, though they were hidden, are now disclosed?

If the historical reality of discoveries inspired by "constructions" is to be used as supporting evidence for the "hidden reality" view, then, as a corollary, we should have to reject a "construction" when the "postdiction" about such past events proves false. But are "constructions" rejected as unsound in such cases? Not at all. They may be relabeled, but their therapeutic validity is not thereby denied.

The classic instance of this logic was provided by Freud himself. I refer to Freud's famous and crucial discovery that, contrary to what his patients had reported and Freud had at first believed, a considerable number of his patients had not in fact been seduced during their childhood.[27] Did he reject his therapeutic interpretations premised on the "seduction"? Quite properly not. He classified the seductions as fantasies. He then asserted that fantasies, conscious or unconscious, could be postulated as having "psychic reality." Thus his interpretative comments based on the supposition of a seduction were still, in essentials, retained as justified. As he later said, the unconscious is characterized by its failure to distinguish between psychic reality and "external" reality. A fantasy seduction counts psychically as a real event. Freud's additional use of the notion of "phylogenetically inherited schemata," though not generally accepted, is one more way of asserting the primacy of meaning over behavior.[28]

The principle was thus established that psychoanalytic interpretations are systems of effective *meanings* rather than temporal events. This was essentially a conservative maneuver for Freud, even though it involved a radical change in his therapeutic *theory*. For it was designed to provide a rational context within which to conserve his therapeutic *methods,* and it also preserved the essentials of Freud's psychoanalytic language. And this is exactly the point of the present discussion: the generative context of Freud's insight, and hence the context within which we can test the validity of his method and language, is that of psychic meaning, not atomistic analysis of behavioral phenomena per se. (This is by no means to say that such meaning-organizations can be divorced from the behavioral; as we have seen, they are forms of interpretation of behavior.) This explicit shift of primary orientation to systems of meanings rather than events in their public, objective character was an early and crucial expression of Freud's genius.

Thus we return to our hypothesis that, whatever the differences between the "hidden reality" view and the "meaning-reorganization" view, the two would seem to be "operationally" equivalent with regard to verification of any particular therapeutic interpretation offered the patient by the therapist. To put it otherwise: whichever ontological theory is adopted, the psychoanalytic theory, language, and practice of the therapist need not, in the first instance, be different in any way. But this equivalence is by no means a total equivalence. There remain other good reasons for distinguishing between these alternative ontological interpretations. There are, as I hope to have indicated by the end of this chapter, many questions of theory and of existential illumination which involve important issues other than verification operations in a narrow sense. There are, after all, reasons for discussing ontology: different basic languages and categories ultimately generate shifts in our perspective. We need not lose what we had, but we may see it located on a new and larger map, one which reveals even the familiar regions in a new way by means of a different projection.

The analysis of the operational context of the two views was not undertaken here merely to reveal the equivalences —though this is itself an intrinsically important matter. However, such an analysis also supplies us with the answer to our original question about objectivity. We now see that both views require with equal force and in the same way that psychoanalytic propositions be ultimately linked in complex ways to the behavioral. But neither view calls for confirmation by reference to a single, past event. This ultimate linkage, the "meaning-reorganization" view reveals, is a matter of creative ingenuity as well as objective inquiry. For example, in the case of the woman patient mentioned earlier, generosity was linked to discomfort via a conceptual bridge: "generosity" leads to "temptation," which leads to "fear," which, in turn, leads to "resentment," which finally connects up with "discomfort." The body of therapeutic doctrine makes readily available to the therapist a remarkably wide variety of workable combinations of such motivational or psychodynamic meaning-schemes for various situations.

It is in this connection that we must take notice of the theoretical conception "overdetermination" and the therapeutic problem of tact. The focus upon "psychic reality" implies that, at bottom, the behavioral can never be totally and unambiguously linked to the world of meaning. It is this potential of any behavioral event—that it has an unspecifiable number of meanings—which is the more generalized form of Freud's postulate that any behavior response is always overdetermined. The practical question is always to discover which specific meaning-schemes are at any moment relevant to and appropriate in the dynamic therapeutic context, which ones can be genuinely accepted and used by the patient at that moment.

There are no doubt times when any of several meaning-schemes will have a productive (integrative) impact on the course of therapy, though each would channel the therapy in a different direction. It is well known that different therapists may respond to the same material with different therapeutic interventions. The world is multimeaninged. But the world does not have *all* meanings. This would indeed be the end of objectivity. An act may have many meanings, but there are infinitely more meanings which it can be objectively shown not to have. All of this is not a special truth in connection with psychoanalysis. Rather psychoanalysis offers a peculiarly illuminating special case of a feature of all knowledge and objectivity.

We now turn to the second question concerning psychoanalysis and "suggestion." Does therapeutic interpretation, whether valid or not, necessarily constitute a foisting of the values and outlook of the therapist onto the patient; is the latter merely "trained," "conditioned," or "influenced" to accept the meaning-schemes (whether objectively grounded or not) as proposed by the therapist? Or can the acceptance of the therapist's "interpretation" be a genuine *insight;* i.e., a rational and creative achievement by an autonomous agent? We need only take note here of the frequent charge that patients tend to find in their waking and dream life the very meanings postulated by the theoretical system of the therapist, whatever his "school." This certainly suggests a suspect kind of influence.

It is obvious to all that the therapist "influences" the patient. However this word and its near relations are ambiguous. They have a broad sense compatible with autonomy, and they have a narrower, "mechanistic" sense which is the opposite of autonomy. In order to see the ambiguity more specifically, we shall proceed indirectly and focus our attention first on such concepts as "autonomy," "rational," and "voluntary."

Rational, voluntary action in its most ordinary form has as its core the use by the agent of a meaning-scheme. The scheme is accepted by the agent, and he himself applies it in a particular situation. His action is distinguished as rational and voluntary by its being his response in the situation *as construed by him.*

Once again there is an analogy with the game situation. A person must know and accept a set of rules and principles, and he himself must apply these in individual cases, before we can properly say that *he* is playing the game. Only then is he acting rationally and voluntarily as an autonomous participant. Without some meaning-scheme, some set of rules and principles, there is no game and hence no arena for rational, purposeful action. With a poorly conceived set of rules, the player's power to conceive and carry out a strategy is exerted erratically and in diminished degree. Without the ability to use the rules, whether through ignorance or lack of skill, the person can at best be an instrument executing someone else's strategy.

If I explain the rules to a person, I "influence" him, but I do not act counter to his autonomy; on the contrary, I increase his autonomy. If instead of teaching him the rules, I simply give him commands as to what move to make, I influence him in the sense of "using" him as a nonautonomous extension of my will. And if I teach him the rules and some rudimentary principles but never bring him to a grasp of fundamental strategies, then I keep him from complete, effective autonomy while allowing him limited autonomy as my subordinate. The key issues are these: Does he know and accept and can he use all the relevant meaning-schemes for construing each situation on his own? Can he respond on his own initiative to the situation as thus construed? The meaning-schemes (rules and principles of strategy) do not tell him what to do. They tell him, when properly applied, what is the nature (meaning) of the situation in which he must act. The response is unique, but whether it is autonomous choice or arbitrary and accidental is determined by just this issue of whether he is able, on his own, to construe the situation.

The therapist faces someone without an adequate scheme in terms of which to interpret the data. Neurotic responses are involuntary, not meaningfully related to the rest of his relevant purposes. The therapist suggests the patient modify or even totally switch "games" he had been playing until now. "You thought what you were doing was 'protecting your brother'; try the assumption that it was 'protecting yourself—from seriously hurting him out of jealousy.'" These suggested modifications are, in general, familiar to the patient. He had not been able to see their applicability to the present case. Why not? Because until the therapeutic work, he was unable to bear the anxiety (inner disintegration) of trying to act in terms of two sharply incompatible meaning-schemes—being the "good" brother and being the jealous, "bad" brother. It was easier to use a fuzzy but socially acceptable meaning-scheme—that of the good brother whose childish overzealousness occasions accidental pain to the small brother. The "jealous brother" scheme may now make more sense to the patient in view of the way the cards are stacked. Old memories, current problems, and cherished expectations take on a new look. The therapist does not need to tell the patient specifically what action to take; he does not play the game for the patient; he has suggested a "game" which the patient can play for himself, one he can play better than the old one, and one he now chooses to play. The patient is at last in a position to select and to pursue an intelligent and independent strategy of his own because the game at last corresponds to the pieces on the board; he becomes effective as an autonomous and rational actor. He may, now that the situation is intelligible, decide to quit that game entirely. That is, if I have been able to accept myself as having been the jealous brother, I may now, as an adult, reject this "game" as clearly incompatible with my adult attitudes and commitments. But had I continued to see myself as the protective but frequently awkward brother, I would continue to discover that "accidents" occurred, and I would continue to persist in cultivating that attitude nevertheless.

In principle, insight therapy is, in this way, value-neutral and liberating in its results. It increases my effectiveness and options. What is more, the method of achieving insight as well as the outcome is significant. For the conditions of insight and autonomy are established through the medium of a two-person relationship thoughtfully *lived* through. The method used is thus characteristic of liberal (i.e., liberating) education; it is not rote training, subservient imitation, or information from an authority, no matter how learned and wise.

Yet there is another side to the story. One must qualify fundamentally the assertion that insight therapy is value-free. It is true that the therapist can, at least in principle, avoid injecting into therapy personal values or advice on particular choices. Nevertheless, he does offer the general schemes of meaning. These inherently embody certain highly generalized but fundamental patterns of experience. The therapist may well be loyal to the Reality Principle, but reality in this context is defined to a great extent by social structure, language, ideology, and esthetic tradition as well as by physical environment.

The meaning-schemes suggested by the therapist, if they are to have any reasonably direct use in life, must be pervaded with culture-bound meanings. To empty out the culture-bound content—if this were possible—would be to deal on such a level of abstraction as would bring the drama of therapy to a complete halt. This is true, even though Freud chose as his basic meaning-schemes what are perhaps the most universal ones possible: that web of meanings which is embodied in family relationships. We shall have more to say of this later, but at the moment it is important to note how even such a general scheme fails to free the therapist of bringing to bear a point of view.

A reference, for example, to fear of one's father, if it is to have therapeutic efficacy, cannot be a textbook abstraction. Fear and fathers, it is true, are universal human phenomena. To this extent, the meaning-scheme in question is, for practical purposes, genuinely universal. But Patient X's fear of his father is in good part a quite special and many-faceted constellation of meanings peculiar to Patient X's personal history and to the role of fear in his culture. The image and role of fatherhood also vary widely in different cultures. Fatherhood—as a concept devoid of culture content—is a rather obscure, complex abstraction. It is not the kind of meaning we discover directly in our experience. It has no therapeutic use. The therapist must offer meaning-schemes which are loaded with cultural, subcultural, and personal value-content.

We must also remember that the range of meaning-schemes offered by the psychoanalyst is sharply limited even though, within those limits, it is internally rich and complex. As a professional technician he does not use the religious, political, institutional, sports, literary, and other meaning-schemes brought to him by the patient; these function as data in relation to the therapist's organizing meaning-schemes. They are *raw materials* of free associations and other verbalization. The psychoanalyst is guided by psychoanalytic meaning-schemes. True, the therapist will commonly make therapeutic interpretations which incorporate the *language* of the patient. And insofar as therapy is an "art" rather than a technique, his use of these languages will reflect the genuine, operative use of the patient's meaning-schemes, not their observation as data. But insofar as therapy is based on techniques and theory, on professional skills and a therapeutic point of view, these uses—for the therapist—will be only secondary. Thus the therapist may have to understand and deal with, say, formulations by the patient of religious or political problems. But the therapist is working to construe the problem in psychoanalytic terms. His help to the patient will have as a good part of its source this specific scheme of understanding. He will not offer a religious solution in his capacity as therapist—though he may in some cases feel constrained to offer his help in religious language.

Ekstein's report of the case of an adolescent patient who was disturbed by her blasphemous wish to be Christ on the Cross illustrates how, as far as therapy goes, the material is translated into psychoanalytic meanings, no matter what *words* are used in the therapist-patient dialogue. He reports:

During the many long months of therapy the therapist attempted instantly to follow Elaine in her own way of communicating without trying at first to challenge the rapidly changing ego states or to translate from one level to another. Interpretation and communication thus took place within the context which the child offered, whether a distant religious parable, a medieval fantasy, or a frank delusional experience. . . . [Later the therapist could] call her attention to the distant devices themselves. . . .

One may wonder what forced this child into the use of these protective distance devices of the ego, through which the affective meaning of her transference reaction was projected into the quasi-religious experience and was largely removed from within the range of the secondary process functions of the ego's organization.[29]

Thus the meaning-schemes used in therapy do introduce fundamental orientations of a kind which transcend questions of technical "correctness" or, in the usual sense, of infringement or noninfringement of the patient's moral and spiritual autonomy. I repeat that I refer now to the selectivity inherent in using only some among the possible general categories of meaning-schemes and to the inevitable cultural content incorporated in the ones which are used.

And yet this is not necessarily bias. A meaning-scheme is a framework within which a bias may be shown. The meaning-scheme establishes descriptive categories as well as the rules for the reasonable use and ordering of those categories. The criteria of bias apply to formulations *within* an accepted meaning-scheme, the question being whether these formulations have been properly used or constructed. A meaning-scheme as a whole can only be viewed as "biased" if it is taken as a formulation within a more comprehensive meaning-scheme. Then the larger schema offers the criteria of bias. Although we have here a formal parallelism, we should not lose sight of the vast practical difference connected with the differences in "logical level." Problems of genuine choice on the practical, everyday, concrete level may involve problems of correctness or bias; but where the alternatives are themselves large-scale, highly generalized meaning-schemes, problems of choice are properly spoken of as problems of philosophical, moral, or spiritual decision. The import and the handling of such decisions differ vastly—and rightly so—from everyday decisions involving possible bias.

The therapist needs to be able to make the vital distinction between persons who, in the sense just suggested, struggle with genuine and objectively grounded moral or spiritual problems and those persons who use the language of the spirit but who use it as a disguise for neurotic maneuvers, for biased judgments and actions. Religious psychiatrists are among the first to stress the commonness of the latter.[30]

Our analysis enables us to distinguish problems of countertransference, which is a form of genuine bias *within* a psychodynamic meaning-scheme, from the problem of evaluating alternative, large-scale meaning-schemes. The latter involves psychology no more and no less than it involves, for example, anthropology, philosophy, and art.

V

WE HAVE SEEN THAT THE PSYCHOANALYST NEED NOT INTRO-duce bias or "influence" in the everyday sense by virtue of his psychoanalytic conceptions and that, indeed, he increases the patient's autonomy by the clarifications produced. We have also seen how, in a broader sense, he does offer, by virtue of the general explanatory categories he applies in life, a specific way of looking at the world. And this perspective is only one perspective among many possible ones. Is the psychoanalytic perspective in some sense more "effective" than others? Might not more philosophical, or sociological, or religious meanings integrate the patient's life better? Even more specifically: might not psychoanalysis tend to emphasize the critical, the "analytic," where other schemes might help *resolve* the problems more directly, by using concepts of "will" or perhaps philosophical or religious syntheses?

It has often been argued, lately, for example, by the psychoanalyst Allan Wheelis,[31] that the patient in psychoanalysis is provided with "analysis" but not "synthesis." The patient is supposed to be too passive. He does not make deliberate choices. He does not use "will." He looks "backward," not "forward." These charges involve a serious misconception. The misconception arises when we contrast the *theory* (not the practice) of psychoanalytic therapy with the implicit model of everyday deliberative choice which dominates self-conscious Western thought. The model is derived from a very special context, that of utilitarian, technical decisions of a simple logical, economic, or mechanical kind. The model does not reflect the actualities of *deliberative* choice.

"Choice," for most of us when we think of the matter in our philosophical moments, usually connotes the selection of a means-act to some end. And if we do think of "choice" as referring to the intrinsic ends themselves, then we implicitly assume that there are clearly defined ends toward which our desires, themselves clearly defined, are directed. We like A; we don't like B; therefore we choose A. The desires and tastes and their objects are given, both in quality and quantity. We need only perform the "decisive" "act of will." In body language, we associate choice with the squaring of the shoulders and marching off. Visually, we are dominated by the "crossroads" model of choice: at the time of choice, we stand at the crossroad and must, in order to take the next step, "choose" (with or without reflection) one or the other road. The "crossroads" locate man at the "instant" of decision. These are the stereotypes which tend to dominate reflections about the nature of choice.

But all of this is a distortion of the realities insofar as choice involves moral agency, deliberative autonomy, the active impact of the entire man. In trivial choices, and in highly technological, routine decisions about economic or physical issues, we have the nearest approximation to a single, momentary "act of will." Go left or go right; sell or buy; move the lever up or down. And the closer we get to the clear case of a pure, momentary "act of will," the less do we ordinarily refer to will and refer instead to habit, routine, the reflex, or the trivial. Either what we choose in these cases does not matter or it is effectively governed by pre-existing rules, goals, techniques. The rare case of a genuinely momentous choice which does remain in the balance until a particular instant when the "switch must be flicked," and without a rule to decide, is a dramatic and misleading exception which dominates our thinking about these matters. It draws our attention away from the significant and common cases of deliberative choice. It is because of this model of the crucial crossroads moment calling for a single act of initiative that we read words like "contemplate," "reflect," "analyze," "perceive," "esthetic," "passivity," "free-associate," as if they referred to the very antithesis of choice. However, if we turn to our own important private deliberations, and certainly if we turn to the crucial deliberations which take place in psychotherapy, we see that responsible choice by no means consists simply in decisively "taking the initiative" at some crucial instant. On the contrary, significant choice involves the "free" production of thoughts, feelings, fantasies, and memories; it involves the willingness to contemplate these, to "savor" them, to explore them, to give them scope to operate, if only within limits and in tentative fashion. Memories of the past, fantasies of the future, and the checking of these against hard facts—this is the kind of "passivity" and analytical activity which are the stuff of creative deliberation and choice. Finally, serious choices, the choices which make one a new person in a new world, involve that sometimes sudden, sometimes gradual, but always involuntary, fusion of the whole into a meaningful pattern which then "takes over." "*Now* I see how I must act." "Now I understand what I must do." We *discover*, when deliberation is successful, that "this is it." Commitment is the nonwillable last phase of the deliberative process. We do not stand, a hovering "free will" or a *deus ex machina,* outside the deliberative process and then, when it is over, provide a "decision." We shall have occasion again to explore the point that the sense that "I can do no other" is precisely the mark of the genuinely autonomous free agent in his most profound actions.

Things "come" to the one who is profoundly, sensitively "open." Yet when the completed process is looked at by the observer and described in ordinary language, he says, correctly and idiomatically, that important decisions have been *made.* This language tends to support the myth of the crossroads "instant of choice." But we need not be confused by the misleading idiom, "make a decision"; we no more make a decision than it is made for us. Decisions *take place* where there is a genuine encounter between the person and his situation.

We need not go from one oversimplification to its opposite, however. It still remains that language explicitly centered around concepts such as "will," "decision," and "creativeness" are entirely appropriate in many contexts. What is the nature of these contexts? Do they include the context of psychotherapy? How do they compare to those contexts in which it is useful to use and stress the more "passive" and "analytical" language characteristic of psychoanalysis?

In raising such questions there is a natural confusion which we must avoid. The question as to whether the language of "hidden reality" or the language of "meaning-reorganization" is more effective *in* therapy is quite different from the question as to which is more adequate as an onto-logical interpretation *of* therapy. There is no reason to sup-pose that the language in which we interpret therapy is necessarily the best language in which to carry on therapy and interpret the patient's conduct. Indeed I think there are good reasons to suppose that it is usually better to present insight psychotherapy as an attempt to *discover* what is present but hidden in one's life rather than as a task of *making* a new world for oneself by "creative choice," by the mobilization of will and purpose. But we need to explore this choice of therapeutic languages more fully.

Regardless of doctrinal differences, most dynamic thera-pists agree on the peculiarly intimate relation of stereotypy and neurosis. The neurotic is one who willfully, that is to say, systematically and persistently, maneuvers so as to avoid or seek specific types of situations. He may be subtle and flexible at times, but this can be neurotic behavior only in the sense that it is in the service of an ultimate, driving rigidity. To present therapy as, in effect, the search for a "hidden reality" enables the therapist to develop a pure culture of the irrational in the patient. This is because the patient is called upon to respond sensitively and contem-platively, "passively," to the actual events in his therapy, a demand which sets out in bold relief his characteristic in-ability to do this. This framework sets in the clearest pos-sible contrast the appropriate, nonneurotic background be-havior of passivity and undirectedness, and the neurotically motivated single-mindedness, the dogged and unjustified willfulness, of the neurotic symptom and especially of the transference. The latter are thus eventually recognizable for what they are even by the neurotic himself. Were we, on the other hand, to use a meaning-scheme setting in therapy which focused attention on therapy as inherently purposive rather than passive, as a process calling for the mobilization of will and decision, we would lose this element of contrast between the undirected and the rigidly directed.

Furthermore, to use meanings which focus attention on the concepts "choice" and "will" is to bring to mind one special aspect of the deliberative process only—and precisely that aspect of which there is already an excess in the case of the neurotic. Neurosis is precisely the disease of uncontrollable "willfulness." On the other hand, to focus on the search for the unknown—or better, to focus on nothing but "openness" to what comes and to stress the readiness to accept the unknown which will emerge—this cultivates another aspect of the deliberative process. But this aspect, as we now see, is by far the more important aspect of vital and serious deliberation, and it is precisely the aspect which the neurotic, in the area where he is neurotic, has failed to cultivate. The neurotic passivity which jumps to our mind when we see the word "passivity" is in fact a form of obstinate refusal to face anxiety openly and explore its quality and source. Neurotic passivity is a defensive pseudo-passivity: it is passive in the sense of rigidly avoiding something. Therapeutic passivity is openness.

The misdirected charges that Freudian psychoanalysis merely "analyzes" but does not "synthesize" arise out of the failure to appreciate that notions of "synthesis" and "decision" are largely observational terms in which one reports after the fact. The effect and point of psychoanalysis include what, in fact and in its own theoretical terms, is truly a phase of reorganization, of synthesis. Great religions and great artists as well as psychoanalysts[32] have stressed the crucial role of passivity, of being "in-spired" in the creative process. The visitations of the muses and of the other benevolent gods are the universal mythic prototypes of the psychoanalytic language of discovery as a medium for what, *after the fact,* we call creative synthesis.

There is another sense of the vague word "effective" in which we can here only suggest different kinds of effectiveness of the various language-schemes used in the practice of the different schools of therapy. We must recall that the languages used do not consist merely of "methodological" terms like "reality" and "meaning." The psychoanalyst works primarily in terms of such key "content" meanings as "love," "hate," "fear," "mother," "father," "brother," "sister," and so on. In short, he looks at the individual's experience in terms of a selected range of "primary group" relationships. What is more—and this bears on our earlier discussion of cultural content—within the limits of therapeutic efficacy, the psychoanalytic scheme goes about as far as possible in minimizing the specifically cultural component. Cultural attitude-terms of respect, scorn, avoidance, or other special "status" attitudes are inevitable but not central in his scheme. Indeed, strictly speaking, what Freud did was to seize upon the primary group framework in its most general forms and to *de*-emphasize radically even the family as a culturally defined unit. The point of his message was: treat father simply as a strong male, the boy's first rival and model; mother is simply the first source of affection and protection, the first woman. Do not be dominated by the cultural conceptions of the family relations, e.g., that one has only tender, asexual affection and respect for mother who, in turn, adores and always protects the child. He forced us to see *through* the culture to such universal human traits embodied in it as male and female, strong and weak, loved and hated.

In a culture without a shared and vital religion or mythology, the most widely and immediately relevant meaning-schemes are those of primary group relationships generic to the human race. This is not to say that such meaning-schemes are a priori crucial for resolving some particular problem at hand. Nor is it to say that subjectively experienced primary group relationships are the most "real" or "basic" or "profound." There is no set of categories which is inherently, for all purposes, and in all contexts, "basic."

Perhaps, also, in an ideologically heterogeneous culture such as ours, a therapy working in psychoanalytic, "personal" terms is most susceptible to a kind of "nonpartisan" professionalization. In a society with a vital and unquestioned mythology, the local adept can set his fee and perform his works in the context of the myth meaning-schemes.[33] Our information here is scanty.

In contrast to the Freudian approach, other insight therapies, for example, Jungian, Existentialist, and Phenomenological psychotherapies build to greater or lesser degree upon other meaning-schemes for their central content. Religious, mythic, moral, and metaphysical concepts are characteristic. Contrary to the claims of many of these "philosophical" therapists, these different meaning-schemes do not of themselves reflect any greater or lesser "reality" or "profundity." As existential or therapeutic languages, their validity is determined by their impact upon experience and not by their verbalistic or traditional claims of profundity or ultimacy. Certainly, in the case of any patient, his fluent use of traditional "spiritual" or "philosophic" language is no very reliable sign of the profundity of a patient's spiritual insight. And as far as claims of scientific validity go, the fact remains that they are not, in a strict sense, logically organized systems of ideas having routinized and reliable interpretations in practice. Nor do the Existential and Phenomenological therapies aim to be. However, psychoanalysis, for all its deviations from this description, remains far and away the most elaborate theory of the person which points in the direction of science.

The confusion between existential validity and scientific validity is compounded because of the pressure to acquire the honorific term "scientific" as the seal of genuine validity. The confusion is further compounded because proponents of the more "philosophical" therapies have glimpsed the vital role of meaning in therapy. They have supposed, to use our language, that meaning-reorganization is an alternative to psychoanalysis rather than a way of interpreting what psychoanalysis is. They have opposed their analysis and synthesis of life's meaning to what they have supposed to be the mere "analysis of causes" of psychoanalysis. They have failed to see that we are dealing with systems *all* of which evoke analysis and synthesis of life's meaning. The contrast which is central has to do with the different basic meanings which provide the language and the context for that analysis and resynthesis.

I would suggest that a primary reliable clue to profundity of insight, regardless of therapeutic method, is the degree of personal autonomy connected with that insight. To what extent does the person not only talk the game but actually behave with spontaneity and yet with purpose? Does he show sensitivity to facts and claims along with an absence of bondage to them? This is not always an easy thing to observe clearly; but it is possible to judge it reliably in many cases.

Of course one meaning-scheme or another may, for biographical reasons, make the patient "feel good." Making the patient "feel good" is, I take it, a reasonably common concomitant of increased autonomy. Or it may even be a therapeutic goal reflecting a humane, though merely palliative, second choice where the further attainment of autonomy appears impossible. ("Is there one among you who has not at some time caught a glimpse behind the scenes in the causation of a neurosis and had to allow that it was the least of the evils possible in the circumstances?" [34]) But "feeling good" is surely not the crucial test of validity of insight. We have discussed this in connection with the problem of objectivity.

When all is said and done, the practical test is not in a priori claims or philosophical name-throwing, but in practice—sustained, serious, constantly critical, and sensitive practice. The most general criterion in the context of our inquiry is this: What kind of meaning-scheme *does* finally bring control and order along with spontaneity into our experience? Available statistics on different psychotherapies are as yet of no help. The methods of collection, the bases of diagnoses, and the criteria of "cure" are too variable and incommensurable. The very role of statistical information is obscure. As yet we can only judge among the various forms of therapy on the basis of such theoretical considerations as the preceding and on the basis of nonstatistical judgments derived from our personal knowledge.

VI

IN THE ENTIRE DISCUSSION OF MEANING-SCHEMES WHICH HAS proceeded, there has been a critical ambiguity. I have tried to use context and language to avoid confusion, but it is now time to explore this ambiguity. For it is the generative seed of psychoanalysis.

As we know, psychoanalysis has since its inception been considered by some as a new science and by others as a penetratingly new quasi-literary form. Its impact on both the humanities and the psychological sciences of the past generation is profound and unquestionable. On the negative side, it has been rejected as a science by some scientists just by virtue of its being too "literary" or "mythic." And it has been rejected by some in the arts by virtue of its being too "scientific." The paradox is acute and the polemics all the more emotionally charged. Although there are innumerable writings on one or another side of this question, I know of none which systematically asks why such opposing charges should so persistently be made against one and the same defendant. To see the answer to this question, however, is to see the source of the peculiar power of psychoanalysis. And the path to the answer leads us to the ambiguous concept of meaning.

The language of "meaning" can function in scientific theory as a more generalized interpretation of the psychoanalytic language. I have used it this way, especially in the first two sections of this chapter. Or the language of meaning may function expressively, existentially, in the very coming to grips with life. The concept "meaning" is, in short, a point of intersection from which one may move either into living or into theories about living.

This is the ambiguity of function of psychoanalytic ideas which is central to this book and which is, I maintain, the seed of the provocative, illuminating, and liberating twentieth-century "Freudian revolution." It remains to say explicitly how and why this is so.

The notion that we can "reconstruct" our world by reconstruing it is not a new one. In modern times it takes its impetus from the Kantian Critiques and is developed in idealist, positivist-phenomenalist, and naturalist forms. Today we see the notion, in the psychotherapeutic context, in Existentialist and in Phenomenological psychotherapies. There are many other contemporary psychological, philosophical, and cultural theories, which in one form or another stress the role of meaning-reorganization in experience. Such tendencies are illustrated by the works of Tolman, the Gestaltists, the perception theorists and Piaget among the psychologists, Cassirer, Dewey, and Wittgenstein among the philosophers, and Whorf, Benedict, and Lee among the anthropologically oriented. By and large these illustrate the tendency toward the explicit use of meaning as a theoretical concept rather than its use of meaning in the existential mode. And it is worth noting that these theory-oriented tendencies have dominated the English-speaking world of philosophy, psychology, and psychiatry.

There is a widespread superstition that meanings are, in some sense, "private" and hence not suitable as data for a scientific theory. We need not argue this vague assumption. Let us simply note that for a science we do not need either "direct" or absolutely reliable perception of the referenda of our key concepts. Indirect observation and a relative degree of reliability in identifying meanings are all that are needed. That there are public cues to meanings is evident. Before ever there was such a thing as a "clinical" test, the existence of social intercourse was massive proof of our ability to express, detect, and interpret meanings with remarkable precision. For what is social intercourse, any social intercourse, except behavior based on the expression of, discovery of, and response to the meaning of behavior? If there are any facts that we know about human beings as human, they surely include the fact that human beings do reliably, constantly, and publicly grasp meanings by observing the behavior and speech of other human beings.

But the concept "meaning" may be used in another context. When we see our life as the "search for meaning," we may do so not in the framework of an observer's description of life but in the framework of an over-all *appraisal by a participant.* Our usual questions and answers about life's meaning or meaninglessness are not attempts at formulating a public, logically consistent, and prediction-oriented theory; instead they are attempts at expressing a perception, adopting a stance, recommitting ourselves to a new life-strategy. In this context, we learn about meanings as a lover learns about his beloved, not as her physician does. The existential questions about meaning are part of a process of generating a new vision which shall serve as the context of new commitment; the scientific questions about

meaning are part of a process of developing a logical, reliably interpretable, and systematically predictive theory.

The dominating Continental tendency has been to stress
this existential function of meaning. The *language* of meaning, as we have seen, highlights the creative role of the
therapist and the existential decision of the patient. It
stresses that the latter makes the move from anxiety or
meaninglessness through (creative or destructive) vision and
decision toward meaningfulness. It focuses on the relation
between our "private worlds" and the "public world." [35] It
suggests the mythic dimension, the creation of cosmos out
of chaos. It moves us easily and naturally into the language
of responsibility and moral agency. All this is highly dramatic and in certain contexts valid. Yet we cannot allow the
existential capabilities of the language to obscure the quite
different, theoretical ways in which it can function.

The scientific and the existential uses of "meaning" are
thus radically different uses of the concept, yet in both cases
there is an identical conceptual element. And both of these
uses of the concept of meaning, the theoretical and the existential, are "empirical" in the sense that they are primarily
concerned with human experience and are highly discriminating responses to it. Both types of use lead to systematic
and sophisticated "knowledge"—but in two quite different
senses of the latter word. Both senses of the word are profoundly rooted in tradition.

Those original souls who first elaborated the existential
vision took science and technique to be anathema. Their
vision arose precisely out of their liberation from the oppres-
sive theoretical and technological orientation of the West.
They spoke, no matter how "philosophically" or "psychiatri-
cally," to the individual unique in his crises; they spoke *with*
him in the dialogue of commitment. Those who had the
scientific vision, however, felt constrained to avoid man-in-
crisis as lived. They saw liberation as coming from putting

man back into nature, and this, in turn, meant to them treating him as object. They used physical, neurological, and sociological languages, or they invented new conceptions. They could not use their language *with* the person in dialogue; it could only be *about* him as object, specimen. Of those we earlier mentioned as theorists, Dewey and the later Wittgenstein would constitute significant and conscious exceptions, though often unappreciated as such. Yet, compared to Freud, their leaning toward the theoretical rather than the existential is evident.

The felt need—at times the expressed need—was to find ways of fusing these two visions. Freud found a set of categories which function existentially and yet are susceptible of logically coherent systematization. He spoke existentially with the patient in crisis; he wrote theoretically about the patient as specimen and object. Yet in both contexts he was able to use the same language, the language of love and hate, parent and child.

This language was not ready-made: he had to propose a series of inspired extensions of language-use which closed the gap between the existential and the theoretical. Of all the possible notions from the cultural grab bag of physics, biology, psychology, social thought, and religion, he singled out as his major auxiliary concept that of an unconscious personal self. Increasingly of interest in European thought, this notion had never before been applied in a specific and detailed way to the linking of the "abnormal" to the "normal" in human conduct.[36] This concept was indeed a "link," a link which made possible the development of logically coherent and systematically organized propositions about human experience which were close enough to the language of subjective human experience to provide an almost effortless transition. It is true that there is no such thing as a science of self-liberation; in the relevant senses, the terms "science" and "self-liberation" belong to different modes of discourse. But in psychoanalysis Freud brought into the most intimate partnership a science of human change and the art of self-liberation. I have tried in this book to show in some detail how this is so.

Because he focused on meaning rather than mere behavior, Freud provided a relatively easy transition from the moral, religious, and esthetic encounter on the one hand to the scientific description on the other. Indeed, the transition is so "easy" that the literature is filled with failures to see that there *is* a transition, that we deal here with two quite different modes of discourse which share an elementary concept.

No wonder that the artist, the humanist, and later the theologian saw existential insight here; while at the same time and by contrast, no wonder that the physician saw a powerful medical technique and the social scientist a set of fertile theoretical conceptions. No wonder that every move in the direction of technique and scientific theory tended to alienate artists, and, in turn, every existential application, every stress on "understanding" rather than technique, logic, or mathematics, was anathema to many scientists. And no wonder, finally, that psychoanalysis persistently and systematically generated efforts in both directions.

The efforts of the facile "purifiers" and hence oversimplifiers of Freud's views, the efforts toward bringing psychoanalytic conceptions and techniques "up to date," to bring them in line with current fashions in philosophy of science or in line with a "humanistic" antiscientism—all these have failed to destroy the central vitality of psychoanalysis. The main body of psychoanalysts stayed close to the Freudian language and insight and for decades, therefore, rejected either scientific or scholarly "respectability." At times crudely, the early psychoanalysts *used* the seminal ambiguity instead of clarifying it out of existence. In their world, the logic of science and the logic of the human drama were uniquely intertwined. Living with it they knew this, though consciously they might stress one or another side of the ambiguity.[37] This knowledge was undoubtedly a source of the early psychoanalysts' courage in facing the scorn of respectable physicians and scholars.

This ambiguity in its commitment to "Reality" was—and is—a generative source of the power of psychoanalysis. The Reality of the many dimensions of life's drama and the Reality of the many dimensions of science have, when juxtaposed, generated a high-tension equilibrium which has been the basis of the psychological revolution of our age. Psychoanalysis in particular laid the basis for a *systematic* contemporary perspective on the life of the spirit. Like its great cousin-syntheses of other times and places, it infected men's minds while receiving their scorn.[38]

NOTES
(See List of Bibliographical Abbreviations, p. 343.)

1. Freud, S., "Repression," in *CP*, IV, p. 86.
2. *Ibid.*, p. 91.
3. Freud, S., *Outline*, Chap. IV.
4. Bibring, E., "Psychoanalysis and the Dynamic Psychotherapies," *JAP* 2:745–770 (1954).
5. Devereux, G., "Some Criteria for the Timing of Confrontations and Interpretations," *IJP* 32:19–24 (1951).
6. Freud, S., "Constructions in Analysis," in *CP*, V, pp. 358–371.
7. ———, "Identification," in *CPW*, XVIII, p. 105.
8. ———, *New Intro. Lec.*, p. 112.
9. ———, "The Psychoanalytic Method," in *CP*, I, p. 269.
10. ———, "Studies in Hysteria," in *CPW*, II, p. 305.
11. Wolberg, L. R., *The Technique of Psychotherapy*, Grune & Stratton, New York, 1954, pp. 441–442.
12. Freud, S., "The Unconscious," in *CPW*, XIV, p. 167.

13. ——, *Dreams,* in *CPW,* V, p. 610.
14. ——, "The Unconscious," p. 174. Italics added.
15. ——, Cf. *Dreams,* p. 617; *Ego & Id,* p. 21; *Outline,* p. 42.
16. ——, *Outline,* p. 44.
17. ——, "The Unconscious," pp. 202–203.
18. ——, *Outline,* p. 44.
19. I*bid.,* p. 106.
20. *Loc. cit.*
21. Cf. Chapter 1, Part II.
22. Freud, S., "Neurosis and Psychosis," in *CP,* II, p. 252.
23. Kubie, L. S., "Problems and Techniques of Psychoanalytic Validation and Progress," in *Psychoanalysis as Science,* Pumpian-Mindlin, E., ed., Stanford University Press, Stanford, 1952, pp. 88–89.
24. Freud, S., "The Unconscious," p. 166.
25. ——, "From the History of an Infantile Neurosis," in *CP,* III, pp. 520–534.
26. Kris, E., "Psychoanalytic Propositions," in *Psychological Theory,* Marx, M., ed., The Macmillan Co., New York, 1951, pp. 332–351.
27. Freud, S., *Origins,* Letter 69.
28. ——, "From the History of an Infantile Neurosis," p. 603.
29. Ekstein, R., "A Clinical Note on the Therapeutic Use of a Quasi-Religious Experience," *JAP 4* (1956), p. 311.
30. Cf. Stern, K., "Some Spiritual Aspects of Psychotherapy," in *Faith, Reason, and Psychiatry,* Braceland, F. J., ed., P. J. Kenedy & Sons, New York, 1955, pp. 125–140.
31. Wheelis, A., *The Quest for Identity,* W. W. Norton & Co., New York, 1958.
32. Cf. Kris, E., *Psychoanalytic Explorations in Art,* International Universities Press, New York, 1952.
33. Erikson, E. H., "The Nature of Clinical Evidence," *Daedalus* 87:69–70 (1958).
34. Freud, S., "The Future Prospects of Psychoanalytic Therapy," in *CP,* II, p. 295.

35. Fingarette, H., "Freud and the Standard World," *The Review of Metaphysics* 10:258–272 (1956).
36. Whyte, L. L., *The Unconscious Before Freud,* Basic Books, New York, 1960.
37. For a typical emphasis, cf. Fenichel, O., "Some Remarks on Freud's Place in the History of Science," in *The Collected Papers of Otto Fenichel,* Second Series, W. W. Norton & Co., New York, 1954, p. 363.
38. The analysis of "unconscious" in the first portions of this chapter is a slightly revised statement of material originally presented to the Southern California Psychiatric Society in October 1958.

CHAPTER 2

ANXIETY AND DIS-INTEGRATION:

Meaninglessness and Nonbeing

I

JUST AS INSIGHT EARLY BECAME A CENTRAL CONCEPTION IN psychoanalysis, so the concept of anxiety in turn took up a central and complementary role in the later theory. Freud said:

> The problem of anxiety is a nodal point linking up all kinds of most important questions; a riddle, of which the solution must cast a flood of light upon our whole mental life.[1]

Under a variety of names, the notion of anxiety is also at the center of the Existentialist account of human experience, and it is, in one guise or another, ubiquitous among religious techniques. In the detailed examination of self-transformation which we shall undertake in Part II, anxiety will, from various aspects, present itself as a crucial hurdle. The concept of anxiety is at the core of ego-psychology.

In this chapter, I shall attempt to bring out in a new way the nature and role of the concept of anxiety in psychoanalysis. This will in turn locate psychoanalytic theory as a whole within a large scientific and spiritual perspective. In clarifying the concept of anxiety, we shall inevitably be clarifying the concept of the ego as well. And, in the latter portions of the chapter, I shall try to show how all of this helps illuminate a problematic cluster of notions: choice, freedom, and responsibility.

We shall begin the inquiry in this chapter by noting a paradox in psychoanalytic theory. Anxiety is a "nodal point" in psychoanalysis because it is postulated to be the generic and immediate motive for all defense and sublimation.[2] Can it be, then, that anxiety is simply a specific uncomfortable feeling, one feeling among many? Is it "after all," as Freud said, "only a perception?"[3] Do we, for example, accept physical pain at times in order to avoid anxiety because the latter is simply a more "painful" feeling than physical pain? Why should this particular "feeling" be a "nodal point"?

We shall find that, although it was as a conscious perception that anxiety first called attention to itself, the conception of anxiety as "after all only a perception" or a feeling is much too simple. The truth is that, from the very beginning, the concept has been used differently—by implication—in the psychoanalytic literature. Even the early attempts at explaining the nature of anxiety were forced to turn from the clinical phenomena (the affect-anxiety) to such theoretical concepts as instinct, tension, psychic energy. Yet, as will be shown, even these theoretical conceptions were not the right ones. Or perhaps we may say more cautiously: the account of "anxiety" in terms of psychic energy is a fundamental misemphasis.

In this chapter, our first task will be to see why the primary definition of "anxiety" must be cast in terms of psychic structure rather than psychic energy or perceived affect. This kind of definition differs significantly, with one possible exception,[4] from the explicit definitions offered by all parties to the controversies in the psychoanalytic literature about anxiety. Nevertheless, I shall try to show that this structural definition expresses neatly and simply the practical usage of psychoanalysts, the relevant data, and the considerations adduced in theoretical discussions of the nature of anxiety. At least equally important, though less amenable to demonstration, this structural view of anxiety is congenial to the genius of psychoanalytic theory.

I hold that anxiety is the other face of ego. It is not primarily an affect, one among many affects, which the ego must master; rather it *is* ego-disintegration. This thesis expresses explicitly the real point of the psychoanalytic theory of anxiety from Freud's earliest writings to the present. Let us see how and why this is so before considering the central bearing of anxiety on the life of the spirit.

II

KUBIE IN RECENT TIMES CORRECTLY SPEAKS OF THE "SIMPLE, conscious experience" of "uneasy apprehensiveness" as the "primary descriptive sense" of the term "anxiety."[5] He then proposes that

> . . . the use of the term anxiety should again be restricted to its original meaning to characterize the conscious psychic state with which we are all familiar.[6]

For us, however, the key question is whether the "primary *descriptive*" sense should be taken as the primary *theoretical* sense.

Kubie is clearly fighting against a tendency, but it is a *sub rosa* tendency. For, officially, psychoanalysts have continued to agree with Freud's view that "anxiety is an affective state. . . ."[7] Anxiety, said Freud, is "in the first place something that is felt."[8] And, in a major unifying and summarizing paper quite representative of contemporary psychoanalytic thinking in this particular respect, Rangell in 1955 still stresses that we must keep in mind "(a) anxiety as an affect and (b) its seat in the ego." [9] This current view has its roots in the earliest history of psychoanalysis.

Freud early spoke of anxiety as transformed libido. In his first psychoanalytic papers he referred to "a quantum of anxiety" [10] and to anxiety as "somatic sexual excitation (deflected) from the psychical field." [11] This was the economic (energy-quantity) aspect of the matter.

As we have already noted, he also emphasized the affect or perceptual nature of anxiety in his frequent descriptions of it as "anxious expectation," [12] "chronic apprehensiveness," [13] and as the "feeling of anxiety alone." [14] Presumably the economic aspect of the matter was a theoretical explanation of the occurrence of the affect-perception, the anxiety proper.

What is important for our purposes, however, is that the *point* of his discussions was not simply to explain anxiety but to *use* the concept implicitly in a new way, as itself a theoretical and explanatory concept, not a descriptive one. What he wanted to stress was that

> . . . almost every accompanying symptom can alone constitute the (anxiety) attack just as well as the anxiety itself can. There are consequently *rudimentary anxiety-attacks and equivalents of an anxiety-attack* (all probably having the same meaning). . . . [15] [Italics in original]

In short, although Freud was first struck by the specific clinical symptom of apprehensiveness, he soon was thinking fundamentally (though not too clearly or explicitly) in terms of a single *hypothetical process*. This process, he said, provides "the same meaning" for a wide variety of symptoms— feelings, thoughts, motor disturbances, paraesthesias, and physiological disequilibria. What was this "same meaning"? Anxiety, of course. But in what sense? For "anxiety" could no longer refer to the conscious apprehensiveness, this now being only one among a number of "equivalents."

In order to answer this question, let us see how the ego and its early analogues are introduced. Freud asks in his early paper on anxiety neurosis [16] why the "nervous system" takes on the particular affect of anxiety. His answer was that anxiety develops when the psyche feels that it cannot deal adequately with a dangerous task it faces. When the danger is internal, the anxiety neurosis develops. That is, from the very outset Freud saw that the transformation of energy from libido to anxiety was inherently connected with the overwhelming of the controlling "nervous structure"—the overwhelming of what he would later call the ego.

Freud continues to speak of anxiety as coming about through the "direct transformation of libido," [17] but when we ask why this occurs, we are told that

a given quantity of libido has become *unusable,* whether on account of the infantile weakness of the ego, as in the case of children's phobias, or on account of somatic processes in sexual life, as in the case of the anxiety neurosis, or on account of repression, as in the case of hysteria.[18] [Italics added]

And in the same context he allows that the unusable drive which is so transformed may be either libido *or aggression,* i.e., either of the two principal instincts.[19] Thus, at least with regard to traumatic anxiety, Freud's position came finally to this: whenever, *for any reason,* drive energy of *any* sort is "unusable" by the ego, then and there anxiety occurs. In more usual terminology: anxiety occurs whenever the ego is unable to master drive energies pressing for discharge. The point is always that the ego fails in its integrating function; but the explicit definitions always show us the matter through the wrong conceptual lens, those of instinct discharge and affect perception.

A recent statement of Greenson's provides a typical and succinct contemporary example of *almost* making the point:

> Panic anxiety is a state of psychic helplessness. In this state there seems to be a loss of internal object cathexis as well as the loss of cathexis of the external object. As this happens, there seems to occur a loss of ego functions.[20]

But loss of ego function is not a *result* of loss of cathexes; the latter is simply an *aspect* of the ego-function loss. For ego functioning consists precisely in the cathecting of internal or external objects, i.e., in organizing the discharge of instincts upon objects.

It is time to look at the problem more systematically from the standpoint of the ego and its essential nature.

What is the chief, the defining function of that which we call ego? The ego is ordinarily spoken of as the mental system which perceives, judges, synthesizes, and executes.[21] It is, especially as used in the context of this discussion, the set of highest order psychic organizing functions of the human being, Waelder's "human ego." [22] The ego by definition is the set of powers which organizes the discharge of inner-generated drive in such a way as to take account of "external reality" and in such a style as tends to maintain reasonable long-term integrity of the person as autonomous agent.

To postulate the existence of ego is to postulate that these powers do exist in the normal human being, that they do *function*. Where, as in the case of neonates, there is energy but little or no use of it in a psychically organized way, there is no ego and no experience. Ego is the name of these integrating functions, not a mysterious entity which "performs" them.

We can properly ask, "How account for the coming into existence of psychic organizing tendencies (i.e., of ego)?"

But it would be an empty question to ask, "How account for the fact that the ego, once in being, tends to organize the psyche?" The former question is one of ontogenesis, of physics, biology, psychology, and sociology. The latter question amounts to asking in the trivial sense, "How comes it that the ego *is* the ego?"

The assumption that there is just such a drive toward integration, and that it is *autonomous,* was implicit in Freud's early views. He spoke of the "secondary process" (here, roughly, the ego) acting to bind excitations "independently of [the pleasure principle] and to some extent in disregard of it." [23] His later explicit remarks about the ego's primary autonomy [24] and its use of neutralized or desexualized energy [25] have been developed with great impact in the writings of Hartmann, Kris, and Loewenstein.[26, 27] The latter authors have developed the concept of an autonomous ego apparatus to the point of suggesting that it emerges correlatively with the id rather than as an effect of it, both having emerged out of an original undifferentiated state. Hendrick's thesis concerning the "instinct to master" [28] is also pertinent though less satisfactorily formulated. Hendrick argues that there is a primary drive whose direct gratification consists in achieving integration of ego functions and concomitant mastery of environment. Assumptions of these kinds enable us profitably to bypass "obscure and speculative" general questions about more indirect psychic energy sources for the production of anxiety and defense.[29] The energies involved may be any psychic energies which are, in a particular situation, unmastered by the ego. Even more fundamentally, the energy of the ego, so far as its primary autonomy is concerned, is postulated as a psychological "given": "Much evidence and much thinking on this subject point to the idea of an innate, phylogenetically determined pool of such defensive affective energy. . . ." [30]

With this review of the contemporary conception of the

ego, we are now prepared to turn back to considering anxiety itself. Since we know that anxiety is a uniquely provocative threat to or even disruption of the ego, we must now consider what the nature of this threat is.

The denial of food is a threat, but a quite specific one. It is just the sort of well-defined frustration of a goal-oriented action pattern which the ego is normally fitted to master. Rather than a threat, it is a stimulus to normal ego-functioning. So it is with many other frustrations: they are specific and of a kind the ego is prepared to master. But there are threats which go beyond this. They may be threats to specific needs, such as hunger, which have in particular cases become so massive that the over-all integrity of psychic functioning begins to be affected. For example, starvation eventually disrupts not only food-seeking behavior but also the total pattern of relationships to men, to the physical environment, and to oneself. It forces major reconstruction of goals and acts. The synthetic functions of the ego are then themselves undermined psychologically and physiologically. Threats to the ego may be of other kinds, such as those resulting from the concurrent evocation of two or more major modes of functioning of the person which are incompatible, e.g., a father figure evokes aggressive impulses. Intraego conflict involving major ego-segments threatens the highest level integrity of synthetic ego-function.

In short, the threats which produce anxiety are the threats which tend to disrupt central ego integrity; [31] they are not threats to highly specific and relatively autonomous systems of desire or planned action. The ego is like the soldier's weapon: with it, he does not eliminate struggle, he is equipped for struggle; but without a well-functioning weapon, he is simply helpless.

There is no reason to hesitate taking the last small step. Anxiety, the peculiarly central threat to the ego, *is* ego-disorganization. More precisely: where fundamental ego integrity is in process of becoming dis-integrated relative to a prior state of organization, we refer to the ego-disorganization as anxiety. The context of these processes is set by the psychological *sine qua non:* the tendency toward psychic organization. Where it operates successfully we speak of ego; where it is threatened with central failure, we speak of anxiety. Ego and anxiety are the opposite faces of the same coin.

The remarkably pervasive correlation between ego and anxiety is, then, not an empirical relationship but a logical one, although, of course, the complex of concepts in question has profoundly important empirical reference. Thus "anxiety" in its primary sense is to be defined as a theoretical and not as an observational concept. As theoretical, it is to be defined in structural, not economic terms. As such it is defined in terms of ego, not as causally related to ego.

This conception fits neatly into the body of psychoanalytic theory. For example, we can now account very simply for the fact that the form of anxiety occurring in a particular situation is specific to the type of ego-integrity which is affected. For example, during the period when the primary ego orientation is phallic, significant disorganization of the ego (or incipient movement in this direction) is called "castration anxiety." Likewise, when the ego is predominantly oriented around the relationship to the sustaining mother, threats to the integrity of the ego are experienced as "separation anxiety." Thus, as the individual moves through the crucial phases of life which challenge him to new self-integrations, there is always and inevitably the other aspect of this movement—the partial, temporary, or complete failures of the new and dominant pattern of integration of the self. When this happens, the frequent and easy first adjustments consist in falling back to former well-learned patterns of integrated functioning: regression to former fixations.

Although we have not distinguished the two as yet, it is not difficult to show how trauma anxiety and signal anxiety fit into our conceptual system. Let us begin by recalling that Freud, when he introduced his conception of signal anxiety in addition to trauma anxiety, still ambiguously yoked together conscious affect and hypothetical psychic process. Once again, the explicit primacy remained with the affect. In the new view,

> the function of anxiety [is] as a signal indicating the presence of a danger situation. . . .[32] The question of the stuff out of which anxiety is made loses interest for us. . . .[33]

> It is not the repression that creates the anxiety, but the anxiety is there first and creates the repression! [34]

Essentially, according to Freud's new analysis of anxiety, the individual "experimentally" acts out the course of action with "small quantities of energy"—this constitutes "normal thinking." [35] When a danger situation establishes itself, the ego, in its imaginative or fantasy rehearsing of the course of action, sees the danger and produces a small amount of the anxiety. The resultant small amount of displeasure produced thereby acts, like a kind of self-inoculation, as a stimulus to the ego to defend itself against that painful course of action in reality.[36]

There is no difficulty in translating this into the terms of the view that anxiety is ego-disorganization. We make the simplest assumption: signal anxiety and trauma anxiety differ only in degree. Where the threat to the ego is incipient, only just beginning to make itself felt, there is signal anxiety. Where the disintegrative process goes farther toward prompt, massive, and diffuse discharge, we are on the road to trauma anxiety. This provides a unity of theory which coincides with efforts by Rangell and others toward a unitary psychoanalytic theory of anxiety.

It is illuminating to review in this context the controversy over whether signal anxiety is, as Freud said, "produced" by the ego "on its own initiative"[37] or whether, as Schur,[38] Rangell,[39] and others have said, it is passively "experienced" by the ego. Freud's conception coincides with the fact that signal anxiety is indeed "produced" by the ego in the sense that anxiety is by definition an aspect of ego functioning. Schur and Rangell have argued that anxiety is "experienced by" the ego because they have seen the other and equally correct way of describing the very same facts: in an important sense, anxiety occurs *in spite of* the ego's organizing tendencies. To say the ego "produces" anxiety is much like saying "the man stumbles over the rock"; to say the ego "experiences" anxiety corresponds to "the man is tripped by the rock." The question of the passivity or activity of the ego in anxiety is thus not a matter of differences in the facts but in the angle from which we observe the same set of facts.

Fenichel stated the matter soon after Freud's book on anxiety:

> There is no absolute distinction between "anxiety in the traumatic state" and "anxiety signal." They are connected together in the first instance by the fact that the anxiety which is actively developed by the ego as a signal obviously arises because the ego's insight into the presence of danger establishes in the id, or rather, in the somatic apparatus, the same conditions which obtain in the traumatic state, except that they are less in degree.[40]

Fenichel here neatly combines the two views about signal anxiety and shows how "producing" and "automatically experiencing" anxiety are two ways of putting the one process. His point of view is substantially that later argued at length and very effectively by Schur. Furthermore, it is essentially the point of view being argued in this chapter. It leads to the corollary that the process may fail as an adaptive one because, as Fenichel says,

> . . . in the presence of dammed-up libido, the acute signal often has the same effect as a match in a barrel of gunpowder . . . the ego, in giving a signal, has set off something which . . . it can no longer control.[41]

We must now turn explicitly to a central point which has never officially been cleared up in psychoanalytic theory: the problem of "unconscious anxiety" and related concepts. Freud himself felt, but did not face, this problem. He wrote in various places about "unconscious anxiety," [42] "unconscious guilt," [43] and unconscious affects, but always with uneasy reservations or parenthetical qualifications.[44] He urged that we avoid speaking of such things as unconscious guilt and anxiety "if we want to have a cleaner conscience psychologically." [45] Although constantly insisting that affects are conscious phenomena by definition, and insisting that anxiety is, in the first instance, an affect, Freud still found himself "forced" to talk about unconscious anxiety. Why?

His resort to *ad hoc* phrases when he wanted to be ultra-careful in his language is illustrated in the following more complete quotation of the remarks cited previously. Here we see how Freud, in spite of his formal definitions, was in fact moved by an unexpressed conception of anxiety as a hypothesized process "hidden behind" the symptoms.

> Somewhere or other there is always anxiety hidden behind all symptoms; at one moment, however, it sweeps into consciousness, drowning everything else with its clamour, and at the next it secrets itself so completely that we are forced to speak of unconscious anxiety—or if we want to have a cleaner conscience psychologically, since anxiety is after all only a perception—of possibilities of anxiety.[46]

Thus the emphasis on the perceived affect leads Freud to postulate that present real symptoms are often caused not by actualities but by "possibilities"—i.e., by nonexistents!

If we insist upon current causes for current effects, then we must interpret him to mean that, although the anxiety-affect does not exist, some other, present but nonperceived condition exists and that the latter is a cause of the symptoms.

The "possibility" of affect-anxiety is no more nor less than the current metapsychological condition of ego-disintegration. And what about the actual occurrence of the *affects* of guilt and anxiety? The answer is now clear. The metapsychological condition of ego-disintegration, upon certain occasions, produces a characteristic affect—what is usually called free anxiety. When the ego manages to bind the energy in a set of partial integrations, we have the isolated response complexes called symptoms. Guilt as a "form" of anxiety consists in the "criticism" of the ego by the superego, a *metapsychological* condition involving a shift from libidinal toward aggressive and hence disintegrative cathexes of ego by superego. This, in certain circumstances, is capable of evoking the conscious affect we know introspectively as guilt.

The definition of anxiety I propose here does not take refuge in apologetic "manners of speaking" or in postulating nonexistent but "possible" affects as universal motives for defense. Nor does it reach for *ad hoc* concepts such as Schur's "awareness of danger": a "thought process" which "belongs genetically to the affect of anxiety."[47] Instead I propose in effect to make explicit the usage we are in fact "forced" to, the usage which is natural.

I propose, in summary, to use the terms "anxiety" (or "structural anxiety") for the metapsychological process of ego-disintegration. "Anxiety-affect," "free-anxiety," or "anxiety feelings" will be used for the characteristic affect sometimes produced by anxiety. The same terminology, *mutatis mutandis,* should be used for guilt and other forms of anxiety. The phrase "unconscious anxiety" and its analogues then are legitimate ways of referring to structural anxiety when the conscious representations of this state of impending helplessness are repressed. This terminology is in fact that used in practice, although, as we have seen, its theoretical foundations are shaky so long as anxiety is considered to be, in its essence, an affect.

This way of speaking also makes the concept of anxiety "equivalents" entirely rational and clear: they are observable responses, other than anxiety-affect, which are evoked by (structural) anxiety. It now also becomes clear how guilt, shame, and other affects can be "forms" of anxiety. When these are thought of as affects, their nature as "forms of anxiety" is obscure: In what way can *different* conscious qualities at the same time be forms of the *same* quality? This vagueness is removed when we see that guilt-affect is not a form of anxiety-affect; it is quite a different affect qualitatively, but it is produced by a specific form of structural anxiety. We can properly speak of "forms of" anxiety now. The conception of disintegration refers not to a quality perceived but to a highly general, recurrent aspect of a variety of different complex processes.

The response to the various forms of anxiety-*affects* is a secondary, though in practice an important, response. It must be distinguished from the primary response to the structural anxiety. Anxiety-affect often produces the familiar vicious build-up of (structural) anxiety: the anxiety-affect perception itself tends to disrupt ego structure and hence ego discharge mastery. This additional structural disruption generates even more affect, which in turn produces further ego-disruption. Thus anxiety-*affect* is one specific cause among the many causes of *structural* anxiety.

Recent papers on the general theory of affects (e.g., Rapaport,[48] Jacobson[49]) have stressed the structural aspect of anxiety. Rapaport writes of a "hierarchy of motives" which bind and control drive discharges, the specific quality of the affect being determined by the specific character of the binding structures whose thresholds have been reached. This is consistent with the position taken here. While even more elaborate in some ways, the exposition by Rapaport fails to state clearly that this position implies that anxiety-affects are no longer central dynamic features in psychoanalytic theory. Inferred structure and process are now the primary referents of terms which had their historical origins as descriptive, affect terms.

Meltzer[50] has recently attempted to provide a structural conception of anxiety. This is the only such explicit psychoanalytic attempt to my knowledge. What Meltzer says explicitly is that anxiety is a concept having primarily structural reference. But he still is unable to bring himself to dispense with the official notion that anxiety is primarily an affect. He therefore erects in a verbalistic way a complex "anxiety system," a "structure" which is postulated to respond to ego prediction-failures by producing anxiety-affect and thus to "account" for the ego's attempts at reparation of its synthesizing power. This is surely a long way round and succeeds only in introducing a verbalistic scheme having no empirical reference other than that of producing anxiety-affect as a stimulus to the ego, the very notion with which we started. Conceptual economy calls for the usual assumption of the primary autonomy of the ego, of integrating powers which are moved to action by the presence of disintegration and not by some additional affect, system, or other single-function *ad hoc* device.

Of course there is an affective or at least an instinctual aspect to the occurrence of anxiety. Yet we need not suppose that anxiety must be defined in these terms. After all, there are dynamic, instinctual, structural, genetic, topographical, and economic dimensions to *every* psychological process. These are abstract aspects of the concrete process, the process itself being neither simply dynamic nor simply genetic nor simply anything else. We need not be surprised that formulations of the concept "anxiety" in terms of instinctual energy have been plausible and have had a foundation in fact. But not all true statements about a situation are necessarily equally useful in theory-building or clinical suggestiveness. We well know the problem in psychotherapy of deciding which of the many known dimensions of a situation it is appropriate to focus upon at a particular moment. There is an analogous problem of theoretic relevance. In spite of the historical origins of the affect and drive perspectives on anxiety and of their correctness, we are justified in asking whether these are the most useful perspectives for contemporary theory-building.

Before going further, I shall summarize this critique and clarification of the concepts of anxiety and of the ego. Ego-disorganization in the context of the autonomous and generally dominant drive toward integration—this is anxiety in the ego. It is the fundamental condition inciting the ego to new forms of response, either regressive or creative. Although "anxiety" historically preceded "ego" in psychoanalysis, the psychoanalytic concept of anxiety has always been, in its distinctive sense, a logical elaboration of the concept of ego and of the implicit forerunners of the latter concept.

If we now add the gist of Chapter 1, we can say, in summary, that ego is the autonomous drive toward meaning, plus the secondary, learned elaborations of this drive. Anxiety is meaninglessness.

III

WE ARE NOW IN A POSITION TO NOTE, AT LEAST BRIEFLY, HOW the development of a clear and explicit theoretical concept of anxiety enables us to mesh psychoanalytic conceptions with the broader fabric of biologically oriented approaches, with other dynamic psychologies, and with philosophic trends in contemporary thought.

Selye,[51] who has worked primarily on the biological level, and psychoanalysts such as Menninger[52] have been trying to generalize the biological concepts of homeostasis and stress in such a way as to unify both the psychic and biological. Such attempts fit perfectly with the view that the ego is a system of functions oriented toward integrating experience. For ego-integration may plausibly be considered a form of homeostasis; or rather sufficiently similar in some significant formal sense to physiological homeostasis so that some very generalized concept of homeostasis could serve as a unifying principle for both. The distinctive character of ego-integration (the drive toward meaning) as compared to physiological homeostasis has, in effect, been discussed in Chapter 1.

Thus the newer biologically oriented theories tie in directly with classical psychoanalytic theory. The complementary concepts of homeostasis and stress have their psychological analogues in the concepts of ego and anxiety. "Ego" and "anxiety" demarcate the psychic aspects, respectively, of general homeostasis and stress, while biological homeostasis and stress are seen as other specific aspects of the total homeostatic-stress system. Ego-disintegration (i.e., psychic stress, anxiety) may be either a concomitant, or a consequence, or a forerunner of biological stress. Or, to put the matter more precisely: the person suffers stress, and we may place emphasis for diagnostic or therapeutic purposes on biological, psychological, and social conceptions in any appropriate combinations and relative emphases which the situation and our general experience may indicate. Or, if our orientation to the situation is existential, the orientation of the subject rather than that of the observer of a person as object, then we, as I shall soon indicate, use quite a different sort of language and gesture. But, when we are acting as scientists, we choose an angle of attack now broadly based on empirical grounds, not a priori metaphysical ones. The structural conception of anxiety, while more clearly integrated into psychoanalytic theory than the affect-energy concept, at the same time helps integrate psychoanalytic theory itself into a highly general biological, psychological, and social framework of inquiry and therapy.

If we move outside psychoanalytic psychology proper to what are in a broader sense "psychodynamic" ways of thinking, we find that in terms of the structural conception, there is a remarkable amount of agreement on the issue of anxiety. Considering the rampant theoretical disagreements in psychiatry, such a consensus is particularly striking. The notion is almost universal that anxiety has fundamental relevance for self-integrity. Rollo May's book on anxiety saves us the need to provide a general review, but a few "refresher" remarks will help to establish the point in terms of the themes presented here. Rollo May speaks of anxiety as the experience of fundamental "threat to some value which the individual holds essential to his existence as a personality." [53] This is in accord with the view that anxiety is a threat to the integrity of the ego, since the ego is defined in psychoanalytic theory as the integrator of the psychic self.

Sullivan's remarks are consistent with the formulation of anxiety as a generic concept referring to the failure of ego-integration. He says:

> It is evident that anxiety generically tends to interfere with the integration of the interpersonal situation necessary for the satisfaction of a need, and that if anxiety appears at any time in the course of a situation toward resolution, it will tend to disintegrate any such situation. [54]

If you think of this direction of activity toward a goal, which is implied by the tension of need, then you can think of anxiety as exactly, that is, at 180 degrees, opposed to the vector quality of the need.[55]

Although Horney's treatment of anxiety, like Sullivan's, is developed in quite different ways from the Freudian psychoanalytic one, there remains a central feature which is shared. Anxiety, for Horney, is a generalized sense of helplessness, a sense that the fundamental powers to resolve "contradictory tendencies"[56] are lost. Anxiety along with the defenses against it constitute the "one essential factor common to all neuroses. . . ."[57] (Although she speaks of this "basic anxiety" as a "feeling," she manifests the typical ambiguity here since she adds that "there is rarely an awareness . . ." of it in its true weight.[58] Thus, once again we meet the failure to distinguish between anxiety as an affect and as a theoretical entity.)

Horney distinguishes between "normal" anxiety or helplessness and the neurotic kind of anxiety. The distinction is central to her view of human nature, and it points directly to the view of anxiety which I have been presenting. With regard to the two types of helplessness, she says,

Perhaps the differences are to be accounted for by the fact that the healthy person made the bulk of his unfortunate experiences at an age when he could integrate them, while the neurotic person made them at an age when he could not master them, and as a consequence of his helplessness reacted to them with anxiety.[59]

In short—I would translate—anxiety involves in its essence the breakdown of the inner integrity. Where the ego is systematically ineffective in a normal environment, there is "neurotic anxiety"; where the ego falters before the universal fate of man—illness, catastrophe, death—the anxiety is "normal."

Jung's central thesis in connection with the dynamics of neurosis revolves around just the same issue of the integration of psychic energy discharged. He constantly emphasizes as central

that inner disunity so characteristic of a neurosis . . . psychic energy flows off in every conceivable direction, apparently quite uselessly.[60]

The theme of "integration" runs through all Jung's works, and the integration in question is always the over-all, psychic unity of the whole person, precisely that unity which, in psychoanalytic theory, is conceptualized as a function of the ego. Although Jung does not use the word "anxiety" often, and although the descriptions of the psychic elements which need to be integrated frequently differ from those emphasized by Freud, there remains a common thesis: neurosis is a failure of the tendencies toward psychic integration in the person. The characteristic signs of this failure, no one of which is inevitable, are anxiety-affect, somatic anxiety "equivalents," and, eventually, defensive attitudes and actions which preserve a degree of integrity at the expense of over-all integrity.

Rather than pursue this remarkable parallelism among the divergent "schools" of psychotherapy, I will cite a summary statement of Fromm-Reichman's:

In going over the literature on anxiety in children and adults, from M. Klein, Sharpe and Spitz, to Ferenczi and Rank, Freud, Rado, and Sullivan, Fromm, Horney and Silverberg, it seems that the feeling of powerlessness, of helplessness in the presence of inner dangers, which the individual cannot control, constitutes in the last analysis the common background of all further elaborations on the theory of anxiety.[61]

We need only add that this inability to control inner dangers is, by general acknowledgment, not necessarily a "feeling" but an inferred psychic state which only at times evokes the specific feeling. Then unanimity as to the central character of anxiety is indeed striking. Likewise is the tenacity with which so many writers cling to the terminology of "feeling" when all their data, theory, and usage cry for a theoretical concept pointing to hypothetical psychic states. The significance of this persistent confusion of phenomenal data and theoretical concepts emerges when we recall that seminal ambiguity which was discussed in Chapter 1. For the existential dimension of psychotherapy provides a perspective from which we want to talk of the *experience* of anxiety as central. And the more the writer is concerned in fact with this dimension, the more he will cast his views in experiential terms rather than theoretical. But, committed as most psychotherapists (in this country) are to science, too, they also introduce usages which imply theoretical notions and hypothetical processes.

IV

THE ESTABLISHMENT OF THE CONCEPT OF ANXIETY AS A theoretical concept also puts the psychoanalytic theory of personality in direct communication with contemporary Existentialism. This is not to say that the psychoanalyst is thereby committed to the views of any particular "Existentialist"; it is rather that communication on the issues is possible in a new and more systematic way.

The existentialist commentary is an expression, the linguistic aspect of man's response in the world, not a scientific statement *about* his response. As I shall have occasion to argue at length in later chapters, what is vital in the existentialist language is its "pragmatic" point, its impact as "spiritual therapy," not its content as theoretical doctrine. And the point of contemporary existentialism is precisely to help us escape our obsession with doctrines *about* the world in order that we may concentrate on discriminating and responsible action *in* the world.

In some existentialist writings there is an emphasis upon the mythic. This is generally true of the religious existentialists such as Tillich and of literary existentialists such as Sartre and Camus. However, the existentialist does not necessarily use mythic language. The existentialist may use a literary or quasi-psychological language, as do Sartre and Camus when they speak of "nausea" or of the "absurd." Or the existentialist may use what are traditionally thought of as metaphysical terminologies. For example, Heidegger does this, though it is essential to note that, as he himself stresses, he is not doing metaphysics. He is talking to metaphysicians and using their language but in a "therapeutic" way which he hopes will lead them to a radically new way of grasping the world, a nonmetaphysical way. He wishes to "overcome" metaphysics and the "representational thinking of metaphysics," to evoke the "unconcealedness of Being." [62]

For purposes of discussion of these trends, I shall consider some of Tillich's formulations. I propose a little "experiment." The reader is invited to peruse the following words of Paul Tillich. They are stated in his more "metaphysical" rather than his mythic or theological vein. Read them first as they stand.

> Nonbeing is dependent on the being it negates. . . . There could be no negation if there were no preceding affirmation to be negated. . . . Secondly, nonbeing is dependent on the special qualities of being. In itself nonbeing has no quality and no difference of qualities. But it gets them in relation to being. The character of the negation of being is determined by that in being which is negated. This makes it possible to speak of qualities of nonbeing and, consequently, of types of anxiety. [63]

In the following, the statement by Tillich quoted above is reproduced except that the nouns "nonbeing" and "negation" are replaced by the noun "anxiety"; the terms "being" and "affirmation" are replaced by "ego-functions" or "ego."

> Anxiety is dependent on the ego-functions it negates. . . . There could be no anxiety if there were no preceding ego-functioning to be negated. . . . Anxiety is dependent on the special qualities of the ego. In itself anxiety has no quality and no difference of qualities. But it gets them in relation to the ego. The character of the anxiety of the ego is determined by that in the ego which is negated. This makes it possible to speak of qualities of anxiety and, consequently, of types of anxiety.

This statement by Tillich reads as a perfect parallel to the discussion of anxiety in the psychoanalytic sense as proposed in the present chapter. By way of anticipation of later discussions, we might add another parallel: Lao-tse's assertion that "Being and Non-Being are born together." [64]

Having indicated the parallelism, we cannot avoid raising the question which Tillich and other existentialist writers raise: How do we distinguish "pathological" or "neurotic" anxiety, psychological anxiety in general, and "ontological" anxiety (nonbeing, nothingness, etc.)? This question has become of increasing importance to the psychotherapist, to the philosopher, and to the spiritual counselor. To find the dividing line between the "psychological" and the "spiritual" —if there is a line—to recognize this line and respect it, these have become troublesome problems indeed. In informal talk and in practice one today finds a full range of opinions. At one extreme: all "these" problems are technical problems of psychotherapy. At the other extreme: all proper psychotherapy is an existential encounter between two persons. The in-between area is amply populated with opinions urging one or another degree of autonomy for the psychological and spiritual.

Tillich holds that when he speaks of anxiety in the existential sense it is different from "pathological" anxiety as this is understood by the various psychoanalytic and quasi-psychoanalytic theories. Tillich, in effect, denies the parallelism which I have been asserting to hold between the existentialist and the psychoanalytic conceptions of anxiety. Instead he sees a kind of genus-species relationship.

"Pathological anxiety," says Tillich, "is a state of existential anxiety under special conditions." [65] We shall understand this better if we see how he contrasts neurotic reactions with what he calls "courage."

> Courage does not remove anxiety. Since anxiety is existential, it cannot be removed. But courage takes the anxiety of nonbeing into itself. . . . He who does not succeed in taking his anxiety courageously upon himself can succeed in avoiding the extreme situation of despair by escaping into neurosis. He still affirms himself but on a limited scale. *Neurosis is the way of avoiding nonbeing by avoiding being.* In the neurotic state . . . the self which is affirmed is a reduced one.[66] [Italics in original]

Tillich appears to be making a distinction which is analogous to the psychological distinction between the sublimative, drive-neutralizing, mature response and the pathologically regressive response to anxiety. In the defensive response, the breakdown of ego functions (anxiety) is met with a denial of or a surrendering of some portion of those ego powers. Always surrendered to some extent is the sovereignty of the synthetic powers of the ego. Such surrender always involves the abandonment of a portion of reality and, in the neurotic, a repression and distortion of inner impulse through the symptom compromise. It tends to increase automatic, involuntary response. Such more or less radical devices protect (at least temporarily) the remainder of the ego. The anxiety, and the ego-aims which generate it, are thrust out of the autonomous self. This follows the principle:

> And if thy right eye offend thee
> pluck it out, and cast it from thee:
> for it is profitable for thee that
> one of thy members should perish, and
> not that thy whole body should be
> cast into hell.[67]

In the alternative case, the disintegration of ego functions is met with reparative efforts. The person grapples with the reality situation. There are modifications but not amputations of the internal structures of the ego in the area of malfunction. When successful, this eventuates in a realistic solution. If the reality situation allows, this is a healing reorganization; it amplifies and reunifies the formerly threatened ego. Thus we see that anxiety is "taken up into the self" and resolved to whatever extent possible, endured to the extent that it must be endured for the sake of maintaining the growth of ego-powers and the orientation to reality. In the neurotic case, however, anxiety is avoided by "avoiding being," i.e., by surrendering that portion of the reality-oriented ego which has begun to disintegrate.

The concept "neurotic anxiety" is a misemphasis. The adjective "neurotic" more appropriately refers to the *ego's response to anxiety*, not to the anxiety. Ego-disorganization per se (anxiety) is neither neurotic nor creative. It is simply the condition to which the ego responds, and it is the nature of the response which is critical with regard to pathology, health, and creativity.

It is true that anxiety is often called neurotic not in view of the prospective ego response but in the light of the genesis of the anxiety. We say it is neurotic anxiety because it is a tension generated by a prior neurotic ego-maneuver.

When the ego's response to a new environmental stress is neurotic, then we are likely to find we have "frozen" a specific form of anxiety (ego-disintegration) into the psychic structure. Thus the compulsive person is permanently beset by the ego-fragmentation he has found he can bear and had settled for in a crisis. He meets constantly and repetitively a stereotyped anxiety. In terms of the ego-maneuver which was its *genesis,* this is neurotic anxiety. The adjective "neurotic" therefore still has primary reference to the ego response, not to the anxiety per se.[68]

There is no genus-species distinction between neurotic anxiety and ontological or existential anxiety. There is anxiety, and there are the ways we face it and respond to it, and the latter may be analyzed in terms of a variety of dimensions of experience and modes of language use. "Anxiety" may be taken into the existentialist vocabulary or into the psychoanalytic one. When anxiety is taken up in the context of psychological language and theory, it is "psychological" anxiety. When it is taken up in the context of existentialist languages, it is "existential" anxiety. When the response is evasive, we speak, according to our orientation and conceptual scheme, either of psychological defense or of lack of spiritual courage, of the "inauthentic." Where the response is reparative, expansive, realistic, there we speak either in psychological terms (sublimation, realism, maturity) or in existential terms (authenticity, courage).

All this is by no means a merely verbal difference. These different sets of terms enmesh us in different webs of meaning which lead to contrasting styles of thought, ranges of inquiry, modes of response. There is no special mystery here. We know, for example, that though the term "person" may be used in a particular situation by a physician, an anthropologist, or a moralist, the subsequent direction that thought and action take may differ radically depending on which of these perspectives is adopted when using that term.

There are certain crucial confusions to avoid. One, as we have noted, is to suppose that the psychological is a species of the existential,[69] a narrow domain "within it." Another confusion is to suppose that the psychological and the existential are competing alternatives of the same type, one "truer," or "better," or more "real" than the other as judged by the same criteria.[70] In place of these confusions, we must recognize that we are in truth dealing with two different meaning systems, two incommensurable domains, two different perspectives on the human situation. Yet these two both anchor certain key concepts in roughly the same area of experience; and "anxiety" is such a concept.

There is but brief space to remind ourselves now that the oversimple scheme used in terms of which I have argued and illustrated my thesis requires eventual correction. It is essential to make explicit that there are not merely two different perspectives but many. The emphasis on what existentialist languages share should not blind us to the variety of languages within "Existentialism." These languages are no more synonymous with one another than are the various psychological theories synonymous one with another. There is overlapping in places, and in other places there are parallels. But the variety of structure and content is sufficient to require us to think eventually in terms of a whole web of partially overlapping languages.

Surely, however, one of the most remarkable "nodal points" in the contemporary perspective on personality is that one we point to by means of the notion of anxiety. Through the range of languages and orientations, from the biological to the theological, it is central. I have tried to indicate how the psychoanalytic conception ties in directly with the others. This, I believe, provides a more rational basis for psychoanalytic discussion of these other views as well as of problems within psychoanalytic theory. For "anxiety" is a major bridge concept by means of which we can cross over from one orientation to another. This we shall often do in Part II. But we must now turn to a more specific problem and apply our reanalysis of anxiety in depth.

V

CLOSE TO THE HEART OF EXISTENTIALIST THOUGHT IS THE conception of existential choice. This conception embodies the paradoxical thesis that arbitrary choice, "unconditioned" choice, can be the profoundest kind of responsible, "authentic" choice. Although I shall discuss in Chapter 4 the problem of responsibility in the context of therapy, the analysis of anxiety opens up a special and fundamental perspective on the problem. Specifically, the preceding analysis of anxiety can illuminate the vital paradox of the existential choice, i.e., of the arbitrary as the ground of responsibility.

To say that a choice has been made without having been decisively settled by automatic application of any rule, set of rules, or other routinelike deciding device is to say that there is no completely decisive justification of that specific choice. There is an element—a crucial and essential element—of arbitrariness in such choices. On the other hand, if there is no such nonregular aspect to the selection, if the decision flows directly and rigorously from some already accepted rule or method, then the selection being entirely nonarbitrary is of a crucially different kind than the other. Indeed, where principles or customs which are decisive exist and where, therefore, one only executes what was already called for by custom or principle, one ought to put the word "choice" in quotation marks, for it is in such cases that we may also say, "I really have no choice in the matter." But where the choice is not decisively established by rule, custom, or method, where there is the ineradicable element of arbitrariness, where we must, in short, *initiate* a commitment, there the choice may be existential. It is the existential choice which is here of interest, for it is in existential choice that man is most profoundly a person rather than an instrument.

For the sake of the record let us note that there is no point in trying to reduce either type of choice to the other. That we are involved in a life which presents us with both types of choice situations is an experiential datum. We cannot reduce existential choice to routinized choice, for experience is simply not pure routine. And, there is little point, for our purposes, in highly general analyses designed to show that *all* our choices are entirely arbitrary since it is always the case that we could reject the regulative principles by which we have operated and thus are arbitrarily rechoosing them each time we use them. This is to use words wrenched out of any significant context. "Person," "choice," "commitment," "principle"—these terms take on their relevant meaning only against a background of more or less routinized integrity and regularity of behavior. Where we have merely chance, we do not have a person, nor do we have intelligible acts such as choices.

Custom and rule are the essential soil of moral freedom. But moral freedom comes to fruit in the act of existential choice, which has in it the ineradicably arbitrary. Yet existential choice is the profoundest form of responsible choice. We cannot argue away the question: How can arbitrary choice be responsible? For this paradoxical formula expresses the very essence of the morally free choice. Let us look at the matter first from the psychological standpoint and put our revised theoretical formulation of the concept of anxiety to work.

Anxiety refers to the breakdown of the higher integrating powers of the ego. Where, on the moral level, we speak of the person finally making his decision, on the psychological level we must speak of the operation of the synthetic and executive functions of the ego. The moral and the psychological are different dimensions of the same event, different ways of grasping it.

If anxiety is ego-disintegration in some degree and relative to a prior state of integration, then a person's actions while in a state of anxiety are in some degree relatively irregular, unorganized. In moral language, there is an element of arbitrariness. In "existential" language: what is done in anxiety is done in a context of meaninglessness, of nonbeing. The degree and kind of dis-organization (arbitrariness) which infuses the action depend upon the nature of the anxiety, i.e., upon the degree and kind of breakdown of the ego's synthetic powers. "Arbitrary" is always defined in reference to some specific regularity or principle. The behavior in anxiety may be quite lawlike or regular in relation to regressive, genetically more infantile psychic patterns.

The question about responsibility then arises in this special context. Since any response at this level will have an ineradicable element of arbitrariness in it relative to the current ego-organization, where is the responsibility?

It cannot be that in his choice the person has "expressed himself" in any literal sense. For the whole point of the matter is that, with regard to the problem at hand, there is no personal organization to be expressed; the self as related to the crisis situation has disintegrated. It is precisely in the area of the choice that there is a biological organism and a collection of psychic functions but no *person,* no structural and unified self to be expressed. Therefore it will not help here to say that responsibility is the decisive expression of the "true" or "real" person. It is not even an expression of an "ideal" self, for precisely in the area of anxiety, the ideals too are inadequate to guide smoothly the ego's reparative work. We shall not speak, in this context, of responsible choice being an expression of what one "really" or "ideally" was or wanted prior to the choice.

Let us now shift the course of our attack on this problem and probe further in a more existentially oriented language, and then we shall again return to the psychoanalytic version. Responsibility is the readiness to face the absence of meaning, the nonbeing of self. It requires that a self *be* formed, a meaning be instated, a policy adopted. The crisis exists precisely because there is no a priori decisive resolution of the situation.

Responsibility is the willingness to "leap into nothingness." But it is more than this: it is the willingness to accept—and accept in a very special sense—the consequences of one's act. Responsibility is, in its primary sense, commitment, not obligation. Indeed, genuine obligations arise out of such commitments. Hence it is in a derivative sense that we say: "He is responsible about carrying out his obligations." It is this aspect of the matter which is considered more fully in Chapter 4.

We flinch from this leap, this commitment without decisive justification. We would prefer to *know*. We prefer security. And the heart of responsibility is revealed when we see that, faced with anxiety and the need for choice, precisely what we wish to know is what we *cannot* know. We establish meaning and regulative principle by our act— if we have the courage to accept and identify ourselves with the act and its import.

This has seemed to many a dangerous doctrine, an invitation to "immorality" and nihilism. Of course, such situations are dangerous. But this is not a normative "doctrine." It is a description of the way things are. Nor is it nihilism. True, it does not rely on the all-sufficing efficacy of any specific value or principle. But it is not nihilistic precisely because it stresses the need to accept and live by the choices one makes. We create our values. We cannot use the prior self and its world to justify them, but we can live by them.

To commit oneself is not to be chained to a new dogma

or ritual. We must distinguish among such notions as (1) integrity, the willingness to treat one's decisions seriously and to live by them; (2) evasion, the making of decisions without serious concern for or acceptance of the implications of our act; and (3) dogmatism, initial commitment with subsequent refusal to face the recurrence of anxiety and the need for those new acts of commitment which life forces upon us from time to time.

We are now prepared to return to the psychoanalytic account of the matter. We normally expect that where anxiety is due to inner conflict involving infantile portions of the ego, insight will lead to a mature solution of the conflict. But what does this mean? It does not mean that we discover a ready-made solution, one which was hitherto undetected. Insight has its primary psychoanalytic meaning in the context of the psychoanalysis of the neurotic, i.e., the person who is by and large mature but who is immature in relatively specific areas. Insight evokes a mature solution because it involves bringing the mature ego powers to bear upon the anxiety. Insight is based on a more discriminating and realistic perception, at long last, of the poorly integrated component elements in conflict. This in turn means that new commitments will emerge out of this more discriminating and realistic apprehension of facts as well as out of the body of already mature attitudes and tastes. The infantile misperceptions and tastes are ruthlessly exposed, in the very act of operation, in their contrast to the rest of the essentially mature ego contents.

The insightful response which results is not an automatic, regular outcome of the ego's functioning once it has perceived the contrast. For, as we have said, there has been no integrated response on the mature level to this conflict. Therefore there is none to fall back on. Nor can the therapist legitimately tell the patient specifically how to respond. Since the patient is moving to a genuinely new organization of the self, the therapist must either insist on a pseudocontinuity with the past self or foist his own personal commitments and style of life onto the patient or be silent and let the patient grow up. Here it is that Freud's comments were intended to apply:

> After all, analysis does not set out to abolish the possibility of morbid reactions, but to give the patient's ego freedom to *choose* one way or the other.[71] [Italics in original]

> However much the analyst may be tempted to act as teacher, model and ideal to other people and to make men in his own image, he should not forget that that is not his task in the analytic relationship. . . .[72]

No wonder patients are so often perplexed when they pick up a therapeutic interpretation in an "intellectual" way and then ask piteously, "But even if what you say is true, what could I do about it?" In a fundamental sense, although the therapist might guess at what the patient "could" do, he cannot tell him what he *should* do. The therapist does not aim to show that there is something specific that ought to be done on the basis of the facts; his aim is merely to get the patient to see that *something* must be done, *and done without ignoring the relevant data.* When the nature of his anxiety is both experienced *and* understood, the psychoneurotic can devise *a* response which will be personal but which will have as one of its properties that it is realistic. The same is true, given manageable challenges, for the normal individual in the process of maturation. *What* is done is not settled by facts, customs, accepted principles or prior ego organization. It is an existential decision; that is, it emerges out of a genuinely new organization of the ego rather than a repetition of a prior mode of ego functioning.

Since it is an outcome of integration achieved through ego reorganization, the existential choice is a genuinely vol-

untary and total response by the person. It is not an automatic, repetitive response unintegrated with the rest of the
ego nor is it an arbitrary act which remains ego-alien and is
disowned by the person. It is this which throws light on
why authentic existential choice has its roots in integrity—a
new integrity. Pathological defensive choice is dis-integral;
it emerges out of the fragmentation of the ego, and hence
it is in some degree involuntary. Such defensive maneuvers
may be ingenious and novel and in certain respects genuinely creative. But there remains always the fact that they
serve a stereotyped ego-aim and that this ego-aim is itself
not integrated into the core of the mature ego. The unintegrated is the involuntary. It is the fruit of defense against,
instead of openness to, anxiety.

Doctrines of "self-realization" or "self-actualization"
often have [73]—but need not have—a basis in outmoded Aris-
totelianism. These notions have a phenomenological basis
in that, in moments of existential crisis, we do seem to "find"
ourselves, "discover who and what we are." We can already
see a psychological basis for this in what has just been said.
The new organization of the ego when it successfully faces
and resolves anxiety is indeed subjectively perceived as a
"discovery of self." For ego-reorganization is not an act of
conscious "will."

"Self-realization" can legitimately be more than an expressive phenomenological characterization if stripped of
the Aristotelian ontology which is normally wedded to it. In
a theoretically tenable sense, self-actualization is the coming into being of a new self, a more meaningfully integrated
self, a self which had not existed before though many of the
extraego conditions which make it meaningful had existed
before. The new self is, to put it briefly, a self which the
person's life and situation "called for"; but what is "called
for" is not uniquely fixed by the preceding circumstances.
It is something which is in part an invention, a creation. It is

a unique integration, one of a limited but not exhaustively specifiable range of possible selves, any one of which would do what is called for.[74]

Thus, although there is a kind of radical gap between the old self and the new, there is also an essential continuity: the ego in process of dissolution does not resort repetitiously to remnants of tried and true measures (of defense); instead it surrenders itself to a new and unknown form of integrity. It is thus "surrendering to" rather than "fighting against" which is the basis of a continuity by identification. And the new ego takes the old ego and the effects of its acts as a legitimate heritage, a heritage neither rejected as unfair nor considered as alien and repressed.

It is difficult indeed at this point to avoid using either of two languages, the language of karma or the language of parent-offspring relations. For, as will be seen in Chapter 5, the karmic notion is that the old self acts, and the later selves, though they did not commit the acts, legitimately inherit their fruits as those fruits ripen in the course of time. This is an occurrence which need not involve generations or epochs; it may be from moment to moment or day to day: Coomaraswamy summarizes and emphasizes that

> It is constantly overlooked that the majority of references [in Hindu scripture] to . . . repeated birth and repeated death refer to this present life. . . .[75]

And he refers to the concept of *punar bhava* ("becoming") as meaning that "man dies and is reborn daily and hourly in this present life." [76]

Not only is the spiritual logic of karma the same as that of responsible choice, it is also at times explicitly that of parent and child. Coomaraswamy emphasizes that the Aitereya Brahmana explains "to man in categorical terms that 'procreation is rebirth.'" [77] This reference reminds us forcefully that the relation between the old self and the new is psychologically very much like that of parent to child. The latter comes to identify with the parents who bore him even though he had no choice in his being born their child or in the nature which they impart to him. So the psychic "offspring," the newly reorganized ego, must, if it is to maintain its own integrity, function as the continuation of the old ego. There must be not merely causal and temporal continuity; there must also be psychic identification. The old, identifying with and giving itself to the unknown new which it spawns, and the new, identifying itself with the undeserved old which it inherits—here is the arbitrary as the soil of responsibility and freedom. The distinguished psychoanalyst Robert Waelder stressed decades ago the basis of freedom in the arbitrary and the basis of responsibility in freedom.

> . . . it is only possible to make predictions at all insofar as limitations on freedom are present. . . .[78]

> Psychoanalysis comes forward as an appeal to man's freedom itself. . . .[79]

We can say here only a few words bearing explicitly on religion. But they must be said because it is essential to see that the experiences we here have dealt with have a peculiarly religious dimension.

The person undergoing a severe anxiety experience is, after all, not so much a moral agent making a moral choice as he is a human being in the process of losing his status as moral agent. The encounter with anxiety is at least temporarily a de-moralizing blow, and the response, except in the most degenerated psychoses, is one of attempting to remoralize the self, to re-establish the foundations of one's autonomy, of personal integrity. The profound encounter with anxiety is thus not only a moral crisis but a religious one: it is a crisis of suffering and of the movement either toward a saving rebirth of a new self or a self-destroying evasion of the task.

I shall put the issue in nonreligious terms: The religious ordeal is a crisis in which man seeks autonomy, an autonomy which in its concrete reality is inherently unknown because as yet unexperienced or at most dimly glimpsed by him. Though unknown in its content, it must be sought. One must be open to it, ready to receive it. Indeed, one must accept it *before* fully and concretely knowing what one has achieved. The autonomy man seeks is inherently beyond any prior decisive moral justification itself; it is, in this sense, arbitrary. But it is itself the profoundest source of all value. Such an ordeal is known to us in connection with the religious quest. To see this we need only substitute the word "God" for "autonomy" in the preceding.

There is here not only a movement *toward* but also a movement *from*. Ego, and the id and environment which it integrates, all emerge together, differentiating themselves out of the psychologically undifferentiated primary unity. This movement from the undifferentiated state to a state of differentiation and integration is most grossly present in the neonate. But it is always taking place, and it is apprehensible subjectively after infancy in memories and in current experience. Not only the artist in his creative work but all of us, if we will, can at times attend to the movement of our life and perceive inwardly the quality of primal chaos and the presentiment of a future order. In addition, we hear, if we are open and listening, the subterranean workings of the inchoate primal generative powers. This experience—if we are able to or are forced to attend to it—is haunted by an archaic power and by archaic personal images, which are embedded in the Ur-structure of ego and id.

The ego and anxiety, being and nonbeing, these and

their apprehendable manifestations are already within a developed world, the human world. It is true that they are generative poles *within* that world. But we can say in a language which reflects the data of psychoanalysis as well as religious experience that this human world has a genesis of its own which is constantly repeating itself, though it has a temporally original prototype.

We can truly say: Before even being or nonbeing, there is that which fathers forth; not itself human, though in an elusive sense personal, creative, it is at work; until, in an inevitable but miraculous series of acts, there emerges out of archaic chaos the human being and the ordered world. These are propositions of theology. Are we in error if we take seriously their congruence with psychoanalytic theories about the psychic context out of which id, ego, and anxiety mutually emerge and in which they function? [80]

N O T E S
(See List of Bibliographical Abbreviations, p. 343.)

1. Freud, S., *Gen. Intro.*, p. 341.
2. See, for example, Fenichel, O., *Psychoanalytic Theory of Neurosis*, W. W. Norton & Co., New York, 1945, pp. 42–56, 132–134.
3. Freud, S., *Civ.& Disc.*, p. 126.
4. Meltzer, D., "Toward a Structural Concept of Anxiety," *Psychiatry 18*:41–50 (1955).
5. Kubie, L. S., "A Physiological Approach to the Concept of Anxiety," *Psychosomatic Medicine 3* (1941), p. 263.
6. *Ibid.*, p. 265.
7. Freud, S., *Inhibitions*, p. 140.
8. *Ibid.*, p. 132.
9. Rangell, L., "On the Psychoanalytic Theory of Anxiety: A Statement of a Unitary Theory," *JAP 3* (1955), p. 400.
10. Freud, S., "The Justification for Detaching from Neuras-

thenia a Particular Syndrome: The Anxiety-Neurosis," (1894), in *CP*, I, p. 80.

11. *Ibid.*, p. 97.
12. *Ibid.*, p. 79.
13. *Ibid.*, p. 83.
14. *Ibid.*, p. 80.
15. *Ibid.*, pp. 80–81.
16. *Ibid.*, p. 101.
17. Freud, S., *New Intro. Lec.*, p. 116.
18. *Loc. cit.*
19. *Loc. cit.*
20. Greenson, R. R., "Phobia, Anxiety, and Depression," *JAP* 7 (1959), p. 672.
21. See, for example, Freud, S., *Outline*, pp. 15–16.
22. Waelder, R., "The Problem of Freedom in Psychoanalysis and the Problem of Reality Testing," *IJP* 17 (1936), p. 98.
23. Freud, S., *Pleasure*, p. 35.
24. Freud, S., "Analysis Terminable and Interminable," in *CP*, V, pp. 343–344.
25. Freud, S., *Outline*, Chap. VIII.
26. Hartmann, H., *Ego Psychology and the Problem of Adaptation*, International Universities Press, New York, 1958.
27. Hartmann, H., Kris, E., Loewenstein, R. M. See the series of papers by these authors collectively and separately in *The Psychoanalytic Study of the Child*, International Universities Press, New York, Vols. I, II, III, V, VII.
28. Hendrick, I., "Early Development of the Ego: Identification in Infancy," *Psychoanalytic Quarterly* 20:44–61 (1951).
29. Rangell, L., *op. cit.*, pp. 402–403.
30. *Ibid.*, p. 403.
31. Freud, S., *Inhibitions*, Addendum B.
32. ———, *New Intro. Lec.*, p. 119.
33. *Loc. cit.*
34. *Ibid.*, p. 120.

35. *Ibid.*, p. 124.
36. *Loc. cit.*
37. Freud, S., *Inhibitions*, p. 162.
38. Schur, M., "The Ego in Anxiety," in *Drives, Affects, Behavior*, International Universities Press, New York, 1953, pp. 67–103.
39. Rangell, L., *op. cit.*
40. Fenichel, O., "Defense against Anxiety, Particularly by Libidinization," in *Collected Papers*, First Series, W. W. Norton & Co., New York, 1954, p. 303.
41. *Loc. cit.*
42. Freud, S., *Civ. & Disc.*, p. 125.
43. Freud, S., *Ego & Id*, p. 72.
44. Cf. *Ibid.*, p. 77.
45. Freud, S., *Civ. & Disc.*, pp. 125–126.
46. *Loc. cit.*
47. Schur, M., *op. cit.*, p. 79.
48. Rapaport, D., "On the Psychoanalytic Theory of Affects," in *Psychoanalytic Psychiatry and Psychology*, Austen Riggs Center, Vol. I, International Universities Press, New York, 1954. Especially p. 292.
49. Jacobson, E., "The Affects and Their Pleasure-Unpleasure Qualities in Relation to the Psychic Discharge Processes," in *Drives, Affects, Behavior*.
50. Meltzer, D., *op. cit.*
51. Selye, H., *The Stress of Life*, McGraw-Hill Book Co., New York, 1956.
52. Menninger, K. A., "Psychological Aspects of the Organism under Stress," Parts I and II, *JAP* 2:67–106, 280–310 (1954).
53. May, R., *The Meaning of Anxiety*, Ronald Press, New York, 1950, p. 191.
54. Sullivan, H. S., *The Interpersonal Theory of Psychiatry*, W. W. Norton & Co., New York, 1953, p. 94.
55. *Ibid.*, p. 96.
56. Horney, K., *The Neurotic Personality of Our Time*, W. W. Norton & Co., New York, 1937, p. 287.

57. *Ibid.*, p. 23.
58. *Ibid.*, pp. 92–93.
59. *Ibid.*, p. 95.
60. Jung, C., *Two Essays on Analytical Psychology*, Hull, R. F. C., trans., Meridian Books, New York, 1956, p. 138.
61. Fromm-Reichman, F., "Psychoanalytic and General Dynamic Conceptions of Theory and of Therapy," *JAP 2* (1954), p. 718.
62. Heidegger, M., "The Way Back into the Ground of Metaphysics," in *Existentialism from Dostoevsky to Sartre*, Kaufmann, Walter, ed., Meridian Books, New York, 1956, pp. 206–221.
63. Tillich, P., *The Courage to Be*, Yale University Press, New Haven, 1959, p. 40.
64. Lao-tse, Chap. II. (Author's translation.)
65. Tillich, P., *op. cit.*, p. 65.
66. *Ibid.*, p. 66.
67. Matt. 5:29.
68. Fingarette, H., "Real Guilt and Neurotic Guilt," *Journal of Existential Psychiatry* 3:145–158 (1962).
69. See also, for example, May's discussion in *Existence*, Basic Books, New York, 1958.
70. See, for example, van den Berg, J. H., *The Phenomenological Approach to Psychiatry*, Charles C Thomas, Springfield, 1955.
71. Freud, S., *Ego & Id*, p. 72.
72. Freud, S., *Outline*, p. 67.
73. See, for example, Fromm, E., *Man for Himself*, Rinehart & Co., New York, 1947.
74. Fingarette, H., "A Fresh Perspective on a Familiar Landscape," *Journal of Humanistic Psychology* 1:75–89 (1962).
75. Coomaraswamy, A. K., "Eastern Religions and Western Thought," *The Review of Religion* 6 (1942) p. 137.
76. *Ibid.*, p. 137.
77. *Loc. cit.*
78. Waelder, R., *op. cit.*, p. 104.

79. *Ibid.*, p. 106.
80. The central psychoanalytic thesis regarding the concept of anxiety presented in this chapter was originally presented to the Regional Conference on Philosophy, Los Angeles, May 1956.

Part II

THE SELF IN

TRANSFORMATION

CHAPTER 3

THE PREPARATORY PHASE:

Blame

I

THE PRIMARY INTEREST IN THE FOLLOWING CHAPTERS IS DI-
rected to the emergence of the adult, the fruition of a life
with spiritual content. But such a life, of course, has its
roots in the essentially psychological and only rudimentarily
spiritual years of infancy and childhood. Hence we must be
prepared to find that at least a selective study of the moral
life in childhood is necessary to set the stage for the following studies in what is, in a fuller sense, the life of the spirit.
The aspect of child psychology and morality which is of
special interest here is that of blame.

Blame-morality is, of course, found in both the normal
adult as well as in the child. But it is intrinsic to the morality of childhood. To do "right" and be praised, to do "wrong"
and be blamed: these set the context of the child's moral
world. And, generally speaking, the child as well as the
adult who deals with him finds this a congenial framework.
But when it comes to the adult acting in relation to other
adults, the attitude toward blame-morality in both East and
West seems ambiguous. Certainly, in the West it is easy for
us to sense that there is a strong pull toward the view that

our spiritual goal ought to be to "rise above" casting blame. Yet who can deny the pervasiveness of that kind of Old Testament moral righteousness which is so often associated with blame-morality?

We can see in Jesus a paradoxical fusion of various attitudes related to blame: the extreme Hebraic eye-for-an-eye doctrine, the Stoic and Eastern morality of spiritual disinterestedness, and a new, intense cultivation of love and forgiveness. Jesus told his followers to love their fellow men and judge them not; yet in his own life as portrayed in the Gospels—a life which is offered as a model for the Western world—he speaks in righteous wrath, uses moralistic vituperation, and threatens eternal punishment. Indeed, he explicitly enjoins his disciples, "If your brother does wrong, rebuke him." [1]

In the ancient Western non-Christian tradition, Aristotle says, in a context where moral indignation is indicated, that

> the man who is angry at the right things and with the right people, and further, as he ought, when he ought, and as long as he ought, is praised. [2]

Yet Epictetus, the pagan slave, writing several centuries later but developing views already enunciated by contemporaries of Aristotle, tells us that

> the signs of one who is making progress are: he blames none, praises none, complains of none, accuses none. . . . [3]

Similar opposition among views on blame may be observed throughout later Western history in both its secular and religious aspects. Direct discussion of blame is scarce, but implicit attitudes toward blame are not only widespread but often constitute an important part of the characteristic atmosphere. The echoes of "Judge not" mingle with those of the righteous condemnation "Ye are a generation of vipers."

In Eastern thought, particularly of the Hindu and Buddhist varieties, there is a clearer sense of a kind of hierarchical relation between blame-morality and the nonblaming kind. Blame and praise, reward and punishment, merits and defects, all are generally thought of as appropriate, important, and intrinsic to the life of bondage—the "normal" life of most men, after all. But those who reach to another spiritual realm, who taste of liberation, move to a level where they neither need to use nor need to check their use of blame: the entire tendency and its spiritual framework are dissolved.

There is no doubt that, East or West, blame is of the very stuff of everyday moral life, childish and adult. Nevertheless, in the Western philosophical and psychological literature, contemporary or historical, there has been little systematic discussion or analysis of it; we find only intimations of various views and attitudes. The study of blame needs to be approached systematically, and we shall do so here. For not only is blame-morality of intrinsic interest as a major piece of our everyday moral life, but it is also, as will become evident, the crucial developmental phase which sets the stage for the maturation of psyche and spirit. The systematic study of blame places us on a road which leads to the central meanings of the ordeal of spiritual liberation.

II

OUR FIRST TASK IS TO IDENTIFY *in the language of commonsense, conscious experience* that phenomenon we call blame. It is necessary to distinguish the sense of "blame," as that word is used here, from a number of other senses easily confused with it. Only then can we begin a psychological analysis and a philosophical critique.

Blame "proper" can be characterized in terms of such *partially* synonymous notions as "reprimand," "reproof," "censure," "moral indignation," "moral condemnation."

Each of these may be used in other senses, however. Blame is a form of moralistic criticism. It involves an affective tone reminiscent of anger; it is not a dispassionate report of the recognition of a moral "truth." It is an attack directed against a person. It is colored by the sense of objectivity and, specifically, by the sense of moral objectivity; it is not felt to be mere whim or personal anger. There are *grounds* for blaming. The essential ground of the proper exercise of blaming is that the blamer should have reasonable grounds for supposing the person blamed has done that for which he is blamed. Blame is a spontaneous response, not a calculated response. Though it may at times be indirectly encouraged or discouraged in oneself, it is characteristically not directly subject to volition as is, say, the opening or closing of the fist. Possibly the most sober and rounded common-sense discussion of blame is to be found in the classic sermons of the philosopher-bishop, Joseph Butler.[4]

For the purposes of the present discussion, blame proper (as characterized above) must be distinguished from several similar or related kinds of behavior. It is, for example, not identical with the recognition of and opposition to wrong-doing—the making of moral judgments. One can make moral judgments without indulging in blame. This is so even if we take moral judgment, in an extreme "subjectivist" way, as essentially an expression of feelings, for, even if moral judgment is to be taken as the expression of feelings, these "feelings" are introspectively distinguishable from the "feelings" characteristic of the blame process. This difference can also be appreciated through a systematic analysis of the psychology of blame, an analysis to which this chapter is intended as a contribution.

For the present, I shall only suggest, by way of an example of moral judgment and understanding, the realistic firmness of a parent or therapist in the face of delinquent impulses or acting out by a child during late latency. Contrasted with this is that much more commonly to be observed moralistic attack upon the same child which we call blaming.[5]

A second kind of behavior easily confused with blaming is that which I shall here call censure, using the word in a narrow sense. This consists in the delivery by someone in an official status of morally condemnatory judgment upon someone who has violated the laws, rules, or mores. Here an individual, perhaps an emotionally uninvolved magistrate, merely acts as the official interpreter of the group attitude; he may or may not be sufficiently aroused to have impulses to blame on his own account. Censure may be used for educational purposes, but blame is not. For blame is not used for any purpose; it is the spontaneous expression of a moralistic criticism.

Still another kind of behavior which is often called blaming consists in engaging in overt behavior which is often similar in certain gross respects to genuine blaming. This simulation of blame is often used as an educational device, especially with children. The mother who may be inwardly smiling and enchanted will nevertheless reprove Johnny for some childish peccadillo. She recognizes his action as normal, but she feels that such actions must in the normal course of affairs be controlled and finally rejected by him. Her pseudo blame is a calculated, educational device.

There have indeed been attempts by some types of utilitarian moral philosophers to interpret blame and punishment as essentially educational, to be used for their effect upon character. Schlick speaks of punishment as "an educative measure, and as such . . . a means to the formation of motive. . . ."[6] This obscures the distinction between moral justification and a motive, a matter to be discussed in this connection toward the end of this chapter. If there is anything clear about the distinctive phenomenon here called blame proper, it is that, when justly used, it is evoked spontaneously by the perception of wrongdoing. We are not *moved* to it by some calculation concerned with its supposed beneficial influence, though the blaming may in some cases actually have a beneficent influence. Utilitarian considerations are not irrelevant to the problem of blame, but they will not serve to provide an account of the psychology of blame and its role in the moral growth of the individual. The immediate psychological context of blame proper is organized much more in terms of spontaneous, moral, condemnatory impulses than voluntary, rational, and educative ones.

One further kind of behavior easily confused with blame is aggression rationalized as blame. It is not always easy in practice to distinguish such rationalized aggression from blame proper; they are often found together. Yet the phenomena are distinguishable and have different psychological conditions and each a different moral significance. Aggression rationalized as blame is a kind of moral hypocrisy; blame proper is a genuine moral response. Blame proper, as we shall see, stems from the "conscience," and it is recognized as such by the person blamed. It is intimately connected with the inner moral conflicts of the blamer. "Moralized aggression," however, will be misunderstood if it is taken to be anything more than a moralistic façade masking amoral frustration, anger, and attack.

III

WHAT IS BLAME? WE NOW PROCEED WITH A PSYCHOANALYTIC analysis of the phenomenon described in the previous section as blame "proper."

As has been noted previously, practically never is blame explicitly mentioned in the psychoanalytic literature except incidentally, and then more often than not it is in the contexts of therapy or pathology. One of the very few explicit psychoanalytic statements on blame, of which much of this section is elaboration and commentary, is contained in a few cogent sentences in Anna Freud's *The Ego and the Mechanisms of Defense.*[7] Our first problem, however, consists in organizing the various scattered *aperçus* and partial formulations into a systematic exposition under a single heading. I shall then discuss, in subsequent sections, the import of this material in the context of everyday moral life and in the context of the life of the spirit for which blame-morality is—as we shall see—a preparation.

Essential, but not sufficient, to the normal blaming process is the discharge of superego aggression directed toward an external object. There is a concomitant withdrawal of libidinal cathexis from the object. These are the most obvious, characteristic features of blaming behavior. It is clear that, except for the substitution of an external object in place of the ego as object, the superego functions in blame as it does in the case of guilt.

The problem which remains concerns the precise nature of the process by which the superego is activated in the blame situation. This problem we consider at once.

In *Inhibitions, Symptoms, and Anxiety,*[8] Freud made explicit in a decisive and concrete fashion the fact that psychoanalysis is not a one-sided psychology of a purely private, "inner" life. He established psychoanalysis on a transactional (situational, contextual) basis when he enunciated the concept of the *"danger-situation"* as central to anxiety, itself in turn the crux of psychodynamics. At the same time, he elaborated upon what was in effect the rudimentary but growing psychoanalytic theory of perception developed in earlier works.[9] Specifically, he argued that what is *internal* (instinct) is no danger except in an *environment* where the expression of the instinct will bring disaster. On the other hand, the prospect of disaster can be recognized only when it has been "internalized": the danger must have some correlate in the personal history of the individual which makes the situation interpretable on the basis of memory as dangerous. Now, since blaming normally is initiated by a perception—the *perception* of wrongdoing—considerations along the lines outlined in the analysis of the perception of danger may be expected to be relevant in analyzing blame. We shall proceed on this assumption.

What arouses the superego aggression in the blamer? Common sense tells us that in the normal case it is the perception of something which is (a) done by someone else and (b) contrary to the demands of the blamer's superego. (We shall hereafter say in such cases that the blamer perceives someone acting wrongly.) Now, from a psychoanalytic standpoint, we know that an *internal* memory-image must be cathected in order to give psychological meaning, the *interpretation*, to the perception of the action of the other person. Such cathexis of the memory-image initially involves the release of minute quantities of energy (secondary process). The memory-images thus cathected will be those of the id-derivatives, ego ideas, and superego ideas which appear most relevant to the situation, and in particular to the perceived action of the wrongdoer. Loosely speaking, then, we make sense of and deepen our apprehensions of the outer world by activating the memories (and their associated ideas) which appear to correspond to the initial perceptions.

This is a process which easily gets out of hand if the energies mobilized and the ideas cathected have not been successfully integrated into the conflict-free sphere of the ego. "The reproduction of a perception as an image (cathected memory-trace) is not always a faithful one." [10] Where sublimation has not successfully and fully taken place, we may expect the ego countercathexes to weaken, and the slight opening in the dam will become the occasion for a major breakthrough: a full-scale cathexis of the ideas involved and a drive discharge whose energy level is of the order of overt behavior. Thus, what begins as a process of perceptual interpretation may abruptly be transformed into the problem of managing full-scale inner conflict.

It is now possible to review and summarize with some precision the early steps in the process of normal blaming. In doing this, however, I shall stress another aspect of the process, a series of "forks in the road," critical stages, each of which is the setting for crucial alternatives in types of behavior.

Perception of another's action requires interpretation by the observer. Interpretation requires the assigning of meaning based on past experiences of the observer. Such interpretation, therefore, involves the mobilization of small quantities of instinct and of ideas associated by the observer with the action observed.

At this point we come to the first significant "fork in the road." If the action in question is interpreted in terms of neutralized instinctual drives and their derivatives operating within the conflict-free sphere of the ego, then the conditions for blaming are absent, and the perception eventuates in realistic "understanding." This will be discussed in Chapter 6.

However, taking the alternative possibility, we may suppose the drives involved have not been neutralized but only semisuccessfully evaded through conflict and defense. In this case, the observation of someone else acting in a certain way constitutes an object-representation which is fused with self-representations involving the observer's inner conflict; the perception then mobilizes that conflict within the observer. The perception of wrongdoing "infects" the perceiver. I shall call the situation at this stage the "infectious, conflict-arousing situation." [11] At this point we come to the second significant "fork in the road." The turn of events now depends upon the economics of the conflict mobilized, that is, upon the relative balance of forces between id cathexes on the one hand and ego-superego countercathexes on the other.

If, for reasons extraneous to our concerns, the superego can be either overwhelmed or "bought off," then drive-energy may be discharged and tension thereby reduced through overt, imitative commission of the wrongful act. The corruption of the superego in such situations is accounted for from a dynamic standpoint by the observer's identification in the superego with the wrongdoer, thus permitting instinctual discharge through delinquent action. This outcome corresponds precisely, I believe, with what Redl has called delinquent group-formation on the basis of the initiatory act of the central person.[12] Thus conflict arousal through "infectious" imitation may have the "delinquent" outcome. The original wrongdoer plays the role of "central person." The observer becomes, through his imitative action, a member of what is, in this psychological sense, a delinquent group. (Although Redl's analyses [13] of what he calls "contagion" and "shock" are consistent in substance with the present discussion, he defines his concepts in terms of the specific responses. I have focused attention on the generic conditions—the "infectious conflict-arousing situation"—out of which the various specific responses develop.)

The alternative prospect of nondelinquency depends upon the superego's retaining its integrity. If this happens, the outcome will be "moralistic," that is, it will consist either of blaming behavior or guilt feelings or some of both. We shall consider each in turn.

Blame may now be classified as a species of moralistic response to an infectious conflict-arousing situation. The superego aggression aroused by the id-impulse is directed outward. The object of the aggression is the external wrong-doer in his role as an agent whose action is taken to represent and therefore arouse the blamer's id-impulse. Analogously to the process which produces guilt feelings, part of the normal, libidinal object-cathexis of objects in the perceptual world is withdrawn from the external object, which now plays a role analogous to the ego in the dynamics of guilt. Since the ego is not in this case the target of superego condemnation, the libido withdrawn from the object becomes available for additional narcissistic cathexis of the ego. Furthermore, the blamer's preoccupation with the wrongdoing of the other person affords opportunity for partial, fantasy discharge of the id-impulse in question.

The dynamics of blaming thus account for the well-known, although less readily admitted, conscious features of the experience: (1) the emotional, quasi-pleasurable brooding upon the *other's* wrongdoing, (2) the increase in the sense of self-esteem and self-righteousness, (3) the moralistic attack upon the wrongdoer, and (4) the resulting sense of catharsis. The inherently involuntary, spontaneous character of the impulse to blame is accounted for by the fact that the process depends upon the existence and mobilization of inner conflict which remains unconscious. For blame may be viewed as a defense against the anxiety which would accompany insight into the inner conflict.

> What is in question is fear of an infectious example, of the temptation to imitate—that is, of the contagious character of taboo. If one person succeeds to gratifying the repressed desire, the same desire is bound to be kindled in all the other members of the community. In order to keep the temptation down, the envied transgressor must be deprived of the fruit of his enterprise; and the punishment will not infrequently give those who carry it out an opportunity of committing the same outrage under colour of an act of expiation.[14]

An alternative species of moralistic response in the infectious conflict-arousing situation is that which results in guilt. Here, as well as under the numerous other conditions which may evoke it, guilt presents the well-known dynamic pattern. Superego aggression directed toward the ego and withdrawal of superego libido from the ego evoke the moral anxiety in the ego which motivates a successful counter-cathexis against id-instinctual discharge. Thus, whereas blame lowers tension, at least temporarily, guilt establishes an equilibrium with a higher energy level (greater tension) than blame.

There are still other variants of the moralistic response to infectious conflict-arousing situations. They involve displacement: the superego's attack is diverted to other persons or to institutions or other entities. These are often viewed as the indirect causes of the wrongdoer's action. There is not space here in which to consider them further.

We have now accomplished the purpose of this section of the discussion: to present a compact, systematic analysis of the place of blaming within the framework of the psychoanalytic psychology. We have avoided, and shall continue to avoid, the therapeutic orientation in connection with blame. We are now in a position to proceed with the examination of blame within the pragmatic-moral context of everyday life.

IV

IN EVALUATING THE NORMAL BLAMING OF A WRONGDOER, THE first point to note is the element of realism in it.

In normal blame, the other person has, in fact, done something wrong in terms of the values of the blamer. More exactly: the blamer has reasonable grounds for believing that the person blamed is in fact guilty of the wrong with which he is charged. This triggering of blame when there is actual wrongdoing is not only consistent with the healthy ego's reality orientation, it helps, within limits to be mentioned later, to reinforce this reality-orientation.

The realism inherent in normal blaming of a wrongdoer is the basis for a response whose elegance and rationality are morally significant. The external act of wrongdoing, the *occasion* for the conflict, is also a crucial element in the *means* of resolving the conflict: the wrongdoer and his action are used as the lightning rod through which the conflicting drives are discharged. Furthermore, the occasion of the conflict-arousal and blame response is also the explicit moral *ground* (reason, justification) for that response. It is conducive to the spirit of rational conduct that the occasion for making a response should be not only the occasion for the action but also provide a ground for acting so.

Still the question must be asked: is blame not pathological if the response must be mediated by a *conflict* within the self? Is there, perhaps, no way of responding to the wrongdoing via the mediation of some inner but *non*conflictual pattern? The answer is yes. In an area where conflict has been resolved by the individual, there can be no infectious conflict-arousing situation because there is no conflict to be aroused. In such cases the response will be of a different moral and psychological order. It is in contrast to this more mature level of conduct that we seem to see an inherent measure of "pathology" in the blame response. Yet such an interpretation must immediately be qualified, for we cannot assume that all conflict is pathological, nor can we even assume that when a response is mediated by a clearly pathological conflict, the response is itself inherently pathological. There is conflict in the Oedipal situation; yet the Oedipal conflicts are essential stages in the normal development of the individual. Indeed the systematic implications of contemporary psychoanalytical ego-psychology point to the view that conflict is, in itself, neutral as regards pathology or normality. What counts, as is now well-known, is the specific nature of the conflict and its relation to the developmental process.[15] Furthermore, even the neurotic *may* frequently adapt his conflicts, within limits, to produce reasonable and beneficial results as in the case, for example, of a compulsive bookkeeper. We must, therefore, discuss at some length the significance of blaming when viewed in a developmental context. We shall then need to consider it only briefly in certain other contexts.

Let us fix our attention upon that stage in the maturation process when (a) the superego and the ego are established but (b) before there has been achieved a firm and deep integration of ego and superego, instinctual demands and environmental demands. The movement of growth is normally toward such integration. Because of the poverty of content of ego and superego at this stage as well as their dynamic instability relative to the instinctual drives, such normal growth requires the strengthening of the ego and superego repressive capabilities more than the cultivation of insight. At this stage insight tends to dissolve conflict by permitting the weak ego and superego to be confronted with and thus overwhelmed by the instincts. This is, therefore, the period when conflict and lack of insight into those conflicts must normally coexist. It is the period when it is essential for the individual to have the chance to "exercise, via the small conflict situations of the normal daily life of children, piecemeal renunciation of childish ways. . . ."[16] This is, in short, the phase which is normally approximated, to one degree or another, beginning with the passing of the Oedipus complex and lasting through adolescence.[17]

This is also the period of greatest activity for social learning, the learning which refines and enriches the infantile Oedipal core of socialization. Such learning includes constant practice in recognizing, evaluating, and strengthening one's attitudes with respect to moral values and to a larger society than the family.[18]

Blaming is now the natural opportunity to accomplish this learning and to aid the maturing ego and superego without overstraining the uncertain, immature psychic balance.

From the standpoint of the individual doing the blaming, the act of blaming provides a mode of tension reduction which does not involve insight and hence does not constitute a threat to ego or superego. At the same time, this occurs in a context where the content and practical significance of forbidden behavior may be identified and studied, though at a safe psychic distance. The child "learns what is blameworthy but protects itself by means of this defense-mechanism from unpleasant self-criticism."[19] Blaming also is based upon and encourages group loyalty, a point to be mentioned subsequently and in more detail.

Eventually, the very security and social learning which have developed behind the protection of blaming make possible the foregoing of defense and the beginning of insight. This stage is descriptively analyzed by Anna Freud.[20] It is enjoined and interpreted in Matthew 7:2—

> Why do you note the little splinter in your brother's eye, and take not notice of the beam in yours? . . . Hypocrite, begin by removing the beam from your own eye, and then you will see clearly enough to pull the splinter out of your brother's.

The movement from blaming through guilt to insight is the last radical phase in the transition from adolescence to psychological adulthood. It is a movement from (normal) intolerance to (normal) tolerance: "Intolerance is the projection of guilt: tolerance is the identification or at least the partial identification and acceptance of one's own part in every crime."[21]

Blame may function in another and not so happy developmental context. When, for reasons often having no intrinsic connection with blaming, the person fails to achieve the maturity of character which is based on insightful solutions of psychological problems, there may occur a fixation of development at the blaming stage.[22] Blaming becomes not a temporary mode of adjustment but the best and final one. As a preferred defense which actually is tension-reducing, it can become so important that it is no longer possible for the would-be blamer to wait for genuine occurrences of wrongdoing by others. The condition for unrealistic, paranoid blaming then exists. The individual becomes sensitized to the presence in others of those repressed impulses which are pressing for discharge in him. Instead of waiting for the others to act out such impulses—which they might never do—the blamer's own imminent acting out becomes the occasion for neurotic, defensive blaming of the other person as a means of tension-reduction and impulse denial.[23]

Still more insidious is the tendency to *provoke* delinquent behavior in order to provide suitable targets for blame. Parents may do this with their children;[24] societies may do this by ensuring the existence of delinquency in order to have an outlet for their blame.[25]

The public interest in crime and sex and the appetite for "formula" literature and "soap operas" are important borderline responses somewhere between normal blame and the neurotic compulsion to project guilt and obtain vicarious instinctual satisfaction.

From a developmental standpoint, then, we must suppose that after adolescence, blaming as a consistently *favored* mode of response represents a pathology.

In considering blame from a developmental standpoint, we must also consider its impact upon the *other* person, the wrongdoer. From this standpoint, too, the blame response is, within limits, remarkably adaptive. To the wrongdoer, blame represents an externalization of his own characteristic superego response to his wrongdoing. Discussion here must be limited to the wrongdoer who does have a sufficiently well-established superego, one which is similar to the blamer's. Where superego development is deficient, blame is experienced merely as aggression or desertion.[26]

Blame, to have a *moral* meaning to the wrongdoer, must reflect and reaffirm his own superego values. When this is so, as it normally is in everyday life, it is a reflection of the fact that there exists some degree of mutual identification in the superego between blamer and blamed; they share group membership.[27]

From these premises we can infer that blame is internalized by the wrongdoer as a strengthening of his superego. The wrongdoer not only suffers deprivation of narcissistic supplies and aggression from his own superego—a process hitherto insufficient to control his id drive—but he now becomes the object of superego aggression and deprivation of narcissistic cathexis by an "additional" internalized superego akin to his own. Thus, in general, blame is a device for keeping the wrongdoer's unsublimated drives under superego and ego control. So long as there is group identification, blame in the infectious conflict-arousal situation tends to shift the balance of forces in the wrongdoer in the direction of a moralistic response relative to the group superego rather than a delinquent response. The child often wants and needs blame or reproof of some kind rather than insight-oriented interpretation.[28]

Another feature of the blame response as it affects the person blamed is that it stresses and often encourages *responsibility* in the wrongdoer.

This is not the place to enter again into a detailed discussion of responsibility. Suffice it to say that in blaming a person for his acts, we may, it is true, increase his guilt; but we may also increase the tendency for him to face the fact of his wrongdoing and deal with it on the basis of ego-control. Thus, in the normal everyday situation, in contrast to the therapeutic situation, blame provides a limited but bearable insight because it also supplies support for the superego.

It is insight *without* blame which is a threat to the post-

Oedipal but not yet mature individual. This becomes clearer if we contrast blaming the wrongdoer in everyday life with responses such as ignoring wrongdoing or "excusing" him without justification. The latter responses tend to obscure the *fact* of the wrongdoing or the *moral character* of it. The rational assumption which may underlie such an approach is that, because of relative ego-weakness in the wrongdoer, the initiative for handling the moral aspects of the matter in a particular case lies with the observer rather than with the wrongdoer. This is, indeed, a common interim occurrence in therapy. There the therapist *must* at times take certain responsibilities upon himself. The therapist may, with a child, be aiming at a trustful relationship, or in insight therapy he may be aiming to reduce superego countercathexis to the degree necessary for insight without overwhelming anxiety.

As an everyday attitude, suppression of justified blame is, in general, a paternalistic subversion of the other individual's independence and maturity.[29] Indeed it is often part of a consistent pattern of such subversion on the part of the parent. The consistent attempt by a parent to *interpret* the child's "delinquent" action instead of blaming is likely to be a symptom of a similar "delinquent" impulse in the parent; such "interpretations" may in fact act as a seduction of the child to the delinquent response in question.[30]

Under certain circumstances, the amount of guilt aroused by blaming the wrongdoer will so overwhelm his ego that instead of responding with increased insight, self-correction, and responsibility, he will respond defensively and regressively. This is an inevitable danger of blaming. In this respect blame is inherently a rough and ready device. It must be so because it is an *automatic* response. This is true in the sense that, given the occasion of a wrongful act, the response thereafter is mediated by the status of the internal conflicts of the blamer, not of the wrongdoer.

Nevertheless, it is important to remember that in normal children, blame is a basic and adequate socializing device in spite of its rough and ready, automatic character. Most children of the age groups here discussed, and especially those in latency, spend a good deal of their playtime with their peers zestfully blaming and being blamed.

We tend at times to become too much preoccupied with the occasional crisis in the life of the normal child, or with the therapy of the disturbed child—situations in which blame is generally *not* therapeutic. Normally, however, in spite of the inflexibility and insensitivity of the blame response, the child can not only "take it" but needs it and thrives on it.

In review of the childhood functions of blame as a conflict-mediated response, we cannot but be struck by the fact that

> What appears as "pathological" in a cross-section of development may, viewed in the longitudinal dimension of development, represent the best possible solution of a given childhood conflict.[31]

The evaluation of blame has, up to this point, been focused upon the post-Oedipal through adolescent phases of development. It is in these years that we can see in sharpest outline the normal significance of blame. Nevertheless, if we recall that the individual does not ever entirely grow out of his infantilisms, that side by side with the more mature forms of psychic life lie at least residues of the never fully outgrown immature forms, we must be prepared to find that blame normally has a place in the psychic economy of the adult.

Whereas in practice the evaluation of blame in the adult is more complex than in the child, in theory it is simple once we have traced its meaning for the child. For the basic principle would seem to be as follows: just as in general we expect residual infantilisms in the normal adult, so in particular we may expect blame behavior as an occasional response or component of a response in the normal adult. Such behavior will thus *not* be a negligible factor in everyday, normal adult life, but it will be occasional rather than consistent; it will be accepted and experienced fully, yet not sought or cultivated.

There is an important part-exception to these conclusions about adult blaming. It is an exception most readily explained in terms of the parental role. We have already stated that blame has its virtues in the education of the child. Does this imply that the mature parent, the parent who has in general grown out of the constant impulse to blame, will be unable to provide the child with the necessary "discipline"?

There are two reasons why the answer, as we know, is negative. In the first place, the present analysis of blame does not imply that blame is irreplaceable in its constructive effects upon the person blamed. In addition to blaming a child, there are other ways of providing support for his maturing ego and superego. As indicated previously, understanding firmness by the parent—if it is a genuine expression of the basic personality and not founded on the *suppression* of the impulse to blame—is reasonably common and is superior to blame in achieving similar developmental goals.

There is, however, another aspect to the problem. Our concept of adult normality must be readjusted once again when we recall that, in general, "any contact with the child tends to mobilize impulses and desires of the parent's own childhood." [32]

This feature of parent-child relations reminds us that psychological "maturity" is not something achieved at the end of adolescence once and for all; it is a concept that implies growth, constant *new* achievement. The normal adult, mature for his age and station in life, will nevertheless find that parenthood arouses old conflicts within him, conflicts which he wrestled with as a child and which he had in many ways resolved. Wittels [33] has written in a somewhat similar vein on the adolescent. We may even suppose that there is a tendency in the parent to echo in timing and in quality the same generic conflicts that his child goes through from infancy to adult maturity. The nature of the "echo" in the parent will, of course, depend to some extent upon the way he moved as a child through these developmental phases. Yet we may suppose a tendency to a spontaneous symmetry in the development of the child and the simultaneous reworking through of analogous childhood conflicts in the parent. Coleman, Kris, and Provence [34] have stated in a lucid development of this problem that "this mechanism of revival of the past is operative in the mother as well (as in the father) *and constitutes a central point in the experience of parenthood.*" (My italics) While little that is systematic has been written along these lines, we may expect, in general, that the parent will ideally achieve a new level of insight, sublimation, and maturity at just about the point that his child achieves the first level of adult maturity and independence. Indeed, these two simultaneous achievements are better seen as the differentiated end products of a single, symbiotic, maturational process.

This analysis of the parental relation may be generalized, *mutatis mutandis,* to apply to other crucial human relationships into which the mature adult enters. The more important the relationship, the deeper and stronger its roots in the unconscious. The greater the stress or novelty in such a relationship, the greater are the possibilities of regression as well as maturation. The handling of regressive tendencies in a new context of novelty and danger is almost an inevitable ingredient of the process of maturation. Accordingly, under all such circumstances, we may expect even the normal, "mature" adult to show an increased tendency to resort to blame as one among many regressive defenses. Here it is essential to remember that a defense does indeed *defend,* that blame may be a healthy, moralistic version of that general and important phenomenon which Kris has referred to as controlled regression in the service of the ego.[35]

V

IT IS NOW APPROPRIATE TO CONSIDER A PAIR OF IMPORTANT objections to the analysis presented up to this point. Discussion of these objections should help clarify the theses of this chapter.

Both questions have to do with the "legitimacy" of blame. In one sense of "legitimacy," we may ask whether there is not, perhaps, a kind of blaming which is *not* immediately motivated by a diversion of one's own unconscious guilt. Is the psychological analysis outlined herein universally adequate; is it valid for blaming in the context of everyday life and normal use? Or is it characteristic only for abnormal, pathological types of personalities? May there not be "disinterested" blame?

In another sense of legitimacy, we may ask whether, granted that blame is normally motivated by inner conflict and defense against guilt feelings, one is ever *morally* justified in engaging in such behavior? At first blush, it may seem a kind of moral hypocrisy to use another's misdeeds as the occasion for evading and covering up one's own impulses to perform the same misdeeds. This may appear to be so even if the consequences of blaming, from a practical standpoint, are conducive to maturation.

The universal adequacy of our analysis of normal blaming may be substantiated in two ways. Let us consider first the possibility that there may be psychological conditions for blaming which do not coincide with the conditions outlined in Section II. Consider, for example, the fate of an aggressive drive aroused by frustration of some desire. The aggressive drive may be discharged in undisguised aggressive behavior; it may be discharged internally in the form of largely somatic symptomatology; it may be diverted into "irrelevant" activity, e.g., warfare or tennis or debating. Among the numerous possible outcomes, the one which interests us here is that response which consists in repressing the instinctual aggression and diverting it to the superego. It may then be discharged in the service of the superego. The result may then be either guilt feelings, if the object of the aggression is the ego, or blame, if the object is another person. In this process, the blame fits the psychological formula outlined in Section II, yet the genesis of it seems significantly different. In particular, it appears to be intrinsically unjustifiable from the moral standpoint. It lacks the essential condition that the target of blame is really taken to have done a moral wrong; though he is *charged* with having done one when he is blamed. We are supposing here that the blame is merely a diversion of aggressive impulses roused in a nonmoral context. But in fact such a supposition is not compatible with the psychology of the situation. For, either there is only a *pretense* of superego (moralistic) criticism—in which case we have aggression *masquerading* as blame—i.e., we cannot say the energies have been genuinely channeled through the superego. Or else we actually have superego criticism—in which case the situation *must* be perceived as one in which *wrong*doing is taking place. But how can this be supposed if we also suppose that in fact the occasion was merely one which aroused (nonmoral) aggression in the observer?

The person who reacts to frustration with defensive (and unjustified) blame is someone who will be on the lookout for actions or feelings in the frustrating person which are likely to be useful in "justifying" his blame. As in the case of the paranoid process, his sensitivity to such things will be heightened. What is more, the blamer will tend to focus upon just those impulses which he himself is at the time struggling to deny and which, therefore, preoccupy him.

The practical result will be that the blamer will usually be blaming the frustrating person for purportedly carrying out the very forbidden impulses about which he, the blamer, tends to feel most guilty. Thus, while the genesis of the process is different from that of normal blame, the outcome exhibits the very pattern which we have previously described. Insofar as there *is* a difference in genesis, it is in the direction of lack of realism, insight, and responsibility. In childhood, somewhat similar but on the whole constructive responses to frustration take place. At that stage of development we are impressed by the maturational implications of the projection and introjection which constantly take place with regard to the parent figures.

Let us consider forthwith the generic reasons why the infectious conflict-arousing situation, as the occasion for blame, is bound to be ubiquitous in everyday life rather than occasional and abnormal.

From a psychological standpoint, the central question has to do with the conditions under which significant amounts of superego energy will be mobilized. In this context, the question is not one of objective moral values but of available psychic energies. We must recall here the well-known genesis of the superego as the resultant of a series of intense, infantile conflict situations organized in terms of the child's drives, his developing ego, and the significant figures in his family environment. These early conflict patterns foreshadow the later moral, spiritual, and social outlook. We think of these latter as novel in important respects, but as genetically continuous with, and in certain ways modeled upon, the infantile conflicts and their solutions as embodied in the superego.[36]

The less successful the resolution of these early conflicts, the more the psychic energies in later years are devoted to managing the unneutralized, conflicting drives involved. The more the psychic energies are devoted to this task, the more the superego and the personality as a whole develop in later years around the infantile conflicts instead of moving on into genuine maturity. Rather than new forms of ever subtler integration, there is an equilibrium based in a tension of gross force and counterforce. "Where there is a prohibition there must be an underlying desire." [37] Superego aggression will be mobilized with increasing intensity as there arise provocations to those infantile forms of behavior representative of unresolved infantile conflicts. The intensity will vary directly with the degree of provocation and the failure to achieve conflict-resolution.

Now, except for the perfectly mature person (a theoretical ideal), everyone else (i.e., everyone) retains greater or lesser, but in any case noticeable, degrees of unsuccessfully resolved infantile conflicts in the personality (and, where there is a superego at all, in the superego). It is possible to deduce in general, then, that for any observed case of human action involving the expression of infantile modes of behavior, there will be in the observer a noticeable "echo" of an analogous impulse with accompanying increase in countercathexis. The infectiousness of infantile behavior is universal, although varying substantially in degree both as among individuals and, intra-individually, as to specific areas of behavior.

There is, indeed, room for supposing a kind of generalized infectiousness about infantile behavior in the sense that the human being is able to perceive its generic character *as* infantile. As such, it constitutes a threat to the superego. Thus, to some extent or other, any rebellion against the superego is perceived by an onlooker in this general aspect as a temptation (to the id) and a threat (to the superego). As such, it tends to mobilize superego aggression with consequent guilt, blame, or a mixture of both. This effect will vary, of course, from individual to individual as previously indicated.

If we now take it for granted that the psychological pattern of normal, everyday blame is properly to be understood in terms of infectious conflict-arousal, the question next presents itself as to the legitimacy of blaming in the second sense mentioned earlier. We must ask: Is it *morally* legitimate to blame someone else in view of the fact that, when I do so, I am, in effect, using the other person as a "lightning rod" to carry off energies which would otherwise be experienced as guilt? Is this not moral hypocrisy?

The analogy of blame behavior with games will be a useful device for clarifying the point. Of course the game analogy is just that: a comparison having limited application. But since it is used here not as proof but for the purpose of illuminating a thesis, its use need not be objectionable.

In one important sense, the question as to the justification for blaming is akin to that of justifying the taking of an opponent's piece in chess. It is the rules of chess which establish the legitimacy of certain moves. Analogously, we may say that the "rules" of blame-morality establish the justification for blaming someone if the person blamed has in fact done that for which he is blamed, and what he has done is a wrong, and if he has no excuses acceptable under the rules. It is important to add that, in this connection, the question of the *motives* for blaming are, generally speaking, irrelevant. The question is only whether one has *grounds* for blaming. We must consider briefly this often obscured distinction.

It is important to know that a surgeon is justified, in doing surgery, by therapeutic considerations, even though he may be largely motivated by the desire for fame, money, or even, perhaps, by sublimated sadistic tendencies. Of course it is important that, regardless of his motives, the surgeon not perform the surgery without the therapeutic indications. Likewise, it is an essential condition for justified blaming that the person who blames not do so if the object of blame has not done (or is sincerely believed not to have done) wrong. Blaming which is only accidentally in conformity with the rules is no more justified than is surgery performed only accidentally in accordance with the therapeutic indications or the moving of a chess piece only accidentally in accordance with the rules.

Neurotics often tend to evade insight into their motives by focusing attention on the grounds which to them appear to justify their action. They "moralize." Perhaps for this very reason, the psychotherapist tends to stress motives and to be suspicious of arguments concerning the justification of an act. But in the last analysis, neither perspective can substitute for the other; they center in independent issues. The proper question is which of the two it is more profitable to consider in a particular situation. There are times when what we are interested in is whether what a man did was justified, not what his personal motives were; and there are times (psychotherapy being a good illustration) when we are interested in his motives more often than we are concerned with the justification of his acts.

We now must turn, however, to the question as to whether the "game" of blaming is, as a whole, justified. The rules of chess tell us what moves are permitted, but they do not tell us whether it is worth playing chess. Analogously, the rules of blaming tell us when one is and when one is not justified in blaming *if* one is engaged in the "game" of blaming. But the rules do not tell us whether the entire practice is justified. Those rules do not tell us the consequences of engaging in blame; nor do they tell us anything of the intrinsic value of the acts or the practice. Though we know what is justified within the game, we do not know whether the game is worth the candle.

This question has partly been answered, in effect, by our discussion of the role which blaming plays in socializing the child, in developing his reality sense, and in providing him with the materials of a moral life while not burdening him with the unmanageable tensions of deep insight. We must also recall the inevitable residue of the infantile in the normal adult and the consequent palliative effects of occasional blame-behavior in this connection.

In general, it is the lesson of our analysis of blame that the psychic strength and the objective social learning which are nourished by normal blaming are essential to the later tasks of maturation. This estimate cannot be confirmed until we have looked at those tasks. To evaluate a game or a system of law or a moral practice requires a large-scale examination of its prior conditions and of its fruits in addition to noting the intrinsic values generated within the functioning system itself. And, of course, such complex evaluations, even after the available evidence is in, cannot be demonstratively established, though in some cases they may be inescapable to the reasonable man. We cannot here go into the developmental phases which precede blame-behavior. But the following chapters will examine in detail the fruits of a personality whose seed has germinated under blame-morality's protective canopy and whose leaf and bud, at the appropriate time, were exposed to the full glare of the sun.

It is the training in the school of blaming and being blamed which prepares us for the first step toward achieving full insight: the acknowledgment of our own guilt and the acceptance of responsibility for what it represents.

NOTES

(See List of Bibliographical Abbreviations, p. 343.)

1. *New Testament: The Four Gospels,* Rieu, E. V., trans., Penguin Books, Baltimore, 1953.
2. Aristotle, *Nicomachean Ethics,* in *The Basic Works of Aristotle,* McKeon, Richard, ed., Random House, New York, 1941, p. 996.
3. Epictetus, "The Manual," in *The Stoic and Epicurean Philosophers,* Oates, W. J., ed., Random House, New York, 1940, pp. 468–490.
4. Butler, J., Sermon VIII: "Resentment," in *The Analogy of Religion,* Henry G. Bohn, London, 1856.
5. Buxbaum, E., "Technique of Child Therapy," in *The Psychoanalytic Study of the Child,* Vol. IX, International Universities Press, New York, 1954, pp. 297–333.
6. Schlick, M., *Problems of Ethics,* Rynin, D., trans., Prentice-Hall, New York, 1939, p. 152.
7. Freud, A., *The Ego and the Mechanisms of Defence,* Hogarth Press, London, 1947, p. 128.
8. Freud, S., *Inhibitions.*
9. ———, *Dreams,* Chap. VII E.
   ———, "Formulations Regarding the Two Principles in Mental Functioning" (1911), in *CP,* IV, pp. 13–21.
   ———, "Negation" (1925), in *CP,* V, pp. 181–185.
10. ———, "Negation," p. 184.
11. ———, *Totem,* pp. 71–72.
12. Redl, F., "Group Emotion and Leadership," *Psychiatry* 5:573–596 (1942).
13. ———, "Contagion and Shock Effect," in *Searchlights on Delinquency,* Eissler, K. R., ed., International Universities Press, New York, 1949.
14. See note 11 above.
15. Hartmann, H., "Comments on Problems of Infantile Neurosis," in *The Psychoanalytic Study of the Child,* Vol. IX, pp. 16–74.

16. Mahler, M. S., "Ego Psychology Applied to Behavior Problems," in *Modern Trends in Child Psychiatry*, Lewis, N. D. C., and Pacella, B. L., eds., International Universities Press, New York, 1945, p. 52.

17. Bornstein, B., "On Latency," in *The Psychoanalytic Study of the Child*, Vol. VI, International Universities Press, New York, 1951, pp. 279–285.
    Spiegel, L. A., "A Review of Contributions to a Psychoanalytic Theory of Adolescence," in *The Psychoanalytic Study of the Child*, Vol. VI, pp. 375–393.

18. Pearson, G. H. J., *Psychoanalysis and the Education of the Child*, W. W. Norton & Co., New York, 1954, pp. 315–319.

19. See note 7 above.

20. See note 7 above.

21. Grotjahn, M., "The Primal Crime and the Unconscious," in *Searchlights on Delinquency*, pp. 306–314.

22. Freud, A., *op. cit.*, p. 129.

23. Flugel, J. C., *Man, Morals, and Society*, International Universities Press, New York, 1945, Chap. 12.

24. Johnson, A., "Sanctions for Superego Lacunae," in *Searchlights on Delinquency*, pp. 225–245.

25. Eissler, R., "Scapegoats of Society," in *Searchlights on Delinquency*, pp. 288–305.

26. Bettelheim, B., "Somatic Symptoms in Superego Formation," *American Journal of Orthopsychiatry* 18:649–658 (1948).

27. Freud, S., *Group Psych.*

28. Kris, E., "On Psychoanalysis and Education," in *American Journal of Orthopsychiatry* 18:630–649 (1948).

29. Sterba, E., "Interpretation and Education," in *The Psychoanalytic Study of the Child*, Vol. I, International Universities Press, New York, 1946, pp. 309–317.

30. Kris, E., "On Psychoanalysis and Education," *op. cit.*

31. Hartmann, H., "Comments on Problems of Infantile Neurosis," *op. cit.*, p. 34.

32. Kris, E., "On Psychoanalysis and Education," *op. cit.*, p. 630. Cf. also Wolfenstein, M., "Some Variants in Moral

Training of Children," in *The Psychoanalytic Study of the Child,* Vol. V, International Universities Press, New York, 1950, pp. 310–328.

33. Wittels, F., "The Ego of the Adolescent," in *Searchlights on Delinquency,* pp. 256–262.

34. Coleman, R. W., Kris, E., and Provence, S., "The Study of Variations in Early Parental Attitudes," in *The Psychoanalytic Study of the Child,* Vol. VIII, International Universities Press, 1953, p. 23.

35. Kris, E., "On Preconscious Mental Processes," *Psychoanalytic Quarterly* 19:540–560 (1950).

36. Freud, S., *New Intro. Lec.,* Chap. III.

37. ——, *Totem,* p. 70.

CHAPTER 4

THE INITIAL PHASE:

Guilt and Responsibility

THE MOVE FROM THE MORAL LEVEL CHARACTERISTIC OF CHILD-hood to that characteristic of the mature adult comes when one faces one's own guilt and assumes responsibility. This transformation we shall examine in a systematic way. There is, however, such a pervasive background of misinterpretation of psychoanalysis in this connection that our first steps in this chapter will be critical rather than systematic exposition.

In this connection, the tendency in the nonpsychoanalytic literature has been to find that the rational implications of psychoanalysis are twofold. On the one hand, psychoanalysis is conceived of as antipathetic to the Calvinistic type of religious morality, the psychoanalytic war cry presumably being "Down with the repressive, burdensome conscience!" The corollary of this attitude toward guilt and conscience is a supposed bent inherent in psychoanalysis toward a more relaxed, hedonistic morality.

A specific aim of this chapter will be to show that (1) there is a moral outlook with respect to guilt and responsibility which is compatible with the data and theories of

146 / **PART II**

psychoanalysis but that (2) this moral outlook is different from the anticonscience, hedonistic one suggested above. In the first portion of this chapter, we shall therefore consider a typical (but mistaken) interpretation of psychoanalysis; though it is a philosophically responsible account, it puts things in a fundamentally incorrect way. Then, in the second section of the chapter, I shall present a brief but systematic account of what I consider to be the correct interpretation of the psychoanalytic material. And, finally, we shall examine and develop more fully a number of moral questions directly related to the material discussed. Here again we shall consider a ubiquitous form of misinterpretation of the implications of psychoanalysis.

I

G. A. PAUL, IN DISCUSSING THE MORAL SIGNIFICANCE OF PSYchoanalytic therapy, states that the analyst helps the neurotic "[see that he] has not done what troubles him and could hardly have avoided the wish to do it, and that therefore he has no ground for his feeling of desolation and so in part to escape it." [1]

Paul's statement implies that the feeling of guilt (feeling of desolation) is reduced by showing the patient, among other things, that he has *done* no wrong act but simply has *wished* to do one. (The assertion that the wish, in turn, could hardly have been avoided and is therefore a ground for guilt reduction, will be discussed, in substance, in Section III.)

Paul's statement raises the questions: (1) Do wishes merit less guilt than acts, all other things being equal? (2) Is the guilt in such cases as Paul indicates therefore unwarranted, disproportionate? (3) Is the primary object of such therapy to reduce or eliminate guilt?

Of course, the answer to (2) rests in part upon the answer to (1). Although it may not at first be obvious, it also rests upon the answer to (3), since our object is to take the facts of therapy as our primary data and discover what moral judgments are suggested by them.

Does an evil wish merit less guilt than the same wish put into action, all other things being equal? My answer is No. It is my aim in this first part of my discussion to show that, morally speaking, wishes count as acts so far as guilt is concerned, though putting the wish into action has consequences which may *in their own right* be morally bad. The wish to kill, for example, merits a certain guilt. It is the character of the wish and the degree of its acceptance which are relevant to the person's guilt.[2] Executing that wish adds of itself no guilt, though it is a very rough practical indication of the degree of acceptance of the wish by the person. The deed ordinarily adds to the guilt a series of bad consequences, e.g., pain and mental suffering. It also acts as a symbol and, short of psychosis, an inescapable reminder of the guilty wish; it presents dramatically and enduringly the fact that the guilty wish is a deep-rooted part of the self. The act may produce *legal* guilt and social sanctions. It thus prolongs and makes relatively more permanent the *conscious* horror and guilt. But the spiritual guilt is in fact no greater for having executed the wish.

Let us leave, for the moment, this dogmatic statement of my thesis and proceed to a consideration of question (3) for further light on the matter. Is the aim of therapy to remove guilt or at least to alleviate it? It is often supposed that this is so, but the point needs careful examination. From the psychological standpoint, said Freud, "we have from the very beginning attributed the function of instigating repression to the moral and esthetic tendencies in the ego. . . ."[3] From this it follows that to reduce the sense of guilt would be to weaken the repressive (i.e., moral) forces. *But to do this alone would make it more probable than before that the evil wish would in fact be expressed in a deed.* This is therapeutically *and* morally bad.

Even when we recognize that repression is often an irrational means of suppressing evil impulses and that, as a consequence, the objective of analysis is to remove (some) repressions, this does not imply the removal of guilt. For where irrational repression is given up as a means of keeping evil impulses from being directly expressed, a substitute rational suppressive guilt mechanism is used.

> Analysis replaces the process of repression, which is an automatic and excessive one, by a temperate and purposeful control on the part of the highest mental faculties. In a word, *analysis replaces repression by condemnation*.[4] [Italics in original]

In the previous quotation, "excessive" refers, as we shall see, not to the degree of guilt but to the scope and rigidity of the repressive process.

From the preceding, it is apparent that it could not be the objective of therapy simply to remove the sense of guilt for evil wishes. From a therapeutic standpoint and from a moral standpoint, such a result could be disastrous.

The doctrine that the deed merits greater guilt than the wish, however plausible a doctrine to the modern, "rational" mind, requires reconsideration in the light of this psychological analysis. Here I return to the earlier point suggested but undeveloped: he who identifies himself with some act, i.e., either wishes to do it or purposefully does it, merits the appropriate guilt. I do not, of course, mean to minimize the social consequences of the actual deed and *additional* values or disvalues produced.

I do not mean to deny that there is a significant relationship between the moral character of a certain type of wish and the consequences of actual instances of it, either as wish or overt action. There is a relationship, but it is not simple. It is certainly not that guilt is in direct proportion to the actual value-consequences of any one instance of the wish. It is not my purpose to go into this question here, since, for practical purposes, in this study, it suffices to recognize the substantial autonomy, with regard to consequences, of the relation between guilt and wish in any particular case.

We have noted that, from the psychoanalytic standpoint, the guilt associated with an evil wish is an important element tending to prevent the realization of that wish. Thus, from the psychotherapeutic standpoint, guilt plays its constructive role in relation to wishes and prior to acts. This is congruent with the (Christian) moral view that it is no moral excuse to have wished but not acted.

> Ye have heard that it was said by them of old time, Thou shalt not commit adultery; But I say unto you, That whosoever looketh on a woman to lust after her hath committed adultery with her already in his heart.[5]

And as we shall see in some detail in subsequent chapters, it is a similar emphasis on the wish rather than the deed which lies at the heart of the Hindu and Buddhist outlooks. Thus, the thesis I am now arguing may strike the reader as harsh or unreasonable, but it cannot be charged that it is eccentric. And, of course, it is not only my aim to recall that it is the thesis of the Judaeo-Christian and Hindu-Buddhist outlooks; it is also my aim to show that it is a thesis implicit in psychoanalysis.

We can perhaps get a better perspective on the matter if we note that the objective of psychoanalytic therapy, and of morality, is to remove both the wish *and* its attendant guilt. This is accomplished in the final analysis *by removing the evil wish*. Removal of the wish brings with it removal of the guilt. The relationship between the wish and the guilt is left essentially unchanged. They appear together and disappear together.

We must now consider whether the position expounded

by Paul can be saved by holding that the guilt felt, though to some extent justified, is *disproportionate* to the circumstances. Is the psychoanalyst trying to reduce the intensity of the guilt-feeling rather than to remove it? Is the guilt "excessive"?

There is a sense in which neurotic guilt-feelings are indeed disproportionate. There is a sense in which, as Paul suggests, the therapist points out a mistake on the part of the neurotic. Here we must ask, however: disproportionate to what? Mistaken in what way? Surely the wish, say, to destroy someone who is near and dear to one is evil in high degree. Yet this wish is typical of the unconscious wishes which trouble the neurotic.

The "disproportion" here is not in the guilt but in the *wish*. It is the wish which is childish, irrational, unwarranted in its context of activation. What is characteristic of the neurotic is his reaction to some situations with just such childishly intense and wild feelings or impulses, with patterns of behavior which are too gross, extreme, or misdirected to achieve any rational objective. What is necessary —from either a moral or a psychoanalytic standpoint—is to modify or to eliminate the wish.

Superficial consideration might suggest that a neurotic will sometimes feel tremendous guilt for some ordinary and respectable wish, say the wish to disagree with a parent. In such very common cases, inquiry ordinarily reveals that there is indeed a neurotic mistake here, but the mistake consists in supposing that the guilt felt by the neurotic has its ground in the conscious, relatively "innocent" wish. Such an "innocent" wish is in fact a cover-up for an unconscious wish which does merit the guilt in question. Freud tells of a person who

> . . . told me that the only thing that had kept him going at that time had been the consolation given him by

his friend, who had always brushed his self-reproaches aside on the ground that they were grossly exaggerated. Hearing this, I took the opportunity of giving him a first glance at the underlying principles of psychoanalytic therapy. When there is a *mésalliance*, I began, between an affect and its ideational content (in this instance, between the intensity of the self-reproach and the occasion for it), a layman will say that the affect is too great for the occasion—that it is exaggerated—and that consequently the inference following from the self-reproach (the inference, that is, that the patient is a criminal) is false. On the contrary, the physician says: "No. The affect is justified. The sense of guilt cannot in itself be further criticized. But it belongs to another content, which is unknown (*unconscious*), and which requires to be looked for. The known ideational content has only got into its actual position owing to a mistaken association." [6]

It is perhaps because of this extremely common phenomenon that the casual observer or reader of case histories gets the impression that the guilt felt is disproportionate to the wish. The psychoanalyst in general assumes the guilt has a ground and looks further.

It is plausible to argue that there are at least some cases where we can find the wish which actually is the ground of the guilt and where, in the light of contemporary knowledge, we recognize that the guilt *is* disproportionate because the standards determining guilt are unrealistic. Typical of such cases is masturbation. For anyone familiar with the contemporary data in connection with the physiological innocuousness of masturbation, it is tempting to argue that masturbation is the real cause of intense and widespread guilt-feeling, but that such guilt should be reduced by a relaxation of our standards.

Psychoanalytic inquiry reveals, however, that the physical and physiological aspects of masturbation are not, per se, the grounds of the frequent guilt-feelings associated with masturbatory practices. The source of the major part of the guilt-feeling is the fantasying which accompanies the masturbation. It is the unconscious and conscious wishes and daydreams, which the act of masturbation helps to express, that are relevant to the guilt-feelings. These fantasies are likely to be incestuous, sadistic, masochistic, or in other ways morally evil (although ubiquitous in so-called Western culture). Here again, then, we can see that the solution indicated is not a "loosening up" of inner standards or conscience with respect to masturbation—though to the guilt-burden of the masturbating child we need not add *another* burden by making violent attacks upon him. On the other hand, neither psychoanalyst nor moralist would argue that our taboos against incest or sadism need to be eliminated. The ultimate solution is to modify or eliminate the wishes; it is not to give them moral approval nor to turn our wrath upon the person and blame him.

Freud spoke of the "omnipotence of thought," by which he meant that the wish is psychologically equivalent to the deed. That is to say, a person often has many of the typical feelings associated with having done a deed, even when he has only wished it were done. Not only his feelings but his behavior may be characteristic in key respects to one who has done the deed. Among the phenomena which consistently follow this pattern, guilt stands out as one of the most important.

Psychologically, an evil wish, because of the omnipotence of thought, is like an evil deed, and guilt accrues. This phenomenon may be viewed in a moral light, and if we take the psychological facts as a reflection of the moral facts, what we have is the moral omnipotence of wishes. That is, we find that the wish is enough to merit moral judgment with respect to guilt.

Freud himself spoke of the "equivalence of wicked acts and wicked intentions." [7] When the superego is established, he said, there ceases "once and for all any difference between doing evil and wishing it." [8] It is clear that not only the content of my thesis but even the "moralistic" language in which it is cast is consistent with Freud's own usage.

Thus, irrational as it may seem to the twentieth-century "enlightened" mind, if psychoanalysis is taken seriously, it supports the position taken so far in this chapter, a position also taken by many moral seers in both West and East.

We are now able to see, in something of a proper perspective, how essentially alien it is to the major objectives of psychoanalytic therapy to loosen conscience, weaken ideals or reduce guilt by reminding the patient that he has not done what he unconsciously wished. Nor are comments to the effect that everyone has such wishes and that they can hardly be helped the sort of comments appropriate to therapy. If this latter approach were correct, then psychoanalysts would indeed merely "loosen" up the conscience. In fact, however, the psychoanalyst does not tamper so lightly with our basic moral standards. His practice and theory show that the wish must be taken seriously, that the guilt is appropriate, and that the rational aim of therapy is, where possible, to eliminate or modify the wish. From this it is clear that the psychoanalyst, far from relaxing our moral judgments in fundamental questions is, in fact, aiming at helping us to be moral (and rational).

Yet we cannot ignore the fact that the psychoanalyst is not usually found *calling* these things morally evil. This absence of moralizing language and manner may give the impression that he has a morally neutral attitude toward them. It would be a mistake to assume this, however. The moral implications which I have stressed are often overlooked because we are impressed by the ways in which psychoanalysis is *not* puritanical: for example, psychoanalysis does not call for the puritanical rejection of persons having evil impulses. These persons and their impulses may be accepted and treated as human beings, especially where present techniques do not enable us to help them rid themselves of the impulses. In short, the analyst does not hold out for either perfection or damnation. For though he does not indulge in blaming the person with evil impulses, and indeed respects his dignity as a human being, we need not suppose that he must *approve*, morally or psychologically, of these impulses. The psychotherapist is like any reasonable person here: he tries to make the best of a bad bargain at times and, *faute de mieux*, to be tolerant of evil impulses in order to avoid the even worse evil which may result from irrational repression or social contempt.

Another reason why we often overlook the fundamental implications of psychoanalytic therapy has to do with questions of technique rather than ultimate objectives. Frequently the objective of the therapist is to reduce guilt-feelings independently of removing the wish. But, when this is so, it is a *technical* objective, with strictly limited and temporary scope, during some special phase of a psychoanalysis. It is because the repressive force associated with the feeling of guilt is what operates to keep the evil wish unconscious, because this repression prevents expression of the wish in open and undistorted form, because, in short, the guilt *hides* the wish. Therefore the analyst must, at times, reduce the guilt *feeling* and its repressive character. This allows the wish itself to come to consciousness. Rational (ego) criticism of our evil wishes, especially when they stem from a systematic irrationality (neurosis), requires ordinarily that we become conscious of the wish. Reduction of guilt feelings with this purpose in view is thus a temporary therapeutic technique, not a therapeutic or moral goal. One device used for such technical guilt-reduction is the abstention from *explicit* moral judgments by the analyst during therapy. It is this, then, which accounts in part for the lack of moralizing language in psychoanalysis.

Even aside from such technical, therapeutic devices, the analyst's lack of moral comment in his writings and therapy should not be taken as an indication that there is no moral judgment implicit in psychoanalytic theory. We must distinguish the objective fact of evil and guilt from the psychological shock, surprise, and horror which the layman often experiences upon suddenly discovering that evil and guilt. The therapist is under less compulsion to *talk* about the evilness because, psychologically, he is accustomed to finding it and observing it. (Needless to say, he may be apt to forget at times that it *is* evil because of this; but this is a human error, not an implication of the data and theory.)

Still another reason for the systematic avoidance of moralizing language is the simple fact that the psychoanalyst is, along with other careful observers of the human scene, all too aware of the confusion and dogma liberally sprinkled through the body of our moral language and theory. He cannot help but see the general tendency to rationalize and otherwise to disguise one's motives by invoking moral doctrines. As we saw in the previous chapter, the neurotic patient is often only too prone to evade insight into motives by concentrating on problems of moral justification, even when it is the former which are the source of his trouble. It is not that moral analysis is irrelevant but that it is appropriate only *after* the relevant features of the situation, including motives, are known. Premature moral analysis too often hinders inquiry into the facts of the inner life. Such neurotic defenses cannot help but make the psychoanalyst wary of introducing moral doctrine into his examination and therapy of the psychically disturbed.

Finally, let it suffice merely to mention here that the objective of therapy is not to indoctrinate the patient with the psychoanalyst's particular moral judgments but to let the patient make his own moral judgments as he discovers his unconscious wishes and their relation to his life circumstances. We have discussed this in a previous chapter, and we shall shortly turn again to further comment on this particular point. In general we may simply note that we must distinguish comment and indoctrination on moral issues from the moral issues themselves. The latter exist and are inherent in the therapeutic process.

II

PSYCHOANALYTC THERAPY IS NOT AIMED AT "LOOSENING UP" the conscience or minimizing or eliminating guilt from human experience. What, then, is the objective and method of therapy with respect to this problem of guilt? And where does responsibility enter the picture?

The first step in the therapeutic situation where guilt-feelings dominate is to reduce temporarily the total feeling of threat and danger which encourages repressive forces, forces directed toward keeping out of consciousness a variety of ideas, affects, and impulses which are felt as threatening by the patient. This reduction of the sense of threat (anxiety-feelings) produces a reduction in the repressive pressure. This, in turn, is automatically followed by the appearance in conscious form of some of these hitherto repressed mental phenomena. (The technical means of accomplishing this are irrelevant to our purposes. The ontological interpretation of these formulations in terms of meaning, ego-disorganization, and the related ideas in Part I is not our concern here nor anywhere in Part II. It must suffice to suggest that we are dealing here with reduction of anxiety-*feelings* which arise when areas of ego-disorganization (anxiety) are pointed out by the therapist and new forms of ego-organization (insight) are proposed. The reduction of these and related feelings aids in permitting the patient to pay attention with relative composure to the task.)

Surprisingly enough for those unacquainted with psychiatric theory and practice, one of the first phenomena to show itself in the patient's consciousness is his guilt-feeling. For it is very frequently the case that the guilt (a specific form of anxiety) is unconscious. Thus the first step often consists in *making the person sharply aware of, making him feel intensely, his profound guilt.* Notice that this is the contrary of what is suggested by the philosophic view previously criticized, namely that the objective of therapy is to remove guilt-feelings.

If we were to put this into more common-sense, moralistic terminology, we might say that the patient is enabled to face his guilt rather than to run away from it as he has in the past.

When the patient has faced his guilt, the next objective is to discover the ground of the guilt. Where there is neurosis, the ground of the guilt will be unconscious, although a *supposed* ground may be present in consciousness. This supposed ground may be obviously inadequate as a ground for the guilt, or it may appear plausible. Still, analyst and patient must look behind it.

In order to discover the actual ground for the guilt, however, it is often necessary, at this stage, to reduce temporarily the burden of *felt* guilt. (The method used here is not, of course, repression of the guilt-feelings; for to encourage repression would be to reinstitute the original neurotic condition.) Reducing the burden of guilt-feelings weakens still further the repressive forces at work and allows additional mental activity to come to consciousness. Eventually the actual ground of the guilt becomes conscious. The struggle by the patient to hide, disguise, and repress this actual ground is ordinarily a long and painful one, and it is only resolved by constant, patient, and skillful exposure on the part of the analyst of each of the strategies used by the patient. Where the problem is major, as in neurosis, the real guilty wish will be found to be deeply rooted in the patient's response to some fundamental human relationship. It is likely to be at the "core" of his personality.

Thus, and again from the moral perspective, the patient may be said to have been forced to face not only his guilt but, in addition, the evil within him which is the reason for his guilt.

There is an aspect of this process which is psychologically and morally crucial but which is too often ignored in lay discussion. To become conscious of the wish is not the same thing as to learn, as from reading or observing others, that one has the wish. It is not, in short, merely an intellectual process. In the latter sense of "becoming conscious," the patient can often be easily made "conscious" of what his repressed wishes are. He can simply be told what they are. If he has confidence in the authoritativeness of the information, he will then believe it. Indeed, evidence can often be furnished which will "prove" to him that he has the wish. None of this is what is meant by "becoming conscious" of the wish in the therapeutic sense of that phrase.

Becoming conscious of the wish, in the psychoanalytic sense in question, is not so much a question of authoritative information or empirical proof as it is of consciously *experiencing himself as wishing* the wish.

The psychological and moral significance of this is profound. It means that the patient has not merely made an intellectual discovery; he has come to acknowledge in the fullest emotional and moral sense that the wish in question is *his*. It is no longer a something believed to be somehow, somewhere within him; *he consciously, vividly wishes it*. In the most literal moral sense, and as perceived introspectively, it is an acknowledged part of his Self, no longer alien to that Self. In psychoanalytic terminology, the patient has *insight*.

At this stage of the process, the patient is facing fully

and frankly his evil wish. He is at last able to reflect upon it in the context of his present life circumstances and fundamental ideals. This context he has in turn learned, in the course of therapy, to recognize in a more realistic and balanced way than when his perception was distorted by neurosis. Being able to appraise his wish realistically in an accurately perceived life context, he at last is able to reject the wish, to modify it, or to retain it, and to do these in a manner harmonious with, and expressive of, his Self. He no longer responds with uncontrollable, irrational reactions.

Let us emphasize that it is not so much that the analyst *tells* him about the attendant guilt; he now sees this fact himself. It is not that the analyst *tells* him about the consequences of his having the wish; he has now appraised these consequences on his own and perceived through life experience and vivid imagination their intimate connection with his wish.

So far as therapy is concerned, the ordinary outcome, if successful, would be the rejection or modification of the evil wish. The reason is essentially simple. The roots of the neurotic suffering which brings the neurotic to the therapist are seen to be the wish, the attendant guilt, and the psychological and external consequences of repressing the wish and expressing it in distorted forms. The rational mind, the mind capable of appraising these factors, will attempt to restructure the wish in such a way as to minimize guilt and other painful consequences. The wish will be altered to harmonize with the basic personality of the patient. In some cases of thorough and deep analysis, the patient may even be able to modify some rather fundamental ideal of his; but this is not so much a purposeful and controlled objective as it is an occasional outcome, a recommitment. This aspect of the matter we have explored more intensively in connection with the chapter on anxiety.

Such a restructuring or rejection of a deep-rooted wish is

not easy. It requires much energy; it requires much in the way of creating—by rational deliberation, experience-testing, and anxiety-fraught moves toward recommitment—a better resolution of the patient's problems. It can be as difficult to create a constructive solution as it has been to discover the previous inadequate solution. At least it is done, however, without the tremendous tension which burdened the patient when under the full sway of his neurosis.

A deeply rooted wish is likely to have certain general features which cannot be eradicated: the sexuality, aggressiveness, or other quasi-biological or cultural characteristics. Such wishes can be *modified,* however, and often in a wide variety of ways. The most fundamental and enduring modification is likely to be sublimation and drive-neutralization: a retention of certain generic features of the wish along with a substantial modification of the specific quality and aim of the wish. The wish is then not merely "added" to the ego but is intimately and harmoniously integrated with the rest of the personality. A typical example of such sublimations is the normal transformation of infantile homosexual motives into brotherly, humanitarian love and into various forms of friendship.

There are, of course, a variety of interesting types of cases which may at times appear to be exceptions to the general principles mentioned here. For example, it is possible to *feign* guilt-feeling as a disguise for some other feeling. In this case, the "guilt-feeling" may of course disappear with insight but prior to the disappearance of a wish. Or again, it is possible to identify oneself with someone (consciously or unconsciously) and to make a part of oneself, as a consequence of this identification, the guilty wishes of that person. In this latter case, guilt may be eradicated by undoing the identification and thereby actually removing the guilty wish from one's personality. It is not appropriate here, however, to go into the byways of these matters.

III

WE ARE NOW PREPARED TO DEVELOP MORE FULLY THE MORAL implications of the previous discussions. I shall begin by presenting some excerpts from a contemporary and exceedingly clear exposition of the kind of philosophic interpretation of psychoanalysis which I hold to be wrong. In this way we can set off most sharply the correct perspective on moral responsibility seen from a psychoanalytic standpoint. John Hospers says,

> In a deeper sense we cannot hold the person responsible: we can hold his neurosis responsible, but *he is not responsible for his neurosis,* particularly since the age at which its onset was inevitable was an age before he could even speak.[9] [Italics in original]

Of course, Hospers admits, the neurosis is a part of the person; but what people mean when they talk about freedom (and hence responsibility) is that the *conscious* will is the master of their destiny.

> Between an unconscious that willy-nilly determines your actions, and an external force which pushes you, there is little if anything to choose. The unconscious is just *as if* it were an outside force. . . .[10] [Italics in original]

Hospers presents a deductive argument to support his position. During the course of it, he makes two assumptions of a moral nature. He assumes (1) that we cannot be held responsible for an event over which we have no control. Such an event, he says, is the neurosis we acquire in childhood. (The childhood neuroses are the roots of the adult neuroses.) He further assumes (2) that we cannot be held responsible for anything which happens as an inevitable result of an uncontrollable event. His conclusion is that we cannot be held responsible as adults for the actions which stem from our adult neuroses, since these are, he says, by the psychoanalytic hypothesis, inevitable consequences of our childhood neuroses. While we could question his formulation of the psychoanalytic hypotheses, we need not consider the matter here. For his version provides us with what ought to be the most difficult form of the argument with which to deal.

Granted, then, at least for the sake of argument, that adult neuroses are inevitable results of these early unconscious patterns, Hospers' argument seems highly plausible. But what can we make of it in the light of our analysis of psychoanalysis in the preceding sections of this chapter?

We have seen that the essence of therapeutic and moral progress is (1) to acknowledge (2) as a part of one's Self (3) guilty wishes (and disguised actions expressive thereof). To do this is to accept responsibility, i.e., to accept as *ours* the task of doing something about these wishes or suffering the moral and psychological consequences. In spite of Hospers' assumption that we cannot be held responsible for the inevitable consequences of uncontrollable events, we seem to see in therapy an acceptance of responsibility for just such events. We also see a new way of looking at responsibility.

If we are to discover the moral viewpoint consistent with psychoanalysis (which is a principal purpose of this study), we must give up the postulate which conflicts with what we know to be psychoanalytic practice. Apparently the patient *must* accept responsibility for traits and actions of his which are the inevitable results of events over which he had no control and of actions which he did not consciously will.

I hold that, paradoxical as it may at first *seem*, this is precisely the case.

As do so many moralists, Hospers looks to the antecedents of the act in order to settle responsibility. The real issue as revealed by our present perspective, however, is this: What is the (moral-therapeutic) *solution* to the present human predicament, granted that what happens now is a consequence of what happened when we could not control what happened?

The solution is, as I have already indicated, that moral man must *accept* responsibility for what he is at some point in his life and go on from there. He must face himself as he *is*, in toto; and as an adult, being able now in some measure to control what happens, he must endeavor so to control things that he is, insofar as possible, guiltless in the future. The neurotic, of course, cannot ordinarily do this without the preliminary aid of therapy.

This may seem a harsh view of life, an arbitrary and inhumane one. In fact it *is* harsh to a degree, but it is *not* arbitrary or inhumane. It is the brute fact which mature human beings and immature ones with moral insight have long recognized in their practice and at times in their theory.

It is not arbitrary, for there *is* a reason for accepting responsibility. The temptation is to ask: "But *why* should I accept responsibility for that which I could not help?" The implication of this rhetorical question is that this is an unjustifiable burden. And it will always appear unjustifiable so long as one looks to the past for the reason. It is to the *future*, however, that we must look for the justification of this profound moral demand. It is not that we *were* children and thus nonresponsible but rather that we are *aiming to become* mature persons. This *ideal*, and not the past, is the ground for the harsh demand that we accept responsibility for what we are, even though we are in many ways morally evil and even though we could not help ourselves.

Guilt is retrospective, but responsibility is prospective. Responsibility is based on a willingness to face the world as it is *now* and to proceed to do what we can to make it the world as we would like it to be. To accept responsibility is to be responsible for what shall be done. The matter is as simple and direct as in the case of a "natural disaster." I am a member of the community. I face the disaster and say, "I had no control over what happened. (Indeed, I am in this instance guilty for none of it.) Nevertheless, I accept responsibility for it; I will clear up and repair this area. What else can I do except run away from reality like a child?"

It is only in a derivative sense that we are responsible for what *has* happened. The common emphasis upon responsibility as pertaining to things past is understandable from a practical standpoint, but it has obscured the essentials of the matter. Being responsible for what *has* happened implies that one accepted responsibility, tacitly or explicitly, in the *doing* of it. Thus we do not hold a person responsible for what he has done till he has reached an appropriate "age of responsibility." And this is presumptive evidence that he accepts responsibility in cases where it is normally accepted. If in fact the person shows no confirming signs of such acceptance of responsibility, we take him to be stunted in his development. We treat him as nonresponsible, a "moral child." In clear-cut cases, we provide a guardian.

The acceptance of responsibility is not a matter of public announcement in each instance of action. Indeed, where a person has reached the "age" and "state" of being responsible, it is the tacit assumption that he does generally accept responsibility for what he is doing—and his mere denial is no more than prima-facie evidence that he had really not done so. We look to his conduct, his general bearing and his utterances on the whole. And then we may well say, in effect, "You disclaim responsibility, but it is evident that you did know, you must have known, what you were doing, and you still went ahead with it. You knew it was *your* action which would produce such results, and you chose to do it. Don't pretend now that you were not involved as an agent, as a *doer* of the act rather than as a mere sufferer of the consequences."

Thus it may seem that individuals can be held responsible though they had not accepted responsibility. But in truth the presumption of such acceptance is a prerequisite to holding a person responsible. When a person is accepted for treatment, the evidence in the particular case is weighty that he had not, until now, accepted responsibility in certain areas of his life. Hence we allow his claim to *therapy* rather than moral judgment and response. In successful psychoanalytic therapy, the patient at last *becomes* responsible; he achieves autonomy by his acceptance of responsibility, and he takes on the burdens of being held responsible.

To say, as some do, that we are automatically responsible for our adult past, for the guilt and merit, is, then, to miss the point of responsibility. It is not that we *are* responsible, but that, by an act of will, of deliberate choice, we shoulder the burden of responsibility from henceforth; we proclaim ourselves responsible for the future, honestly acknowledging our present inadequacies and handicaps for this task, ready to accept the full burden of possible failure even though it be in fact the result of an unfortunate past, not consciously or responsibly willed.

To face the world and oneself as they truly are and to accept responsibility for what in each of these one can control are the necessary conditions of maturity. It is not a penance for the past but the price of the future. Humility is of the essence.

Honest humility reveals that to accept responsibility, considering what we start with, is a heavy burden. To say, as criticism, that this is not "fair" or "just" is to suppose that the world is fair and just. This is precisely what the world is not. It has no design leading to some inevitable, built-in moral future. It is we human beings who can reach humanity only by accepting the challenge to *make* the world just.

Without getting into metaphysical issues, it is perhaps worth noting that it is irrelevant to the present view whether one holds that the accepting of responsibility is itself "inevitable," "caused," or "free" in any of the traditional metaphysical senses of these terms. In any case, it is a *fact* that accepting responsibility is a necessary condition of maturity, and those who do not, or "cannot," do so, for whatever reason, are in fact doomed never to have psychological and moral integrity.

It is possible at this point to see how, in a passage previously cited, Hospers is correct in his facts but incorrect in his interpretation. He suggests that the unconscious, insofar as uncontrollable, is *alien* to us, as alien as the external environment which "pushes" us. He is correct in saying they are comparable but incorrect in his suggestion that they are in all relevant respects alike in being inherently "alien" to the Self. The purport of psychoanalytic therapy is that we must come to acknowledge the unconscious as part of the Self, not as alien to it. I capitalize Self because I do not mean what Hospers does when he admits, of course, that the unconscious or the neurosis is part of ourself. He means that it is part of us, but not part of that Self which we think of as the subject of guilt, freedom, and responsibility. It is in this latter sense, however, that I mean that we must acknowledge the unconscious, with its neuroses, as part of us. We learn from psychoanalysis that to treat the unconscious as alien to the Self, in the morally significant sense, is to *subvert* the Self. It is to remove important parts of it from rational control. It is a surrender of integrity.

Indeed, even with regard to our dream wishes, Freud said,

> Obviously one must hold oneself responsible for the evil impulses of one's dreams. In what other way can one deal with them? . . . If, in defence, I say that what is unknown, unconscious and repressed in me is

not in my "ego," then . . . I shall perhaps learn that
what I am repudiating not only "is" in me but sometimes "acts" from out of me as well." [11]

Hospers is correct, I have said, in presenting a parallel between the unconscious and external environmental
"forces." But what I have said about the unconscious, I
would also say about external forces. Insofar as either of
these can be made harmonious with our Self, we must accept responsibility to make them so. Once again, I would
emphasize that it is pointless to say that we *are* responsible
for integrating so much of our world as we can into the
pattern of human purposes; it is rather that *we must accept*
such responsibility as the price of maturation. This is the
ground of our saying in ordinary language that we can be
responsible for physical happenings as well as for actions.
We can be responsible for the machinery subject to our control or for the social organization subject to our control just
as we can be responsible for our personal actions. This is
common knowledge, but the justification of it is often sought
in the past, and it will not be found there.

It is important to note that, if we follow the lead given
us by psychoanalysis with regard to guilt, we are led to the
view that guilt accrues according to the moral character of
a wish or an act and that this is not limited to acts or wishes
for which we have assumed responsibility. Responsibility
comes relatively late in life; guilt appears very early in life.
Thus we can be guilty where we are not responsible. Indeed, Freud said that so soon as the superego is established,
there ceases to be "once and for all any difference between
doing evil and wishing to do it." [12] In this sense, at least, we
are born into sin. For we are involved with evil and guilt
before we are able to assume that responsibility for our self
which might, at least ideally, keep us from having the wishes
which constitute morally the fact of the spirit's corruption.

Thus it is easy to see that our argument is consistent not only with psychoanalytic doctrine but also with a large segment of traditional morality as found embedded in religious views. It is common in Christian thought to argue that we are born sinners, but not to argue that we are responsible beings when we are children. And it is central to Buddhist thought that it is moral corruption and spiritual illusion into which we are born, but that responsibility and illumination are the eventual means of achieving purity and sanity. The implausibility of this view, insofar as it seems implausible, results not from evidence to the contrary but from *assuming* that the world is in some sense already moral and that, therefore, it would be unjust to suppose a person guilty unless he were responsible for his acts. It must be added that the guilt of a responsible person has a different quality, or at least a different significance, from that of a non-responsible person.

There is much more we might say about this phase of individual development which I have called the assumption of responsibility.[13] Indeed, the present chapter provides only a kind of basic orientation and framework. This orientation is that of therapy rather than, as in Chapter II, psychoanalytic theory. And it is the therapeutic framework which is the relevant one in this chapter and the rest of Part II. For we are concerned with a tracing out of the self in transformation rather than with static theoretical formulations in connection with moral or spiritual conceptions. The framework of this chapter, then, must be filled in by the material in the next two, material which shows in depth the significance of insight and responsibility as these are achieved in therapy. Then, in the final chapter, we shall look in depth at the consummatory phase of this transformation.

NOTES

(See List of Bibliographical Abbreviations, p. 343.)

1. Paul, G. A., "Symposium on the Problem of Guilt," in *Aristotelian Society*, Supplement, Vol. XXI, London, 1947, p. 214.
2. Fingarette, H., "Real Guilt and Neurotic Guilt," *Journal of Existential Psychiatry* 3: 145–158 (1962).
3. Freud, S., *Ego & Id*, p. 47.
4. ———, "Analysis of a Phobia in a Five-Year-Old Boy," in *CP*, III, p. 285.
5. *New Testament*, Matt. 5:27–28.
6. Freud, S., "Notes Upon a Case of Obsessional Neurosis," in *CP*, III, pp. 313–314.
7. ———, *Civ. & Disc.*, p. 113.
8. *Ibid.*, p. 108.
9. Hospers, J., "Free-Will and Psychoanalysis." Reprinted in part in *Readings in Ethical Theory*, Sellars, W., and Hospers, J., eds., Appleton-Century-Crofts, New York, 1952, p. 571.
10. *Loc. cit.*
11. Freud, S., "Moral Responsibility for the Content of Dreams," in *CP*, V, p. 156.
12. ———, *Civ. & Disc.*, p. 108.
13. See Fingarette, H., "Responsibility," *Mind* (in press).

CHAPTER *5*

THE MID-PHASES (1):

Karma and the Inner World

THE DOCTRINE OF KARMA, WHETHER WE ACCEPT IT OR NOT, poses profound questions about the structure, transformation, and transcendence of the Self. It raises in new ways general questions of ontology. We may be parochial and dismiss the doctrine, especially its theses on reincarnation, as obvious superstition. Or we may recall that it was not any self-evident spiritual superficiality but the historical accident of official Christian opposition which stamped it out as an important Greek and Roman doctrine, a doctrine profoundly meaningful to a Plato as well as to the masses. Perhaps more significant, it has remained, from the first millennium B.C. until the present, an almost universal belief in the East, even among most of the highly trained and Western-educated contemporary thinkers. As one Western student of the subject quite properly says,

> A theory which has been embraced by so large a part of mankind, of many races and religions, and has commended itself to some of the most profound thinkers of all time, cannot be lightly dismissed.[1]

In any case, an investigation of the doctrine will force us to examine from a fresh perspective both the nature of the self and the ontological question, What is Reality?

Certainly we can avoid some irrelevant psychological hurdles if it be stressed at once that, in our discussion of karma and reincarnation, we will not have jumped into an antiscientific position, nor will we be treating reincarnation as "pseudo" or as "super" science. The real issues are philosophical. They have nothing to do with amassing reports of *wunderkinder,* Indian yogis, or the periodic newspaper sensationalisms exploiting fakes or unfortunates claiming inexplicable knowledge of past events. These "marvels" are as philosophically uninteresting to us as it turns out that they are to the great prophets of karma.

The assumption in this chapter is that joining a fresh examination of karmic doctrine to an examination of certain aspects of psychoanalytic therapy will throw a new light on therapy, on the meaning of the karmic doctrine, and on certain of our major philosophical and cultural commitments. The task of the reader in such a discussion is to see what the evidence and the argument say rather than to read into the words the Westerner's stock interpretation of "esoteric" doctrines.

I
Some Suggestive Illustrations

LET US SET THE STAGE BY INTRODUCING ILLUSTRATIVE MATErial out of two contexts, one the ancient East, the other the contemporary West.

We are told in the Tibetan *Book of the Dead* that, upon entering a womb (for a new birth):

> If [about] to be born as a male, the feeling of itself being a male dawneth upon the Knower, and a feeling of

intense hatred towards the father and of jealousy and attraction towards the mother is begotten. If [about] to be born as a female, the feeling of itself being a female dawneth upon the Knower, and a feeling of intense hatred towards the mother and of intense attraction and fondness towards the father is begotten.[2]

An early Indian sutra states:

Finally, as the time of [the human being's] death approaches he sees a bright light, and being unaccustomed to it at the time of his death he is perplexed and confused. He sees all sorts of things such as are seen in dreams, because his mind is confused. He sees his [future] father and mother making love, and seeing them a thought arises in him. If he is going to be reborn as a man he sees himself making love with his mother and being hindered by his father; or if he is going to be reborn as a woman, he sees himself hindered by his mother. It is at that moment that the Intermediate Existence is destroyed and life and consciousness arise and causality begins once more to work. It is like the imprint made by a die; the die is destroyed, but the pattern has been imprinted.[3]

It takes little effort to "transpose" such passages into the analogous psychoanalytic language; indeed they can be read as poetic accounts of the nature and import of the Oedipal phase in individual maturation. The "birth" of a unified self and personality, the profound "imprint" which this Oedipal birth into selfhood places upon the fundamental character of the person, the "womb" or dreamlike "Intermediate Existence" of the infantile, pre-Oedipal period, the beginning of life, consciousness, and "causality" on the new level of a psyche now essentially complete and integrated, the central role of intrafamilial sexuality, aggression, and anxiety in this process at its crisis—all these need only be mentioned once the juxtaposition is made. It will be no great surprise after this to learn that, according to the detailed Tibetan accounts, the "Intermediate Existence" before "entering the womb in order to be born" is a complex one, an existence fraught with openly id-like experiences, an existence which has a definite genetic continuity, however, with the eventual "birth" and with the specific spiritual nature of the being which thus comes to life.

In such discussion of birth and rebirth, the three driving forces which must be overcome in the inner man are, of course, Anger, Lust, and Stupidity.[4] These are mentioned in varying terminologies, but nowhere can we mistake the broad intention. These three "cravings" at the root of all suffering are remarkably reminiscent of certain basic psychoanalytic conceptions. I refer to libidinal drive and aggressive drive and to the neurotic self-deception or psychotic delusions which are the generic consequences of unsublimated libido and aggression. The anxiety which prevails is vividly expressed in images of monstrous horrors and cataclysms, terror-inspiring precipices. ("Fear these not . . . O nobly-born, they are not really precipices; they are Anger, Lust, and Stupidity."[5])

A teacher has a frustrating, unsuccessful day in class. He knows that there have been successful days, that things cannot always go well. Nevertheless, he feels resentful, guilty, shameful, and impotent. That night, asleep, he dreams. He is addressing a class, teaching them of the wonderful nature and powers of the Sun. It is evident that he is not merely teaching about the Sun's great power, he is in that very act the transmitter of that power, its medium, the agent and offspring of the Sun. He is—an anxiety-fraught pun—the son. The students, however, have difficulty appreciating the magnificence of the whole subject, the wonder of the Sun's power.

The dream may be looked at as an obvious reaction to

the frustration and impotence felt during the day. It is a fantasy of omnipotence lived out in a manic dream world, with only the nagging tag ends of frustration caused by an unforgivably dense group of students. But the dream is not only a reaction to the day's events. For both dream and the preceding day's events are expressions of a more enduring, underlying fantasy. The day-feelings of guilt and impotence are in substantial part the natural psychomoral consequences of archaic unconscious fantasies of pride and omnipotence. The dream is then understood as a particular plastic manifestation during sleep of an enduring, unconscious "drama" operating continuously, day and night. The night-dream, as Freud said, is simply a special form of expression of a deep, unconscious wish.

Let us "stretch" our language a bit. We may say that the teacher in question lives a secret "life," a colorful, quasi-mythological life, a life aimed at glorious domination over others while acting as the protected agent of the All-Powerful. Garbed in twentieth-century attire, the dream-teacher is a twentieth-century Sun-priest. This secret life has, as we have noted, an intimate relation to his public life. Yet the teacher does not know of its existence as a continuous life; he directly encounters it erratically, only in the form of isolated dreams. He forgets even these, or he ignores them. Immediately the dream ceases and he awakes, that life is "alien" to him, "unreal."

There is, then, an "occult" influence upon the teacher's "real" (waking and conscious) life. It is not a fantastic occultism to say that the teacher lives two lives: in secret he is a sun-priest intoxicated with his powers; in public, he lives a life in which he tastes the bitter moral fruits of his pride: he is no longer a glorious and charismatic preacher but a prosaic, impotent teacher. With insight, the teacher himself might come to experience fully and acknowledge consciously the reality of both his lives.

I spoke of "stretching" our language. In truth, the language just used is quite simple and direct; it would be recognizable as a quite natural description of the situation if we had not previously "stretched" our language into the more technical terminology of "fantasy," "unconscious wish," and similar psychoanalytic conceptions which have themselves only relatively recently come to feel familiar rather than "stretched."

Let us put aside for the moment, then, such technical terms as "fantasy" (which the dream is) and "unconscious fantasy" (which the dream represents in a distorted way). Let us put aside for the moment the notion of reality in the physical, biological, or even psychological senses of systematic theory or historical reportage. Instead let us focus upon the teacher's *experience*, the meaning and character of life *as lived*, as perceived, apprehended, prehended—but not as conceived, observed by the outsider, or theorized about. Then we may say, based on his own reports and our inferences, that his secret sun-priest life is among the important realities intimately affecting his life as teacher, though he does not know that it is or why it is.

The psychologist, and the dreamer himself, may do well for *some* purposes to distinguish between "fantasy" and "reality." The dreamer, however, as the psychoanalyst knows, must in another sense of these terms experience the *reality* of his secret life if he is ever to be liberated from his bewildered and unknowing bondage to it. For him to label it facilely as "fantasy" is to dismiss it; here is the seed of neurosis. To confuse it with public, waking, conscious life is to be psychotic. The person who, on the one hand, can live through this secret life, perceive it as real, and explore it with complete seriousness and who, on the other hand, does not confuse it with the structure of public, waking reality—he is the one who moves in the dimension of normality-creativity.

II
The Doctrine of Karma

WITH THESE INTRODUCTORY COMMENTS AND ILLUSTRATIONS
as background, it is now appropriate to review briefly but
more systematically the doctrine of karma and reincarnation as traditionally expounded.

Although familiar to the ancient Greek world, and
stressed in Orphic, Pythagorean, and Platonic teachings, the
most elaborate and sophisticated forms of karmic doctrine
known to us are to be found in the Upanishadic and Buddhist texts. Avoiding the many specific differences among
the sects, the general notion of reincarnation may be
sketched along the following lines. My present life is only
one of a set of lives. These lives are in certain respects entirely separate: their social, geographic, and physical characters may be quite unrelated to one another. Yet they form
an interdependent series by virtue of a peculiar continuity:
karma, "action." This karmic continuity is a psychomoral
one. In Christian terms: "Whatsoever a man soweth that
shall he reap"—if not in this life, then in some other one.
In Upanishadic and Buddhist language:

As a man acts, so does he become. . . .
As a man's desire is, so is his destiny.[6]

Beings, O monks, are responsible for their deeds.
Their actions mould them and are their parents. . . .[7]

The deeds of this life, and the impressions
they leave behind, follow [the dying man].[8]

This continuity is not ordinarily known to us. We are—or
ordinarily appear to ourselves to be—tossed at random into
a world of haphazard delights and miseries, the latter pre-
ponderant as is evident to those who will but look. We are
alive only insofar as we strive and struggle, and hence these

lives are at their root generative of dissatisfaction, of suffering. The more one strives and struggles in the usual way, the tighter one's chains become. There is no evading spiritual cause and effect: what does not ripen in one life will ripen in another. This is the law of karma, of action and its consequences.

In the West, we tend to think of heaven and hell as analogues to our penological practices: the punishment is physical discomfort and psychic isolation (prison) regardless of the specific nature of the criminal act. The karmic law is much closer to the old Greek notion of cosmic justice, or to the notion of "poetic justice." The punishment exactly fits the crime. But poetic justice must operate within a life, if not this one, then another one. It cannot be realized if life terminates in an essentially static heaven or hell. It is utterly alien to the idea of nondiscriminating spiritual awards (hell fire regardless of the individual's specific crime, amorphous heavenly joy regardless of the specific virtues of the individual).

Karmic law is not the edict of an All-Powerful Disciplinarian, not an expression of will accompanied by the threat of sanctions. It purports to be factual description: Somehow or other, things do eventually "balance out" in the moral realm; each moral action produces, eventually, its quite specific moral reaction. And our constant strivings are constantly producing new "karma" as well as bringing past karma to fruition; the weary round of births and deaths is perpetuated.

In the course of spiritual progress toward freedom from the round of births and rebirths one eventually achieves the power of remembering past lives. One then sees their connection with the present life. The ordinary person can neither remember nor understand: "And what happened to you in your mother's womb, all that you have quite forgotten."[9] The greater the spiritual progress, the greater the ability and the easier the task. Knowledge of one's former lives is one of the "five kinds of superknowledge." [10] In achieving this "superknowledge," one is concurrently achieving liberation from the karmic bonds. As in psychoanalysis, this knowledge is not the goal, but it is a distinctive ingredient in the achievement of freedom. Spiritual knowledge and spiritual freedom are born as one. (Compare Lao-tse, II: "Being and Non-being grow out of one another." [11])

Siwek has expressed the view that the doctrine of reincarnation is morally enervating: for not only are we assured of an indefinite number of lives in which to rectify our ways, but the widespread desire to keep on living on earth is a powerful motive to "sin" *in order* to assure rebirth. [12]

This view is understandable as "external," a result of seeing the words of the doctrine rather than its meaning as it functions in the appropriate context. From this "external" standpoint there have also been defenses of the karmic doctrine. Such late nineteenth-century metaphysicians as McTaggart and Moore have argued that the doctrine of reincarnation is more just and humane than, e.g., the Christian doctrine. [13, 14] Karma, after all, faces one only with deserts proportionate to one's acts, not with eternal damnation for the finite acts of a relatively brief life. The door to reform is never absolutely cut off by karma as it is by Christianity. Such legalistic arguments pro and con, while of some interest in other contexts, divert one from the spiritual core of the karmic doctrine.

The doctrine of reincarnation does not receive its spiritual impulse and quality from theoretical discussion. I have tried to set the stage for detailed analysis by suggesting that karmic insight emerges in the situation of one who is driven by anxiety and suffering, who seeks self-awareness, and who is grappling in a highly personal and direct way with the fragmented, enslaving lives which he has lived, is living, and hopes to escape. For one who is not urgently concerned with suffering and illusion, who does not feel despair and the need for illumination, the doctrine of reincarnation is indeed a devilish snare. Although it has other meanings too, the Christian way can at least be used to *threaten* the ignorant with future massive suffering, thus acting, it is hoped, as a spur to the regenerative processes. But the way of reincarnation must begin where there is already an awareness of *present* suffering and enslavement. Life *is* suffering: This was the first of the Buddha's Four Noble Truths and the generative postulate of his teaching.

My karma is the body of all my deeds and thoughts as viewed from the moral perspective, all of them seeds guaranteed to bear their proper sorts of fruit. But we must ask who is the person represented by "my"? The reference here is to the unity which transcends the various phenomenal selves. The Buddhists, in contrast with Upanishadic orthodoxy, deny that this unity is to be identified with anything like a substantial soul. All, however, recognize that we are dealing with two different orders of existence, the phenomenal and noumenal, the latter being characterized either as Atman, Purusha, or Self, or as nonego, the Emptiness which is full, Nirvana.

Even in this first sketch of the karmic doctrine, we must pause to note parallels with the more detailed version of psychoanalysis.

We become responsible agents when we can face the moral continuity of the familiar, conscious self with other strange, "alien" psychic entities—our "other selves." We should perhaps speak of an "identity" with other selves rather than a "continuity." For we must accept responsibility for the "acts" of these other selves; we must see these acts as *ours*. As Freud said of our dream lives, they are not only in me but act "from out of me as well." [15]

Yet identity is, in another way, too strong a term. There is a genuine difference between, say, the infantile, archaic (unconscious) mother-hater and the adult, humane, and filial (conscious) self, between the primitive, fantastic brother-murderer and the sophisticated fair-minded business competitor, between the archaic sun-priest and the teacher. Indeed, it is the assumption that there *is* a *genuinely* civilized self which is the prerequisite for classical psychoanalysis as a therapy. The adult, realistic self is the "therapeutic" *sine qua non* of the therapist. The hope in the psychotherapy of the neurotic is that his neurotic guilt is engendered by a "self" which *is* in a profound sense alien to his adult, civilized, realistic self. "For whosoever hath, to him shall be given. . . ." Insight only helps those who already have a realistic ego.

The psychoanalytic quest for autonomy reveals the Self in greater depth; it reveals it as a *community* of selves. The genuinely startling thing in this quest is not simply the discovery that these other, archaic selves exist, nor even that they have an impact in the present. What startles is the detailed analysis of the peculiarly close, subtle, and complex texture of the threads which weave these other selves and the adult conscious self into a single great pattern.

It is a special, startling kind of intimacy with which we deal. It calls for me to recognize that I suffer, whether I will or no, for the deeds of those other selves. It is an intimacy which, when encountered, makes it self-evident that I must assume responsibility for the acts and thoughts of those other persons as if they were I. Finally and paradoxically, in the morally clear vision which thus occurs, there emerges, as in a montage, a new Self, a Self free of bondage to the old deeds of the old selves. For it is a Self which sees and therefore sees through the old illusions which passed for reality. Yet this Self is the Seer who is not seen, the Hearer not heard. It is a no-self.

We shall study this "selflessness" in detail in the final chapter, but it will be helpful to note here briefly what this involves as seen through the lens of psychoanalytic theory. With the dissolution of anxiety-motivated, conscious and unconscious stereotyped self-images, there is left of the Self only the id-ego-superego triad. The self thus conceived is a "metapsychological" or theoretical concept, not anything which is observed or experienced directly. Thus there is left only the *non*phenomenal dynamic unity which manifests itself phenomenally in the rich flux of thoughts, feelings, fantasies, and actions. The self moving through the rich flux of experience is now not blinded and hobbled by the old superimposed and stereotyped fantasies which formed a tightly and dynamically interrelated community of selves generating its own repetitive destiny.

Freud uses the very imagery of karma when he says that "analysis sets the neurotic free from the chains of his sexuality." [16] It is the links which tie unconscious and archaic fantasy lives to conscious act, will, feeling, and thought which are our chains. It is insight which dissolves them and releases us from bondage.

In such broad terms, then, there seems to be a noticeable consistency in language when we compare the psychoanalytic conceptions, either figuratively or precisely formulated, and the karmic doctrines. One may suspect, however, that a more detailed and precise look at the matter would show important divergences, particularly of an ontological sort. The principal divergence which comes to mind is this: Is not the karmic doctrine, after all, quite unlike psychoanalytic notions in that it has to do with separate human lives in different times in history?

Karma requires the continuity of moral properties through space and time independent of physical continuity. This suggests a kind of quasi-substantial, self-identical soul capable of dwelling in different bodies. Indeed Upanishadic orthodoxy holds to such a belief, and even the more popular Chinese Buddhist discussions [17] have seemed to hold to the doctrine of such a continuously existent soul in place of the more subtle and proper Buddhist doctrine on the matter.

One can approach this directly as a traditional form of metaphysical question. McTaggart[18] has noted that reincarnationism is entirely consistent with the conception of an immortal soul so fundamental to the West's official ideology. Yet, important as this direction of argument may be for those who already accept the theological dogma of immortality in its scholastic, Western forms, it will not be pursued in this study.

In contrast to this rather scholastic approach, we might settle the ontological question by adopting the current fashion, that of viewing the karmic doctrine as a characteristically superstitious doctrine embodying some psychological insights. Freud himself said, in a closely related context, that "behind this superstition there lies concealed a vein of ethical sensitiveness which has been lost by us civilized men."[19]

Today, however, this is too easy a way out, and it is an unproductive one.

The question then arises as to how we are to interpret but not "psychologize" the karmic doctrine and yet be consistent with physical and biological science and with an acceptably empirical philosophy.

There is no doubt that vast numbers of Asians, including many who are highly sophisticated in Western ways of thought, believe in the karmic doctrine. We may ask: Do they believe in it neither as metaphysics, nor psychology, but *literally*? This question only raises the prior question: What do we mean by "literal"? When we deal with a radically foreign culture, such questions need not be mere verbal fussiness.

It is not my purpose to evade the ontological issue as to the "literal" truth of the doctrine of reincarnation. Quite the contrary. The question of the reality of karma lies at the heart of my inquiry. However, this *is* a philosophical question, as I have said. Does a "literal" belief depend for its proper verification on scientific or protoscientific methods? Can we proceed to the ontological question by examining "evidence" that Mr. X or Mr. Y displayed information about the historical past which he "could not have known" from his experience in this life? This approach begs all the crucial questions and assumes that the karmic doctrine has the same ontological status as a historical hypothesis.

The best way to approach the ontological questions is to do so indirectly. This I shall do, temporarily avoiding explicit or extended treatment of the issue. Therefore until we have explored the psychological aspects of the matter in some detail, the ontological issue must be thrust to the back of the reader's mind. There is a conceptual bridge which will lead us from West to East, but that bridge is erected not with the concepts of physics and history but with the concepts of psychology.

III
Fantasy and the Language of "Many Selves"

I HAVE INDICATED ROUGHLY THE SPIRIT IN WHICH I PROPOSE to approach the doctrine of reincarnation from a psychological standpoint. During the following discussion, the purpose is to interweave a variety of types of sources, Western and Eastern, literary and scientific, religious and ethical, in order to identify and analyze the mode of human experience which is in question. In this section, and in the following one, we shall elaborate certain themes by exploring the language of "many selves."

The notion that each Self has in some sense many selves is not elaborated systematically in any contemporary language in the West. But it is inherently congenial to the description of the human condition. It is as congenial a way of informal speaking for the psychoanalyst as it is for the novelist. For example when the distinguished psychoanalyst Lawrence Kubie talks informally about the human meaning of the psychotherapeutic experience, he says about one of his patients:

> With the elimination of certain of these inner blinders, it suddenly became clear that *a wholly different person was hidden* behind this façade of hostility and rage and hatred and meanness.[20] [Italics added]

In the very same paragraph, Kubie also reverts to the language of mythology. He describes the same woman as having behaved "like one of the ancient furies." This perfectly natural way of describing the situation in clear and universally understandable English has been for the most part preempted by the technical language. The technical language is useful, but for purposes other than those which concern us at the moment. The language of hidden selves, however, is not only perfectly clear and apt today, it was partly embodied in the once accepted doctrine of "possession," for millennia the nearest thing to a Western "psychological" language. The doctrines of possession by such alien, quasi persons as demons and of inspiration from within by the gods have a long history as antecedents and analogues of the concepts of regressive and sublimative eruptions of the unconscious.

There have been some fragmentary attempts at a more systematic use of such language even within the psychoanalytic stream of thought. Fritz Wittels [21] has remarked that psychoanalytic language would much more suggest the true state of things if we spoke less of having an Oedipus complex or introjecting father images and instead spoke of *being* Oedipus, of *being* father. What Wittels refers to here is, of course, the inner quality of the experience. After all, as Freud showed, in the life of the mind it is *psychic* reality which counts; the fantasy of introjecting father, of incorporating father into oneself, of becoming father is a psychic *reality*. The phrase "in fantasy" is a way of stressing that this experience is not a revelation of physical, physiological, or social reality. This emphasis is essential in some contexts, but in the present one we need to emphasize that "being father" *is* a psychic reality.

Within the Freudian tradition, the technical language which both most directly suggests and also strictly refers to these "many selves" is the language of "identification," "introjection," and of such special clinical phenomena as multiple personality ("a climax of multiple identifications"[22]) and hysterical identification.[23]

In psychoanalytic terms we can characterize the infantile aspects of the superego as consisting of "the internalized parental figures dressed in the variable garb of one's childhood mythology."[24] The ego, too, is from certain relevant vantage points "the precipitate of abandoned drive-objects, that is, of *identifications*. . . ."[25]

What is more, the genuinely "personal" quality of these "sub-selves," especially when operating with some degree of autonomy, is particularly evident in situations where ego-control is for any reason lessened. Rapaport reports, for example:

> In recording various thought formations of my own, ranging from those in hypnagogic to those in dream states, I obtained material suggesting that the closer the state approximates that of the dream, the more "me-ness" recedes . . . though formations resembling those of multiple personality begin to occur.[26]

An example of this "many self" language from other than the Freudian standpoint is H. S. Sullivan's usage. He directs much attention to what he calls "self-dynamisms," each of which is, as the very language suggests, a self-like configuration of dispositions. Indeed, as soon as Sullivan lapses into more informal discussion, he drops the word "dynamism" and simply speaks of different selves, of different "me's" and "you's," of the various "persons," either real or illusory, who are involved in a specific interpersonal transaction.[27]

All of this is, of course, no secret to the literary artists of the West. Using neither the language of psychology nor of Eastern "metaphysics," they have known that, as Virginia Woolf's Mrs. Dalloway says, "our apparitions, the part of us which appears, are so momentary compared with the other, the unseen part of us, which spreads wide."[28]

By way of returning the compliment, psychoanalysts soon perceived a specific and related truth about art. According to Freud, the artist is one who not only perceives the truth about the many selves, his very art rests upon evoking them. To use Freud's own words:

> In the realm of fiction we find the plurality of lives which we need. We die with the hero with whom we have identified ourselves; yet we survive him, and are ready to die again just as safely with another hero.[29]

This statement of Freud's expresses the important point that we can discriminate not merely other selves but also other *lives*, the lives lived through by these dynamic selves. Here Freud refers specifically to the living through (in fantasy) of other lives by means of literary techniques. It is this aspect of the matter in particular, the current and "vicarious" living through of many lives, to which we shall address ourselves in the pages to follow. And we may begin by noting that, although this participation in many lives is accounted for in the East within a religious or quasi-religious framework, in the modern West its institutionalized form has been that of the arts.

It is the creative artist who has provided us with opportunities to body forth these unseen selves, to *see* them (literally, in the case of the visual arts), and more than this, to *live* them. Art, quite properly, *object*ifies, makes concrete and evident what has previously been fugitive and subjective.

> To create *King Lear* [says Wyndham Lewis], or to believe that you have held communion with some historic personage—those are much the same thing.[30]

Henry James thought of literature as involving that "mystical other world that might have flourished," and the acute French critic, Poulet, quoting the previous, remarks:

> James plunges himself with delight into the memories of his former life only to discover in them the possibilities of other lives; and if he chooses to journey by memory to such and such a place in the past, it is often because from that point of departure he can imagine a different sort of existence for himself. Thus the past becomes the place where one can also recapture "the possible development of one's own nature one mayn't have missed." [31]

Poulet's remarks on Proust are equally apropos. For Proust, each sleep, each change, is a "death"—followed, it is true, by a resurrection, but in a different ego.[32] (Note Coomaraswamy's comment about the Hindu scriptures:

> . . . the majority of references to repeated birth and repeated death refer to this present life. . . .[33])

According to the psychology of art as developed in psychoanalytic theory, essentially this same process goes on in all the arts. The artist evokes highly charged fantasies in a controlled fashion—controlled as to the pattern, the relative intensity of the drives mobilized, and the degree of consciousness of the fantasy. Baudelaire, like some other artists, intensified the temporal and hallucinatory quality of the experience by the very special method of taking drugs. In opium-induced states, he said, one "lives several lives in the space of an hour." [34] The recovery of the past takes place in sharp and poignant vividness, and yet, he reported, it seems to reveal events and images as in the very depths of the horizon. This is a partly spatial image, but it is used to report a paradoxical temporal quality. We shall shortly return to this sense of temporal immediacy fused with radical pastness.

The secularization and isolation of the arts in the West reflects our ideological orientation. It is an orientation which excludes the acceptance of the world revealed by art as a real world. Instead of being conceived as an elaboration of worlds and lives which, in some mysterious way, really belong to us, the arts are subordinated to the waking, utilitarian world. In that context they tend to be seen as disruptive or at best as an "escape valve." They are disarmed by being classified as "play," "diversion," and "imagination," rather than as real life. Their professional practitioners are alienated and neutralized by being typed as outsiders, significantly enough as either homosexuals or libertines.

Thus genuinely creative art is insulated from "life" for most Westerners. It is, for the regnant ideology, a dis-ease. And there are no other institutionalized and deeply accepted alternatives for the adult. To expect the Western adult, alone and unaided, to evoke and to live out creatively his own secret lives is ordinarily to expect too much. For the Westerner in bondage to the technological outlook, other worlds, other lives than the accepted public life, are fragile and eccentric "fantasies." Aside from the arts, it is only in psychotherapy that these are raised to a level of consciousness and substantiality such that they can be vividly felt and understood. But for most Westerners they are too tenuous to be noticed in other than an occasional disquieting moment.

There are probably just as vast differences in the individual ability to undertake such a spiritual odyssey in the East as in the West. But a great difference in capacity may be supposed generated when the culture supports, strengthens, and deepens the capacity rather than rejecting it. There is little doubt that aside from the arts, themselves in a shaky and ambiguous position, the modern West has consistently been antagonistic to the flowering of the life of fantasy. The very term "fantasy" says "unreal," "fantastic." The East, on the contrary, has encouraged the most intensive and full development of what we call fantasy. The East has focused upon the central role of what we call "fantasy" in human life-as-experienced. They do not use a terminology expressing a negative bias; they do not speak here of fantasy but of insight into deeper realities.

The vicarious living of other lives is not merely a desirable experience, it is essential. There can be no development into a *human* being without the incorporation into the total Self of a variety of lives and part-lives. The more these are fully lived, the more rich and deep a Self. Indeed, we know from psychoanalysis that we must live the lives of others around us as we perceive them (identification) in order to develop even that minimum unique blend of lives and part-lives which can establish us as individuals. Hence we may look with confidence to childhood as an area in which there must be institutionalized patterns of "fantasy" or "vicarious" living of lives.

It is now generally accepted that the play of children is not play in the trivial sense of that word. Indeed there is no trivial sense except as a reflection of our adult unawareness of what play is. Play is *playing-at*. It is the rehearsal of various roles and the practicing of these roles in a variety of situations. The very words "rehearsal" and "practicing" are misleading; they derive from the adult, retrospective view of the matter. From the standpoint of the child, play is the serious business of life. It is merely a life partly out of gear with his "official" self. Of course, the normal child can soon distinguish easily and quickly between what adults call "real life" and "play." The more psychological way of stating the matter is to say that the child acts out his fantasies and seriously tries, through the play-situation, to resolve conflicts in which these fantasies play a part. But he normally recognizes reasonably well which of these selves and lives are *defined* as real by the adults around him; and he learns to go along with their game—until finally he is quite unaware that it was *their* game, for it is now his, too.

The lives which the child lives through in play are not entirely distinct from one another. Situations, conflicts, and roles may be repeated, but the conflicts may be resolved either in a compulsively repetitive way or in different ways on different occasions. Sometimes the same "play" role and situation are carried on with continuity as in a "continued story." For months at a time, two girls will be rival queens of different planets. These lives and situations are evidently and at a glance (for the adult) closely related psychically. Though the nine-year-old girl may be queen of a planet in the distant future of space travel, this space-queen's problems are, to the observing adult, remarkably like those of the "English queen" of a month ago; and all these royal problems are, in turn, remarkably reminiscent of the child's present tensions and problems, the dynamic conflicts which dominate her present family life and "real" social life. There is a remarkable ability—which we tend to take for granted until we recall the case of the psychotic—to keep a variety of conscious and closely interrelated lives entirely unconfused.

Thus the child is daily, hourly "reincarnated"; not in the physical sense, but in the psychically, humanly important sense: the experienced reality of the moment is that of another person in another body in another life, yet a person whose destiny is strangely yet intimately connected with that of the young girl of today.

That the human being has the potentiality to live *this* kind of "reincarnation" is, then, a fact. It does not necessarily disappear in the adult. It is only a fact local to technological Western culture that, aside from art (and its debased form, "entertainment"), adults who are "normal" do not exhibit such capacities. But in earlier periods in the West and in most other cultures at all times, this capacity is commonly found well integrated into the values and norms of the culture.

Although the normal Westerner does not exhibit a sophisticated capacity to take fantasy seriously, this does not mean he does not have and use the capacity in a variety of unsophisticated forms. In a good number of cases it flourishes in open conflict with the social norms. Undisciplined and unsanctified, it is openly significant in the lives of the roughly one tenth of the U.S. population which requires hospitalization for mental illness. We can only surmise the great role fantasy plays in criminal actions which are either themselves the acting-out of fantasy or are committed in order to finance the narcotic and alcoholic addictions so intimately related to unsublimated fantasy.

To our discussion of art and play as forms of vicarious lives, we must add a discussion of the universal fantasy-life of the dream. In childhood play and in art, too, our fantasies are very largely externally controlled. Culture shapes the child's play forms rather rigidly, and in art the audience experiences the control of a genuine creator acting through his artifact. But the dream, although influenced by culture and local circumstances, still remains, for the Westerner, the single freest and most personal fantasy experience to which he normally has access.

In dreams we live other lives both explicitly and implicitly. We openly appear in different times, places, and roles, while remaining recognizably ourself. We *implicitly* live still more lives. For, after all, the other persons in our dreams are *our* creatures; we live their lives for them. And this becomes evident to one who understands his dreams, whether he be Hindu, Buddhist, or psychoanalyzed Westerner.

". . . the dreamer striving against his own wishes is like a combination of two persons, separate and yet somehow intimately united. . . ."[35] Freud's words express the very essence of the reincarnation notion: a plurality of persons "separate and yet somehow intimately united." We need only remind ourselves that, taken collectively, our dream-world is a world infinitely rich in persons. In a dream we *are* sun-priests, gangsters, kings, warriors, lovers, haters, children, animals. Dream experience is not waking experience —but it is genuine experience, a part of our life, indeed of our most intimate life. Viewed in terms of its own inner life, the time-order of the dream experience is incommensurate with the time-order of the current waking life: our life as king or as slave is lived in a different time, a different place, a different world from our current waking life. One may be satisfied to locate the dream-life in past or future, or in some other region in the present world; or one may emphasize (as some reincarnationists have done) that these other lives are radically out of gear with the waking order of space-time and belong to different epochs or "cycles" of space and time. The role of the dream as profoundly revelatory of a reality is accepted in our oldest cultural wisdom. Aeschylus' Clytemnestra expresses the point succinctly:

> . . . For the sense
> When shut in sleep hath then the spirit sight,
> But in the day the inward eye is blind.[36]

And we know the profound import of the dream in Biblical times and lands.

More apposite to the specific theme of dreams and reincarnation, however, is the attitude expressed in the Upanishads, the first Eastern texts to elaborate the reincarnation doctrine. Two notions in particular are conjoined in the Upanishadic references to the dream; both notions suggest the theses of this chapter. First, we are told that the dream experience is a creation of the inner Self; it is not contact as usual with the world it portrays, but a construction entirely of our own out of the materials of our waking experience— it is the "play" of the inner Self. Second, discussion of the dream state is intimately related to discussions of the self as reincarnated, of the transcending of the everyday world of bondage, and of the "forms of death." The dream state is intermediate between the karmic world of birth-and-death and the "other" world which is the home of him who has become enlightened and free of karma. It is important to present at least one representative passage at length:

'Which is the self?' 'The person here who consists of knowledge among the senses, the light within the heart. He remaining the same, wanders along the two worlds seeming to think, seeming to move about. He on becoming asleep (getting into dream condition), transcends this world and the forms of death.

'Verily, this person, when he is born and obtains a body, becomes connected with evils. When he departs, on dying he leaves all evils behind.

'Verily, there are just two states of this person (the state of being in) this world and the state of being in the other world. There is an intermediate third state, that of being in sleep (dream). By standing in this intermediate state one sees both those states, of being in this world and of being in the other world. Now whatever the way is to the state of being in the other world, having obtained that way one sees both the evils (of this world) and the joys (of the other world). When he goes to sleep he takes along the material of this all-embracing world, himself tears it apart, himself builds it up; he sleeps (dreams) by his own brightness, by his own light. In that state, the person becomes self-illuminated.

'There are no chariots there, nor animals to be yoked to them, no roads but he creates (projects from himself) chariots, animals to be yoked to them and roads. There are no joys there, no pleasures, no delights, but he creates joys, pleasures and delights. There are no tanks there, no lotus-pools, no rivers, but he creates tanks, lotus-pools and rivers. He, indeed, is the agent (maker or creator).'[37]

Radhakrishnan makes the point that "in the dream state the self is identified with the subtle body."[38] It is the "subtle body" which, according to Upanishadic texts, transmigrates.[39]

Bergson[40] explicitly compared the essential processes of the dream to Plotinus' account of the transmigration of the soul as a swooping down of the spirit into a new material body. The dream, Bergson argued, occurs when the dreamer's deeply submerged memory seizes upon the sense-perceptions of the day as "material" to form the manifest dream. Thus, says Bergson, the "spirit" (the submerged memory) is "embodied" in the day's "matter" and a new life, the dream-self, is given birth.

Aside from the "sophisticated" civilizations of the Orient and Europe, the role of the dream as a form of genuine life-experience has been recognized widely if not universally in other cultures. It is hardly necessary to develop this at length, but Devereux's[41] detailed psychoanalytic studies of the Plains Indian have furnished a remarkably useful treatment of the subject for our purposes.

> The manifest content of dreams [says Devereux concerning his psychotherapy of a Plains Indian] was, for the greatest part, treated as a *real* incident. . . . This mode of interpreting . . . resembled in every respect traditional Plains Indian patterns of dream interpretations.[42]

Devereux stresses the function of the dream in the Indian culture as a way of reinforcing "through anticipatory gratification, certain culturally sanctioned and standardized wishes. . . ." [43] He also reports that success dreams are considered by the Indian as "trial actions." [44] The Indians feel "morally and otherwise responsible for their dreamed behavior," [45] although not in quite the same way as for their waking behavior. (Freud: "Obviously one must hold oneself responsible for the evil impulses of one's dreams." [46]) Devereux mentions in a footnote the report that Papuans converted to Catholicism confessed to adultery which, upon further questioning, turns out to have been dreamed. But it must also be remembered that, like Devereux's Indian patient, the tribesman is "perfectly able to differentiate between reality and dream." [47] The dream is real life but not quite the same life as the day-life. "It is true that in the metapsychological sense this bad repressed content does not belong to my 'ego.' . . ." [48]

Devereux states that the dreams reported in the therapy of his Indian patient corresponded closely to the traditional stylized Plains Indian dreams. [49] This confirms the tenacity of the cultural influence (as well as the immediate therapeutic context) in shaping the feature of the dream fantasy as reported.

The genuine skill with which the "native" dream specialist operates is seen as analogous with the psychoanalytic mode of dream interpretation by Erikson [50] as well as by Devereux. Indeed, reincarnation itself was originally held to be an exclusively shamanistic affair, the shaman being the very person most versed in dream lore and exploration.

I do not present the widespread interest and concern with dreams as a novel datum. However I have wanted to stress the intimate connection that it has with the notion of reincarnation in the classic literature and the close relation of both to the process of self-exploration and self re-creation, whether in psychotherapy or indigenous ideologies. By virtue of its offering a dramatic and varied life experience, the dream is a cognitive revelation of a complex realm of being which has a "deeper, firmer, and more commanding meaning."[51] That the words just quoted were originally written by Quinn in reference to the actual role of the dream in the artistic experience of such men as Poe and Baudelaire only re-emphasizes the universality of the dream's potential as a profoundly genuine spiritual experience.

Lord Raglan, in his study of death and rebirth,[52] argues that the dream could not be a basis for the belief in reincarnation since *any* sane man (in whatever culture) can distinguish between waking ("real") life and dream experiences. Of course it is precisely because of this obvious distinction that so many dreamers in human history have been led to suppose that their dream lives are *eruptions* of *other* lives into current life rather than elements within current life.

Having begun this discussion of the reality of dreams with the words of Freud, I shall conclude it with the words of a psychiatrist writing from the phenomenological standpoint. Medard Boss writes in his book on dream analysis that:

> We exist no less in dreams than we do in waking life. We "exist" in the sense that even in the dream we are always within a world, the reality of which we had best not deny too hastily.[53]

> . . . man can realize his existence in dreams, just as in waking life, through the most varied relationships and attitudes.[54]

To summarize: the "living out" of fantasies, whether in play, art, or dream, is one major process which, I suggest, is an analogue to reincarnation. Through each of these experience forms we glimpse one transcending moral-psychic unity manifesting itself in a variety of discrete, phenomenal lives. The living of many lives enables the Self to work through, existentially and creatively, various moral tendencies potential in its nature. To "learn by experience" and eventually to profit by insight into these experiences: this is the way to spiritual progress and human freedom.

Of course, the living out of fantasies can boomerang. In neurotic play, in "formula" entertainment, in "acting out" during therapy and in various forms of psychopathology we see the fantasy enslaving the person, dulling and stereotyping his perceptions, subverting his freedom through the bribe of quick gratification. In constructive play, art, therapy, and spiritual exploration, we postpone gratifications, and we suffer. We suffer in the sense of having pain, and we suffer in the more philosophical sense that we are exposed, acted upon, *open* to the impact of the inner and outer worlds. In neurotic play or cheap entertainment, for example, we do not, in the corresponding sense, suffer. We neither tolerate pain nor do we remain open. Instead we *impose* our cliché fantasies upon the world; we buy immediate gratification and relief at the expense of insight and liberation. Every action is the forging of a new link in the chain which binds us. (Of course we suffer *neurotically*. There is pain, but its meaning is uncomprehended; there is passivity, but it is a stereotyped response to stimuli interpreted in clichés.)

IV
Memory, Hallucination, and the Language of "Many Selves"

THE LIVING-THROUGH OF FANTASIES IN ART, PLAY, DREAM, and psychosis is only one major parallel to the "recollection of former lives." This living-through is *current*, "vicarious" exploration of new experience. It contrasts with recollection in the strict sense, the coming to consciousness of *memories* of fantasies already lived out in waking life or dream, in fantasy or "fact," in consciousness or "in the unconscious."

Let us turn our attention now to the "recollection of former lives" in the modality of memory-experience proper. An important aspect of such "memory" experiences, one we shall also consider here, is the vividness, liveliness, and "reality" of the experience. The person who has the experience must, in short, be struck by its having three properties: it has dramatic vividness and reality; it is "really" an experience of *his;* and, finally, it is perceived as having happened in the past, the distant past, in fact the past of *another* life.

The evidence of clinical and theoretical psychoanalysis suggests that just such experiences could and do occur under conditions of intensive self-exploration. The occurrence of early memories during the course of deep insight is associated with a peculiar "liveness." [55]

But even prior to genuine insight, the "screen" memory is a common pseudo-memory or quasi-memory experience. In addition to noting, with Freud, their predominantly visual character, Greenacre speaks of the "peculiar peripheral luminosity and general intensity of screen memories." [56] She also refers to screen memories which do not have the brightness quality but instead have a persistent stubbornness. [57] This I interpret as implying, among other things, a radical sense of their reality, their tangibility.

Such memories have another typical characteristic: they are isolated, they stand apart. [58] But this isolation from the rest of experience is not characteristic only of screen memories. It is in general a characteristic of all important derivatives of the unconscious when these suddenly break through, whether in the context of creative activity of an artistic or scientific kind or in a more personal form. Thus Rapaport remarks upon the fact that the central idea in the moment of creative insight "is characterized by a paucity of relationships to other contents of consciousness."[59] Schachtel, too, stresses the "alienness" of early memory recovery.[60] The vividness and isolation of such erupting unconscious material comes to an intense peak in hallucinatory phenomena. Ferenczi reports that in rare though not unique cases of his, the patient's response to associations just prior to insight is a hallucinatory experience.[61] Hutchinson in his studies of insight remarks upon the hallucinatory vividness which often characterizes the new idea at the moment of inspiration. He distinguishes between such nonpathological hallucination and the kind associated with psychopathology. In the former case, the experience is "specific and final." That is, it occurs only once and is worked into the fabric of experience; its content is specific to the particular situation. By contrast, the pathological hallucination repeats itself and is not integrated into the fabric of experience.[62] It "clings" to the person and the person to it. As for the "alien" or "isolated" quality, Hutchinson refers to this in somewhat different language. He uses in an incidental way language which, though cast in terms of divine possession, is closely related to the language of reincarnation doctrines:

> If one had the least vestige of superstition, it is easy to see how he might suppose himself to be merely the incarnation . . . of higher forces.[63]

In short, we conclude that this kind of eruption of the unconscious has a phenomenological quality which naturally evokes a variety of different but closely related languages. The language used depends probably upon local tradition and upon personal, idiosyncratic ideas and emphases. One person may conceptualize the experience as possession by a divine or demonic being, thereby stressing the "alien" quality. Another person may conceive the experience as a memory from a former life, thus acknowledging the alienness and uncanniness but also stressing the quality of direct experience, of self-belongingness, of personal participation. It is important to remember that in the Pythagorean, Hindu, and Buddhist traditions of learning, the memory is a highly valued and strenuously cultivated faculty among spiritual adepts.

Even for peculiarly talented and industrious Western inquirers into the inner world (e.g., Marcel Proust, Thomas Wolfe), the actual memories of such significant early events in life take on a vividness suggestive of the eidetic or hallucinatory.[64] The general intensity of sensibility in the spiritually gifted must also be borne in mind in understanding the experience of the great prophets who have accepted the reincarnation doctrine.

We know that hallucinatory material, whether healthy or pathological, is relatively easily generated when external perceptual stimulation is reduced sharply.[65] This reduction of external stimuli is typical in Eastern "meditational" exercises. Goldberger and Holt have reported that increasing duration of such isolation tends to increase the "vividness" and "structure" of the perception. More to the point, however, is their report that the quality of *realism* depends on the perception's plausibility in terms of the beliefs of the normal "ego." [66] This is suggestive when we recall that vivid recollections of former lives are usually reported by ascetics operating within a cultural context normally permeated by reincarnationist ideas.

Déjà vu is a phenomenon closely related to memory and hallucination. In *déjà vu* the individual has a distinct and startling perception of the event now taking place as a duplicate of what has taken place before. In typical modern Western fashion, we may take one of two courses in interpreting *déjà vu*. We either dismiss it as an "illusion," a "psychological aberration," or we may try to defend its legitimacy by arguing that the experience must actually have taken place (or at least one very like it) but that we cannot quite remember when and where. Unfortunately, it is rare that we can discover such an actual resembling event in our acknowledged past. We remain satisfied with a verbalistic, unverified "explanation."

"Folk" explanations, even in the West, take the phenomenon more seriously. And for the reincarnationist, the whole falls into place: he supposes that an essentially similar event did take place in his experience—but not in this life. In this case, the reincarnationist stresses the fact that there is no evidence of such an event having occurred in this current life. Taking into account the lack of memory of such an event in our present life and the uncannily realistic quality of the experience, he may well be receptive to interpreting the data as dramatically consistent with the dominant world view of his culture. And indeed such *déjà vu* experiences are among the common types of evidence offered to support the doctrine of reincarnation.

If we consider the psychoanalytical explanation of the *déjà vu* experience, we find that, once again, the psychological conditions of its occurrence are precisely those we should expect on the basis of the theses of this chapter. The *déjà vu* is, psychologically, the eruption of a formerly unconscious fantasy into consciousness, the stimulus being a real current situation which in certain crucial respects resembles the fantasy situation. In the current situation, the fantasy, if somewhat disguised, evokes less anxiety than usual and thus can be tolerated within limits by the ego. Freud mentions the *déjà vu* experience of a young woman while visiting at a home in which one of the brothers in the family is dying. He traces her *déjà vu* back to the fact that some months earlier her own brother was very ill but did not die. Her fantasy that her brother would die, repressed at the time, is now evoked. Freud cites Ferenczi's language; the sense of familiarity in the *déjà vu* situation is referrable to the unconscious fantasy of which the girl was reminded.[67] Schilder makes essentially the same point.[68] With embellishments, the explanation has remained valid, and it accounts, with appropriate variations, for related phenomena such as "*fausse reconnaissance*" and "*déjà raconté.*" Thus, we may say with a kind of psychological-metaphorical truth: the *déjà vu* experience is a "recollection" of an event in another (i.e., a secret) life, an event which can be re-evoked via the memory modality of experience, though it is not a memory of any event in my conscious life.

To this list of vivid "recollections" of what was in fact never conscious [69] we should, no doubt, add what Freud called "constructions." [70] Here we have to do with profoundly repressed infantile memory. These are reconstructions of what "must" have happened as inferred on the basis of the analytic material. The reconstruction evokes belief, eventually compels belief, and yet is never perceived as an actual memory of an event in the person's life. In short, on the basis of self-exploration, the person achieves a rocklike sense of the reality of an event which bears crucially on his current life, but which is not recalled via any memorylike modality to have actually happened in the "real" life, i.e., the waking, conscious life. Again, the reincarnationist language stands ready-made, perfectly suited to characterize the experience without awkward straining of the facts in question.

I should perhaps repeat that the data and comments offered here are not intended merely to provide psychological "explanations" of the belief in reincarnation. The crucial point is this: the psychological accounts help bring forcefully to our attention that the reincarnationist view is not merely an "effect" of certain psychological processes; it is itself a keen and accurate *expression* of the precise structure and quality of the very experiences with regard to which it is evoked. I do not call it a description of those experiences because I do not wish to beg the question of its literal or ontological truth.

V
Time, the Transcendent Self, and the Many Selves

TIME, THE SELF, AND THE SELVES ARE INTIMATELY RELATED. For it is out of this perception of the co-presence of many selves in a dynamic equilibrium that is generated the sense of an immanent Self, an apprehending Subject who stands "out of time" and "out of process," who apprehends in a different mode and exists in a different mode, who is the eternal (nontemporal) subject of all temporal experience.

We can adumbrate this Self in three different relevant languages. Poulet, in his great study of time in literature, summarizes one outcome of Proust's exploration of his memories as the manifesting of an "essential" Self which is

> not a present self, without content, at the disposal of time and death; and not a past self, lost and hardly retrievable; but an essential self, liberated from time and contingency, a primal and perpetual being, the creator of itself, the author of an eternal song immediately recognized. . . .[71]

This is the Self which, in the Proustian world, contemplates the many selves that

> stud with their presences the depth of temporal space and render it visible by their shining multiplicity.[72]

This "essential" self, this "primal author" and transcendent subject which Proust's spiritual explorations revealed can be juxtaposed with the Atman of the Upanishads, the *purusha:*

> You cannot see the seer of seeing;
> You cannot hear the hearer of hearing;

You cannot think of the thinker of thinking;
You cannot know the knower of knowing.
This is your self that is within all;
Everything else but this is perishable.[73]

Everyone sees his sport but him no one sees.[74]

"Atman," says Radhakrishnan, "is the foundational reality underlying the conscious powers of the individual, the inward ground of the human soul." [75]

I have noted in the discussion of the doctrine of karma that the Buddha rejected the idea of such a transcendent soul. For him, we "cannot know the knower of knowing" because there is no knower; there are only the knowing, the seeing, the hearing, and the thinking themselves. It is the "collections" of these which form "selves," and it is the *moral* continuity from life to life of such individual complexes of thought-feeling-desire which replaces the enduring substantial Self. Moral character and destiny neither begins with birth nor ends with death.

Likewise, we have noted in the same context that the psychoanalytic conception of the person is an echo of these doctrines. The conscious self-perception and the many unconscious complexes of drive-fantasy form a community of selves. Their subtle and intimate interrelations are conceptualized in terms of an overarching, single pattern: the dynamic-structural unity of the forces of id, superego, and external reality. All the phenomenal selves are synthesized, brought into a system in equilibrium by the ego, the ego itself being an inherently theoretical entity. Thus the ego is the inherently nonseeable psychological subject of all seeing, the inherently nonphenomenal subject and unifier of all phenomena. There is a connection here with the logical point that in every act there is the acting "I" who cannot be an object of the action. Although the total action, including the actor-"I," may *later* be an object of study, it is studied by a later "I" which cannot itself also be observed in that very same act.

This Self has a very special relation to time. The Self, being "noumenal" rather than phenomenal, is not *in* phenomenal time, the "subjective" time-order; it is a *source* of the order of (subjective) time. Disturbances of "subjective" time are disturbances of the ego. Fantasies, memories, and perceptions are time-ordered; the ego is not. The ego is their ordering.

The ego exists in calendar time, not in subjective time. But calendar time is as much a theoretical construction as is ego. We observe star positions, clock faces, calendars, or subjective time "feelings." From these we make inferences in terms of the concepts of calendar time. We do not observe calendar time "directly"; it is not a phenomenon. Like the ego, it is not in a phenomenal sense a "thing."

Does the ego really "exist" or not? Does the Atman exist or not? Does there "exist" a transcendent unity? Upanishadic orthodoxy or Buddhist heresy? Metaphysical orthodoxy or positivistic, antimetaphysical heresy? Echoes.

It is important to distinguish the basis of unity of the Self and the basis of unity of each self. The unity of Self is noumenal, but that of the self is phenomenal. Baudelaire, for example, takes *"feeling"* to be the principle of unity for each self.[76] The psychiatrist Boss takes "mood." In speaking of the dream, Boss says:

> The dreamer, on the other hand, is frequently, and intensely, in a very definite mood. . . . Corresponding to this concentrated mood the dreamer can enter into these realms of existence and behavior all the more vividly. It is for this reason that he feels closer to their things and people, and that they can all be united in a single dream world of the moment, however far removed they may be in time and space in his waking life. The unequivocal mood of the dream often man-

ages to bring forth things and people whom the dreamer had long "forgotten." . . . They attain full corporeal reality in the dream world, and appear as if they happened only yesterday.[77]

This underlying and unifying "feeling" or "mood" undoubtedly is a characteristic phenomenal aspect of what Freud describes in theoretical terms as the "wish." In the dynamics of organizing a dream, Freud insists, "this single characteristic, that of fulfilling a wish, is the constant one."[78] "Condensation," "displacement," "visual representation," "secondary elaboration"—these are the powerful and flexible devices used to achieve dynamic unity in the service of an unconscious wish.

The resultant fantasy, with its characteristic "feeling" or "mood," its "personal accent," unifies and fuses related experiences and ideas of past, present, future in a single apprehension, a "self."[79] A memory, says Schilder in his study of the psychopathology of time, "is revived only when the present situation forms a unity with the past situation."[80]

The sense of "presence," of nearness in subjective time, is generated, then, when any object or situation is cathected by the currently mobilized drives and when it plays a significant role in the dominant drive-fantasy complex. Such a "dynamic theme" or "unifying image," once mobilized in waking life or in the dream, is like a magnet. It draws together out of all the realms of the mind—imagination, long-forgotten memory, perception, action, and "involuntary" responses—elements which once functioned or can be made to function within that dominant fantasy. The current perceptions incorporated are then perceived as "real"; the memories, though perhaps locatable in long past (calendar) time, are, in subjective time, "as if it happened yesterday"; the hopes are vividly present: "I can already see it!"

Thus far, it is the unity of the experience which has been

stressed. This generates a specific self and the Self. But what of the other distinctive temporal perceptions in these experiences? Why is there an almost universal tendency to perceive and order the various selves as separate and scattered through time? In Upanishadic Orthodoxy, in Buddhism, and in Greek Orphism, there is as much insistence upon the temporal structure as upon the unity transcending that structure.

As the previous comments suggest, psychic material which does not function within the dominant dynamic theme is perceived as pale, alien, merely verbal, or "theoretical." If past at all, it seems long past, "as if it were years ago, though I know it was only last week." In situations which evoke this kind of statement, we must suppose that the remembered event is not perceived as dynamically relevant to the current dominant theme. This may be due to repression, or simply to a real lack of relevance. From this standpoint, if we consider the unifying image and all it unites as the contents of a "self," then it was another person, another self which took part in that palely remembered event last week. ("I know I was there, but it might just as well have been somebody else for all it means to me right now.") Often enough we even hint at this direct connection between self-identity and dominating theme when we say: "I have changed so since then that it seems like a different world, though it's only been a few months."

In discussing religion specifically, Freud has characterized the repressed as having the quality of "remoteness in time." Even more specifically, he suggests in this context that the idea of reincarnation may be connected with just this striking experience.[81] Furthermore, he states elsewhere that another quality accompanying such "gusts" from the unconscious, a quality no doubt partly due to the shift in time-perception, is that of uncanniness.[82]

One finds in the lore of every culture some archaic

golden or mythic age, the Garden of Eden, the "Dream Country" of the Australian aborigines. Not by coincidence, the mythic always has a special and definite relation to time. The central events of myth always occur in a strange and distant past, a past hospitable to marvelous beings and miraculous doings. Mythic time reflects the very paradoxical quality we have been discussing: it is a time both continuous and discontinuous with the present time-order. The mythic time is connected to historical time by the familiar genealogies of gods, biblical patriarchal lines, royal family descents, and other totemistic identifications. And indeed mythic beings often operate in present time, but always in conformity with their destinies and natures as established in the mythic past. Myth is dramatic yet timeless in the way that the unconscious is: "Gods moving in crystal," [83] "for ever panting, for ever young." [84]

The choice of the mythic language of supernatural transactions, or the karmic language of past personal lives impinging upon present life, or the language of the unconscious is a choice reflecting culture, inner experience, and the specific context of language use. The first language emphasizes that there are forces which operate within the self but which are (in a qualified sense) *not* of the self; the other two emphasize that the operative force *is* indeed (qualifiedly) of the self.

We must conclude our discussion of time with specific reference to the process of self-exploration and self-transformation. Meerloo says:

> . . . in all inner disturbance the time factor is a cardinal point. There is always primarily a search for past time, for the obscure and forgotten crisis or the might-have-been; it is an attempt at recapturing it and working it out differently, usually more happily, or for simply dwelling on it. [85]

If the eruption of the unconscious fantasy is *merely* an eruption, then it remains "alive," "real," but peculiarly isolated from the rest of our reality-experience. Two dynamic themes, the ego-syntonic and the ego-alien, are operative side by side, and the phenomenological quality of two different and incommensurable orders of reality is sharpest. However, where the integration of the two begins, where the ego-alien becomes ego-syntonic by virtue of dynamic insight into the psychic "links," there the quality of temporal contrast begins to dissolve.

The time aspects of the process can be summarized in terms of karmic insight and also in terms of psychoanalytic insight. In karmic terms, (1) he who pursues the path of enlightenment becomes aware of hitherto unknown selves in a strangely remembered past, a past not a part of his ordinary memory's past; (2) he sees how these selves, or rather their moral-psychic "impressions" or karmic effects, are operating in his current life; (3) he becomes aware that, somehow, all this is a perception not governed by the ordinary time-order, it is a structure of separate, hitherto compartmentalized existences perceived in a larger context in which all are interdependent and thus copresent; and, finally, (4) he perceives that all these different realms of time and being are not separate in some ultimate metaphysical way; their radical isolation from one another is illusory (Samsara, Maya). In truth the world is "empty" of such metaphysical distinctions (Nirvana). This is liberation.

The psychological analysis may be stated briefly. The unconscious elements of inner conflict, which have hitherto operated outside the range of direct ego control, outside the range of the voluntary, now have emerged. This means they are once more operating as live, open, direct aspects of experience. To know the events and conflicts of the past in this way is not merely to learn about the past; it is to have the full-blooded experience embodied in the present. Therefore one is able to respond anew to that experience, only this time with all the powers of one's adult reasonableness and autonomy. Thus, instead of being subject to the hidden influence of the unconscious, one experiences it as an open and meaningful element in one's adult life pattern. Instead of being estranged from reality, one becomes a free agent *in this world,* the current, real world. (As we are often told, Nirvana and this world are one.) But this is equally well expressed by the former neurotic's saying that he is indeed living in a different, transcendent world!—for until now he lived in bondage and blindness, and at last he lives in freedom and with realistic vision.

With insight fully achieved, the special, dramatic, temporal quality of unconscious "eruptions" fades away. What then claims the attention is the quality of unity, of interrelatedness, of the presence of a unifying meaning among disparate events. From the focus on the plurality of the selves, we shift to an apprehension of the *single* Self of which they are manifestations. Even this eventually dissolves as a perception, when the new insights are well integrated and woven into the everyday fabric of life.

Such an enlightened person perceives time more clearly than ever. Past, present, and future are no longer *confused;* they have been de-fused. Successful psychoanalysis enables the person to distinguish realistically between past, present, and future instead of repetitively reliving the past in the present.[86] Likewise, the Buddhist says that the enlightened one sees clearly the discreteness and separateness, the uniqueness of phenomena; he sees how they are "ego-less." By the use of this technical term, not to be confused with the psychoanalytic "ego," the Buddhist points to the fact that the doctrine of metaphysical essences ("egos") is a reflection of our inability to see things realistically in their particularity. The belief in essences ("egos") reflects our slavelike attachment to seeing each new situation as merely a repetition of some unchanging theme, an essence which makes time irrelevant by reducing everything to the same, essential pattern.

Time, for the enlightened one, becomes light, indeed transparent; for the unenlightened it is often confused, always a burden. This is the fact whether we take it within a karmic or a psychoanalytic framework.

VI
Toward the Ontological: The Forms of Perceptual Experience

ALTHOUGH WE OFTEN THINK IN TERMS OF THE SIMPLE SET OF distinctions "dream," "waking perception," "hallucination," these are like the political boundary marks on a map. Apparently so sharp and clear when we study the terrain in our armchair, they are distressingly undiscoverable when we set out to explore the actual countryside. The actual geographic "boundaries" are not discontinuities at all; the single-colored territories on the map do not all have some one common physical property. So it is with our conceptual classifications of perceptual phenomena and the phenomena themselves.

Freud himself indicates some awareness of the shading off of one kind of experience into another. He says:

> . . . I thought of introducing a new category of dreams which were not subject to the mechanisms of condensation and displacement but were to be described as "phantasies during sleep." [87]

His sense of the slipperiness of the question is further displayed by his concluding this particular discussion by saying that "I dropped the category of 'dream-phantasies' "— and then, in 1930, adding a footnote, "Whether rightly I am now uncertain." In 1922 he noted the existence of sleep-consciousness in such nontypical "dream" forms as simple repetitions of actual scenes of the day, reproductions of traumatic scenes, "night-phantasies" and perhaps telepathic "dreams." [88] Although these are treated more or less as exceptions, this is a result of his categories, not the data. For one can look at the data as revealing that dream-perception in fact shades into a variety of sleep-perceptions having properties like those of simple memories, waking perceptions, and eidetic imagination. The classical psychoanalytic concept of the dream, a disguised wish-fulfillment based in the repressed infantile wish and occasioned by day-residues and current conflicts, certainly points to an important "psychic" region. But this region merges without discontinuity into other regions and displays even within its "borders" many of the features characteristic of other, neighboring regions.

Brenman, discussing "dream" phenomena influenced by hypnotic suggestion, states that the results range from a "slightly embellished reminiscence of an actual event to a production which at least on the surface resembles a classical night dream." [89] She states that the hypnotized dreamer not only "dreams" but reports out loud the content of the dream and evinces vigorous motor responses. In this connection we should also note such well-known phenomena as somnambulism and the even more common experience of awakening from "normal" sleep with genuine outcries. The vagueness of the dividing lines between dream and waking perception is also attested by the experience of wondering whether one has just dreamed something and then awakened or whether that something "actually" happened.

Sterba discusses a most interesting phenomenon which is surely more common than we have realized. He reports a number of dramatic instances of individuals who, just prior to reporting a dream to him, vividly act out in waking life, and quite unconsciously, the essential content of the dream.[90] Thus what we might call an "experience-content" is actualized both in the dream mode of experience and in a waking mode. For example, Sterba reports that a man who ordinarily never forgot to wear his glasses forgot them on one occasion prior to an appointment with the analyst. The patient offered "reasons" why he had not gone back to get them. Later during the hour he reported a dream of the night before in which, anticipating a fight with another man, he took off his glasses for safety. The reader will surmise the transference relationship at the time of the incident.

Shall this entire range of perception still be labeled "dream" when we see that there is no single characteristic of waking-perception which cannot somewhere be found here? Even the sleep-condition is not clearly shared by all, for the transition from sleep through sleep-under-hypnosis, through hypnotic trance, through "light" hypnotic trance, and, finally, through bemused daydreaming reveals no clear steps corresponding to our categories. Nor is this a series with a sharply defined order: all types of memory, vividness, connectedness, and "reality" qualities may occur in any combinations under any sleep-or-waking conditions.

With regard to unconscious fantasies in general, we have already mentioned Wittels' argument that it would be much more suggestive of the true state of things if we were not to speak of having an Oedipus complex or introjecting father images but rather of *being* Oedipus, of *being* father. Here Wittels is not denying the data which psychoanalysts have uncovered, but he is emphasizing a different aspect of the data. He assimilates the data to a different categorial scheme, one closely related to Freud's concept of "psychic reality." And, of course, it is precisely out of the inward experience, the "realities of the psyche," that the karmic doctrine draws its vital spiritual strength.

We must recall, too, that perceptual processes which are usually considered paradigm instances of pathology need not be considered such at all. Hallucination is a significant case in point, and the entire discussion of hallucinatory and quasi-hallucinatory phenomenon in Section IV of this chapter is directly relevant here.

Szasz and Stevenson [91, 92] have pointed out with particular force in this connection that we must avoid being dominated by the clinical pathology orientation. We must be cautious in interpreting the vast, growing body of reports on chemically and physically induced perceptual "disturbances." These include quantitative changes, e.g., intensification of color and depth, empathic qualities which exhibit a much wider than usual range of reality, and hallucinatory, or depersonalization, qualities. They also include qualitative changes, e.g., disruption of rational thought, perceptions of, for example, intense nausea in the foot or of intense pains which do not annoy. Are these "inherently" abnormal, unnatural? Why?

Surely such perceptual and other functional changes are not abnormal simply because a mechanical or chemical device has been introduced. The interference with perception produced by wearing properly prescribed eyeglasses is not a phenomenon which we assimilate to the category "disturbances of perception" but to "correctness of perception." Why? A plane mirror-image is assimilated by us to the category "accurate reflection" instead of to the categories "perceptual abnormality" or "confusing illustration." Why? Are not "normality" and "abnormality" relative to such matters as context, function, and purpose? Are there ranges of phenomena which are troublesome disturbances in our interpretative and action schemes and which are yet useful elements in other cultural or personal contexts?

Our habit of comfortably assimilating phenomena disturbing to us to a wastebasket "psychological" category, the "abnormal," prevents us from appreciating the remarkable discriminations which have been achieved by those who have studied such experience in terms of "the phases of spiritual insight," or "the power of recollecting clearly one's former lives." Our lack of discrimination may be both cause and effect of our lack of appreciation of the positive possibilities of these experiences. Cultural puritanism and parochialism easily masquerade as hardheaded common sense, even as "scientific." There always remains, in this connection, the peculiarly philosophical act—superficially a verbal one but pregnant with profound human consequences. To what order of existence, to what system of categories, to what "language-game" shall we assimilate a phenomenon which can equally well be assimilated to any of several different quasi-autonomous orders of existence? Does one have a memorylike dream which *represents* a crucial aspect of one's character development? Or does one have a trancelike vision in which divine powers portray symbolically one's fate? Each possibility can be worked out, indeed have already been explicitly and systematically worked out in many variations. Each has its peculiar merits and demerits.

VII
Toward the Ontological: The Contexts of Reincarnationist Beliefs

IS THIS ALL, PERHAPS, A VERBAL "SHELL GAME"? PERHAPS IT would be well to stress at once that I am not going to argue for *identity* of meaning between the doctrine of karma as expressed by the believer and the psychological and poetic-literary comparisons presented in the course of this discussion. I shall subsequently (Section VIII) state more explicitly what I think the relationship between the psychological and ontological formulations is. Let us turn our attention now to evidence which will bear directly upon this issue.

We may get substantial clues as to what the believer in reincarnation "really" ("literally") believes if we study the grounds offered for the correctness of the doctrine and the ways in which the doctrine functions once it is believed. Further, we shall take note of the larger cultural context in which the beliefs are expressed. Such considerations as these cannot be ignored in trying to estimate what a doctrine means to the true believer. Although his explicit verbal pronouncements on the doctrine must be given serious consideration, his words must be tied to behavior, contexts, grounds, and consequences.

As a viewpoint widely accepted in the East "on faith" and on authority, the doctrine of reincarnation plays an important role in popular religion. It provides a language and a complex of imagery for rite and literature and for the totality of myth. One or another language dealing with birth, death, and the meaning of life on earth seems to be ubiquitous in human cultures and is probably an essential condition of culture. Reincarnation and karma are the key concepts of one such language. The doctrine also caters to the popular demand for the miraculous and the superhuman. It offers marvelous chronicles and hopes of finding adepts having superhuman powers. There is little need to belabor this aspect of reincarnationist doctrine and imagery; it offers rich possibilities for the ever-popular miracle, magic, and wonder. Indeed this function of the doctrine is so evident that it has dazzled the eyes of Western observers and blinded us to certain other, subtler functions of the doctrine, those I am attempting to elaborate in this chapter.

As a moral-pedagogical doctrine, its role is equally great. The great literature of the Jataka tales, the so-called birth stories of the Buddha, are reminiscent of Aesop's fables in Western tradition. And, like Aesop's fables in the West, the Jataka fables are part of the everyday lore of the East. The Jataka tales use the fabulous in order to present practical moral instruction, a ubiquitous device in human culture. The connecting theme in Jataka tales is the proposition, in each tale, that we are being told of an event in a previous incarnation of the Buddha and of other beings.

In addition to ritual, magical, mythical, and moralistic functions, the doctrine undoubtedly serves a more personal, though universal, demand: it expresses the universal unconscious denial of personal mortality. Tillich evaluates the reincarnation doctrine as a "dangerously inadequate" symbol of eternal life.[93] This aspect of the doctrine has also been pointed out by a number of other commentators, particularly psychoanalytic writers.[94] It is often suggested that this denial of death is the psychological essence of the reincarnation doctrine, its core function. That such unconscious wishes motivate much belief in reincarnation can no more be denied than that Christian doctrine serves many Christians as an aid to denying their own death.

Let it here be said once for all that these roles in popular myth, magic, moral education, and anxiety-reduction are clearly among the most common functions of the reincarnation doctrine as they are of any great institutionalized religion. Yet we shall put these aside in the present discussion. These functions are all related to reincarnationist and karmic conceptions in an "external" way, as *authoritative*, "received" doctrine rather than as inwardly revealed "reality." They rest upon what, in the language of Upanishadic orthodoxy, is called "*smriti*" (received doctrine) rather than "*sruti*" (intuitively experienced truths).

I am interested here in the karmic doctrine as *sruti*, as an expression of the genuine dialogue of spirit. The latter may be a rare basis for belief. It is no less rare or important, I am sure, in the Christian or Jewish traditions. And, in a related context, it is no less rare than the physicist's interpretations of physical theory as compared with the popular beliefs about science.

I am, of course, urging that the doctrine's spiritual function, a function whose source is in direct experience rather than authoritative teaching, is that of providing a conceptual and action framework within which a person may explore and reorganize the psychomoral community of selves which constitute the person. That is to say, the function which I consider central to the spiritual experience which underlies the Upanishadic, Buddhist, and probably the Orphic karma-reincarnation teaching is a function systematically related to a process which can be described in psychoanalytic language.

The mere listing of various functions of the karmic doctrine, as I have done, does not establish the claim made as to which is the *sruti* meaning. The discussions in preceding sections of this chapter do show that the parallels between psychoanalytic ideas and karmic doctrine are systematic rather than erratically coincidental. What is necessary now is to show that this parallelism is the one which includes the *sruti* meaning of karma and not some other possible meaning. We shall now turn directly to this question.

The reasons offered for belief in reincarnation derive for the most part from reflection upon metaphysical argument, moral experience, the dream and related phenomena, perceptual-memory phenomena (e.g., *déjà vu*), and the occurrence of apparently unlearned skills and character traits.

Such contrasting and yet keenly analytic Western philosophers as the positivist David Hume[95] and the idealist J. M. E. McTaggart[96] have been among those in the West who have held that reincarnationist doctrine is a more plausible metaphysical doctrine than the usual Christian doctrines of the soul.

However, the metaphysical type of argument is not characteristically used as a "proof" by believers; and in particular it is not used in the Ur-texts of reincarnationism. In the great traditions of reincarnationism, the typical metaphysical elaborations have appeared as scholarly elaborations upon the already authoritative intuitive enunciation of doctrine. Metaphysical reasoning has been an attempt to make "rational" or "intellectually comprehensible or plausible" what was already given in the life of the spirit. Even in the early Western Orphic tradition, the belief rarely occurs in a context of logical analysis. It was its relevance to human suffering, to the Orphic and Pythagorean emphasis on memory as a special and marvelous mental power, which dominated. The classical scholar, Dodd, suggests that the belief was probably strengthened by intuitive glimmerings of infantile traumata.[97]

The earliest Upanishadic texts present us with a range of explicitly metaphoric imagery: the continuity of soul is concretely compared to the caterpillar who crawls from leaf (body) to leaf (body). Or the soul or character is portrayed as fashioning its body to its moral needs as the goldsmith fashions gilt.[98] In general, these Ur-texts offer analogies and metaphors to illuminate a view, rather than arguments to prove it "logically."

Furthermore, when more systematic clarification is undertaken, the texts turn immediately and frequently to the problem of the relation of waking states to dream states. In this line of exposition, it is explicitly asserted—in language which seems to be closest in spirit to "literal" statement rather than metaphor, analogy, or symbol—that dream states are the first important experiential step away from the waking state and toward the knowledge of Brahma. In several key passages the dream consciousness is identified with the "subtle body," that which transmigrates. The latter is distinguished from the "gross body" which roughly corresponds to the physical body and to so much of perception as relates to the physical body (i.e., waking-consciousness, roughly speaking).[99]

The subsequent elaboration into an orthodoxy of great and complex metaphysical systems was a chief target of the later "protestant" heresy, Buddhism. In the Buddhist texts there are innumerable variants on the theme that the Buddha is fundamentally antimetaphysical. He again and again turns attention to the individual, his suffering, and his search for the path toward moral and spiritual freedom. In the Pali text of the Majjhima-Nikaya, the Buddha speaks in typical fashion:

> Accordingly, Malunkaputta, bear always in mind what it is that I have not elucidated and what it is that I have elucidated. . . . I have not elucidated, Malunkaputta, that the world is eternal, I have not elucidated that the world is not eternal. . . .
>
> I have not elucidated that the soul and the body are identical, I have not elucidated that the soul is one thing and the body another; I have not elucidated that the saint exists after death, I have not elucidated that the saint does not exist after death, I have not elucidated that the saint both exists and does not exist after death. . . .
>
> And what, Malunkaputta, have I elucidated? Misery . . . the origin of misery . . . the cessation of misery . . . the path leading to the cessation of misery have I elucidated.[100]

In later basic texts of Tibetan Tantrism and in Chinese Ch'an (Zen), this antimetaphysical interpretation is suggested even more directly. The Tibetan *Book of the Dead* is replete with passages along the following lines:

> Apart from one's own hallucinations, in reality there are no such things existing outside oneself as Lord of Death, or god, or demon, or the bull-headed Spirit of Death.[101]

> Indeed, all these are like dreams, like hallucinations, like echoes, like the cities of the Odour-eaters, like mirage, like mirrored forms, like phantasmagoria, not real even for a moment.[102]

And from a major Chinese Ch'an Buddhist source, we learn that

> By letting our minds dwell on evil things, hell arises. By letting our minds dwell upon good acts, paradise is manifested. Dragons and snakes are the transformations of venomous hatred; while Bodhissatvas are compassionate thoughts made manifest.[103]

The great Taoist, Chuang-tse, tells an anecdote which is often quoted in Western literature—but, no doubt because of our Western bias, almost always with the omission of the crucial last two sentences. I add these, in Giles's translation and italicized, to Waley's text:

> Once Chuang Chou dreamt that he was a butterfly. He did not know that he had ever been anything but a butterfly and was content to hover from flower to flower. Suddenly he woke and found to his astonishment that he was Chuang Chou. But it was hard to be sure whether he really was Chou and had only dreamt that he was a butterfly, or was really a butterfly and was only dreaming that he was Chou. *Between a man and a butterfly there is necessarily a barrier. The transition is called metempsychosis.*[104]

Perhaps, finally, the reader should be reminded that *déjà vu* and related phenomena are not uncommonly mentioned in the literature of reincarnation.

The primary discussion in the classic Eastern literature of reincarnation revolves around what we should call moral-psychological themes rather than metaphysical or logical argumentation. The Buddhist scholar, Rhys Davids,[105] has stressed the moral content of the doctrine as central. Moore, in his admirable 1914 Ingersoll lecture on the doctrine of reincarnation, criticized

> . . . the modern rationalizations of the belief in reincarnation which endeavor to give it the semblance of a

scientific hypothesis. . . . The genuine doctrine has never been concerned to demonstrate itself to the finite understanding; it finds its authority in revelation, its verification in ecstatic experience. Its philosophy is an ontology which is above reason, incomprehensible, apprehensible only by intuition.[106]

And Radhakrishnan stresses that *sruti* doctrine "is not a matter of logical demonstration, but an intuitive insight." [107] The Vedic seers, he says, claim only this kind of inspiration and revelation for their hymns.

These intuitional experiences are within the possibility of all men if only they will to have them. . . . What is dogma to the ordinary man is experience to the pure in heart.[108]

Of "evidence" offered in support of reincarnation, the type apparently least tied to spiritual or moral considerations is that based on the observable disparities in human talents and qualities, as well as the occasional remarkable resemblance of persons of one generation to those of preceding generations. The fact that some must struggle to learn or achieve skills or human qualities with which others seem to be "born" has provoked reflection. How neat an accounting to suppose that those who are born with a quality have struggled for it in a previous life and achieved it! But the character of the explanation reveals that the question was not a would-be causal one but a moral one. The primary impulse, even in this area, is to show that the world is not "unfair." The "explanation" does this, for it is couched in moral terms: we "earn" our strengths and weaknesses in one life or another; nothing is morally arbitrary. As Moore suggests, we must be suspicious of reading a quite alien "scientific" curiosity into this matter.

It does seem plausible that this quest for an explanation of human diversity and similarity may have had a premoral impulse which was mythic-magic. Indeed the reincarnation doctrine as a whole probably had its roots in preliterate, stone age culture and is still found in cultures studied by anthropologists. It was probably rooted in dream, trance, and other natural or drug-induced perceptual phenomena, all aided by bits of genuine insight into human relationships. But I have been dealing in this chapter with the doctrine as transformed and spiritualized in the emergence of Upanishadic, Buddhist, and Orphic reincarnation doctrine during the middle of the first millennium B.C. The literature and evidence shows that Western interpretations, implicitly based as they are on the systematic application of the categories of physical space-time and of logical argument, are inapplicable to the karma-reincarnation doctrine in its profoundest spiritual import.

VIII
The Ontological Status of Reincarnation

THE QUESTION WHICH NOW RE-EMERGES WITH ADDITIONAL force is this: if the spiritual sources of reincarnationist doctrine lie so close to the kind of experience touched by psychoanalysis, why is the matter formulated in terms of *bodily* lives in past and future? In part we have answered this in an earlier section of this chapter. The complicated disruption of time perception caused by uprushes of the unconscious, the "living" quality of the new perceptions, their combined "alienness" and yet "belongingness"—all these and more lend themselves wonderfully to expression, at least as "metaphor," in reincarnationist language. But to leave the doctrine as an elaborate metaphor is to fail to learn a fundamental philosophical and existential lesson. For I want to show that whereas it may be viewed as metaphor, it need not be. And to see it as *not* metaphor is to achieve a form of self-liberation.

Let us return to Freud. Among the key ideas which enabled Freud to continue his early explorations was the idea of "psychic reality." This is related to his conception of "the omnipotence of thought." Freud showed that the unconscious mind takes the "thought" for the deed; or, even more correctly, in the unconscious, the thought *is* the deed. To wish death is, for the unconscious mind, already to have killed. Freud was here restating in his own language one of the revolutionary and characteristic insights of Jesus as well as of the Far Eastern traditions.

> You have heard how it used to be said, Do not commit adultery. But I tell you, anyone who even looks with lust at a woman has committed adultery with her already in his heart.[109]

And the Dhammapada opens:

> All that we are is the result of what we have thought: it is founded on our thoughts, it is made up of our thoughts.[110]

Freud, too, took seriously the *entire* inner life, and he postulated that it is all meaningfully interconnected. This postulate of "psychic determinism" is, as I have in effect argued, closely related to the doctrine of karma: no psychic event is a psychic accident: it grew out of its specific seed and bears its specific fruit.

Now such a doctrine emphasizes the importance, the reality and the vitality of the unconscious life. How does it come to be, then, that the psychoanalyst should interpret his discoveries as finally "debunking" visions, prophesy, devils, gods, and reincarnation?

The usual answer would be that the psychoanalyst now sees the true causes for these beliefs. He understands that they are "superstitions," quasi-physicalistic or "para"-physicalistic interpretations of what are really "psychological" phenomena. How else would we understand the charge that these are, for example, "merely" projections of subjective experiences.

This way of putting the matter stems from Freud's having taken a stand at the very beginning of his inquiry which prejudiced the issue. Freud, quite naturally, took the stand of science, technology, the modern West: he oriented himself fundamentally toward the public world, toward reliably interpretable theory when cast in a logically consistent and predictive form. Physical space-time, and the concept of history as rooted in these, frame not only the common-sense Weltanschauung of technological man, they establish the framework of reality for Freud, too. This is a legitimate orientation; it has profound uses. But for Freud it was more than a useful orientation; it was for him, as for most Westerners regardless of professed beliefs, the ultimate orientation.

When Freud discovered the world of inner life and its remarkable degree of autonomy from the social and physical environment at any moment, he was forced to attribute to this nonlogical, nonphysical world a secondary kind of reality—it was "psychological," "subjective," "fantasy," unless reinterpreted in terms of some logical scheme tied to physical space-time events. At least this was his way of looking at it when theoretical and philosophical description was in question. In daily practice, Freud was precisely the man, as I have said, who systematically grasped the *reality* of this realm.

Freud was not alone. All of us in the West are so in bondage to the public, physical orientation that we can only allow ourselves to come to terms with the "inner" world (where it deviates from the physical) by indirection; we do so on various levels of awareness through art, play, or dream, conscious fantasy, neurosis, or psychosis. The limping metaphor "inner" serves to mark how we have crippled ourselves, cut ourselves off from the "outer" world, even in the language we use.

In those cultures which are not so fascinated by the public, the logical, and the physical, it is easier and more common to consider another mode of existence as reality. It is the world of the human being, the drama of men in their relations to each other and to nature, which plays the central role.

In such societies the physical-causal aspect of the world is as vague, shadowy, and crudely understood as is the dream-world in the West. In the modern West, the dream and the hallucination are still perceived by most persons as isolated, largely meaningless eruptions. For those who belong to nontechnological cultures, however, quite the reverse holds: it is the physical object—as physical—which, although recognized, is isolated, meaningless, unconnected with other events. No objects or events are firmly located in a clear structure of physical space-time and causality. Even when the rudiments of operating a Western machine are learned by someone from a nontechnological culture, the machine and its operation are still located by him in the larger structure of a world moved by persons and motives. He is, to the technician, a perversely superstitious and unteachable savage or peasant. In the nontechnological culture, the meaningful world, the real world, the world that binds together, is the highly elaborated and familiar world of human drama, of myth, ritual, dream, hallucination, and daily ritualized work. All these are bound in an essentially *dramatic* unity rather than a technological one.

It is a great discovery of the major civilizations that the person is a plurality-in-unity. The modern Westerner assigns the unity to the body (the reality) and assigns the multi-personal aspects of self, the appearances, to the mind, the psychic, the subjective. By contrast, the Easterner postulates a psychic-spiritual unity, and is quite at ease associating the multiplicity of many selves, the appearances, to a multiplicity of bodily lives. Thus, for each culture, what is familiar, sensitively elaborated, and fundamental is seen as the realm of unity; what is obscure, eccentric, and less important is seen as the realm of plurality, of appearances, illusion, maya, fantasy. East and West show an exact reversal of emphasis and conceptualization.

We must not suppose, however, that the Chinese, for example, were unskilled in the study of numbers, of the physical heavens, or of nature; far from it. The Chinese did have "empirical" achievements. But, as Granet stresses in his study of Chinese thought, the important thing to note is that "the history of Chinese thought is remarkable for the independence which philosophic wisdom manages to maintain in regard to what we call science."[111] "In place of a *Science* having knowledge of the World for its object, the Chinese conceived an *Etiquette* of life which they supposed sufficiently potent to institute a total Order."[112]

In getting at the inner meaning of the classic conceptions held by Chinese thinkers we must keep reminding ourselves that

> When they speak and when they write, the Chinese seek by means of stylized gestures, vocal or other, to shape and to suggest forms of conduct. Their thinkers do not have any other pretentions. They are perfectly satisfied with a traditional system of symbols which are more powerful in orienting action than they are congenial to the formulation of concepts, theories, or dogmas.[113]

When a psychiatrist told a Chinese that Harry Stack Sullivan's psychiatry was based on a study of interpersonal relationships, the Chinese asked with surprise, "What other kind are there?"[114]

Whatever the scholastic superstructure, it is vital to re-

member that the Chinese conception of the universe "proceeds directly from mythic conceptions." [115] Traditional
Eastern empirical knowledge was instrumental to spiritual
demands and categories and to quite limited, practical purposes of a military or agricultural kind. The point of doing
astronomy, for example, was not to develop elaborate logi-
cal-experimental theories; it was to cast better horoscopes,
to adjust oneself to the Tao of the Universe.

The categories of time and history have quite different
import in the East from in the West. Percheron concludes
that the people of India have had an "indifference for historical dating" and, in their legends, no more respect "for
geographical extent than for the duration of time or unity
of aspect." [116]

Lily Abegg in her study of the mind of East Asia provides support for this point as well as insight into it.

When the East Asian surveys his history, he does not
actually look backwards; it is the eternal present that
he contemplates. We therefore do wrong when we say,
for example, that an East Asian 'looks back' towards his
'ancient sages,' for this is a term derived from Western
concepts of time and historical development. He just
regards them as if they were still living.

East Asians have a well-developed sense of history,
inasmuch as the past remains alive and is ever-present
to them. Thanks to their great powers of memory their
historical knowledge is extremely rich. They have, however, little sense of chronological sequence in history
and of the causal relationships between successive happenings; in this sense they are 'history-less.' [117]

We must take such perspectives into account in interpreting the karmic doctrine as it is understood by those indigenous to the Eastern cultures. When they speak of different bodies and different lives, we must inquire whether it
is the moral-psychological-mythic "implications" of their

statements which primarily concern them or the physical-historical ones. We cannot, of course, expect a clear and sharp *avoidance* of physical-historical comments since this aspect of the world, as we have said, is not clearly distinguished from the dramatic aspect in the first place. One cannot *consistently* avoid something of whose existence one is not consistently aware. Bits of what we Westerners would call naïve physicalistic reasoning occur occasionally in the classic texts on reincarnation. What we must do, however, is to look to the preponderance of evidence, argument, applications, and origins. We must see in what framework these are presented and toward what they point.

We might take as our watchword here the amply supported statement of Lord Raglan that "only the smallest fraction of the human race has ever acquired the habit of taking an objective view of the past." [118] And we might add that this "smallest fraction" belongs almost entirely to the cluster of subcultures having their roots in postmedieval Western Europe.

Typically, where the belief in reincarnation is held, there is no serious concern with historical documentation of the series of former lives. If such a remarkable process as transmigration referred to physical time, it is surely simple to see that historical documentation would be relevant. Yet it is the case that although the belief is nearly universal in India *even today*, there is still no serious concern on the part of spiritual leaders with providing or checking physical or historical proof. Why not? These aspects of the matter are sensed to be and are stated to be trivial and irrelevant to the main point of karmic doctrine. If anyone should find what appears to be a case confirmatory of the doctrine as taken in a physicalistic-historical sense, that is interesting. But it is no cause for special joy or increased confidence. Should anyone find disconfirmatory physical or historical evidence, it is ignored. This strongly suggests that the content of the belief, its meaning for the believer, has little or nothing to do with what *we* Westerners mean by physical or historical events as such.

When we of the modern West say, "Jones was alive in 1867," we mean clearly to indicate that our statement is logically tied to propositions about certain physical space-time events, to geographical space and to calendar time. We have an elaborate historiography as well as laboratory science with which to confirm many such statements. Physical time is a beautifully elaborated, solid structure, ever dominating our thoughts. "Subjective time," with all its comparable richness of structure, remains for us the "leftover," the residual, obscure, formless penumbra of our time-consciousness. But just as a few ancient Chinese showed remarkable, though limited, ability to elaborate physical, logical, and mathematical distinctions, so a few Westerners have achieved remarkable discriminations with regard to subjective time. The West can offer the "stream of consciousness" writers to match the Chinese "Dialecticians."

I am not emasculating the reincarnation doctrine by cutting out its physical implications. I am trying to preserve it whole. My aim here is to keep the Western mind from reading an alien, physical-historical meaning *into* it. I am not "psychologizing" it; I am "de-technologizing" it. I want to present it as a reality, not a metaphor.

The late David Roberts wrote:

> From a naturalistic perspective, the language of vision in literature, philosophy and religion, tells us something interesting about the imaginary worlds which human wishes and needs have spun; but only scientific language is accurately geared to the structure of reality. From a theistic perspective, the language of drama and of personal relationships—struggle and triumph, anxiety and fellowship, guilt and forgiveness—will be regarded as fundamental.[119]

Which language reveals Reality? Which *is* "fundamental"? For those inseparably wedded to the physicalistic orientation, to orient oneself toward the dramatic world is a "flight from reality." For those of a more flexible cast of mind (a less question-begging mind?), we may consider such a reorientation as a "shifting of the index-pointer of reality." [120] Chuang-tse's anecdote about the butterfly takes on a more general and profound meaning when we see that his words *wu hua* may also be taken to mean "the ontological transformation of things" as well as "metempsychosis." [121] Where shall we set the "index-pointer of reality"? Things will work out meaningfully, though differently, *either* way.

"Reality" is, as a metaphysical term, an honorific, not a descriptive, term. We call "real" the world as viewed from our preferred orientation. Even could we in principle deduce ("explain") the world of the dramatic from a sufficiently full physicalistic account of the world, this would not settle the issue. For we can, contrariwise, make sense of the physical world in terms of a dramatic account of the world. The truth is that this latter goal has been realized, whereas the former is as yet a moot program. For we have a variety of elaborate and satisfactory accounts of the significance of the physical world within the basic framework of mythic and dramatic images. That there is variety, and that the accounts are not all logically consistent with one another, is irrelevant. The criteria of validity for dramatic unity do not include internal logical coherence, laboratory verification, or consistency with other such accounts. It is such differences in criteria which objectively distinguish the scientific from the dramatic orientation. But to insist that one or another of these orientations is the *reality*-orientation is to express fundamental cultural or personal leanings, and it is not to provide any further information.

Ultimately the question is: Which way do we choose to grasp the world: in dramatic, human images, or in logical-physical-causal conceptions? Each world is "secondary" for the other. For the world of science, the dramatic is, roughly speaking, "subjective"; the imagin*ative* is a portrayal of the imagin*ary*. But for those whose fundamental stance is in the dramatic world, the physical is, so to say, illusion. It is an obstacle which must be seen *through* when it is not a conceptual device to be used.

Whitehead argued that John Locke had misled the rest of us by so stressing scientific abstractions that "we have mistaken our abstraction for concrete realities." [122] The conception of the universe framed in terms of such high abstractions is, says Whitehead, "quite unbelievable." [123] But Wyndham Lewis, in turn critical of Whitehead's critique, has commented bitterly on this modern, condescending anti-Lockianism. Lewis asks

> *Who* has mistaken, or mistook the very practical and useful abstractions of Science for "concrete reality" or for truth?
>
> It is *he,* Dr. Whitehead, who has *believed* in this 'dull,' 'meaningless' picture, quite naïvely, no doubt. And now, with a gesture of enfranchisement and discovery, he announces that it is 'quite unbelievable.' But of *course it is unbelievable*. It has always been unbelievable. But, from certain aspects, and if kept in its own province, it can be extremely useful. So why not let its 'dullness' and evident unreality alone, and allow it to go on doing its work? [124] [Italics in original]

It is unfortunate that our slavery to the physical-causal mode of thought is so great that many attempts to assign "ontological primacy" to the human, the dramatic realities, are beset by charges of mystification, obscurantist irrationalism, even—ironically—antihumanism. It is ironic that the directly graspable world of human beings in dramatic conflict, the world which has been familiar to humankind since the beginnings of the race—all this we now find dark, obstreperous, esoteric, even silly or boring. The *human* world in the West has become peripheral and surreptitious, an "underground" world.

> The things I thought were real are shadows, and the real are what I thought were private shadows.[125]

I know quite well that a discussion such as the present one, if it succeeds at all, can make a person intellectually open to the view that the world of the spirit is "real"; but it cannot bring the conviction that counts. These are not, at bottom, matters of disputation but of the gesture of life, of "forms of life." One cannot accept a new reality-orientation through the medium of a generalized analysis. The response to life is always concrete, dense with meaning.

Until now I have simplified the alternatives to two: the physical orientation and the dramatic. There is, of course, a spectrum of orientations which merge one into another. Even among the "dramatic" orientations classified in the most wholesale terms we have significant choice. The Judaeo-Christian apprehends life on earth as a unique cosmic event, a coming out of nothing, a staking of all on the one chance, and, finally, a reaping of eternal reward or punishment. The Far Eastern image is of a multitude of interconnected lives, a slow and arduous struggle toward spiritual enlightenment. The physicalistic image is of a cosmically meaningless life, beginning and ending in nothingness. None of these views is intrinsically more sentimental or hard-boiled than another. Each can, in its own way, both liberate and burden; and each can be used sentimentally— whether by the infantile optimist or the defensive cynic.

Although we must be specific in life and follow one way or another, there is a sense in which these are no longer mutually exclusive alternatives. It is true each image of man's fate must be taken—when it is taken—as absolute and universal. But, for twentieth-century man, there is no one particular orientation which we must take, indeed no one which is adequate. We can no longer be parochial. The absoluteness of each perspective has validity only as and when a commitment to an orientation is made; and what is suggested by "absolute" can only be precisely interpreted within an orientation. When an orientation is not taken, the claims generated by it are not valid. For the validity of such images comes in their operation. In particular it comes when they function as the central, dominating, organizing images of a man's life. Let such an image cease to dominate a man's life and, as a *spiritual* conception, it ceases to be. The validity or invalidity of such a vision is not like the truth or falsity of a proposition in science; it is like winning or losing a race. But if a man does not enter the race, he can neither be said to win or to lose. So there is no question of the validity of a basic orientation to the world for one who is not at the time committed to that orientation. It is not a question of true or false but of increments of Being. True and false take their meaning *within* the orientation selected.

If we are guided by the scientific orientation to the universe, of course we cannot validly introduce the illogical, the antimathematical. But an analogous prohibition holds true of the Christian conception or the Buddhist: in neither can we properly introduce that which is respectively either anti-Christian or anti-Buddhist. The question is not how to introduce what is alien in spirit into any of these visions of life. It is, rather, when and how to shift from one great vision to another so as to maximize our total vision, to deepen it, to build it in many dimensions, to render what was opaque into that which is never transparent but increasingly translucent.

What each conception, each vision demands is that it be the genuine organizing and generative seed, that its integrity be respected and enhanced, that it receive the utter commitment which guarantees the dominance of its spirit and excludes that which is alien to its spirit. We cannot toy with the idea of reincarnation as an intellectual or cultural curiosity having a certain piquant and quaint validity and still discover its power and its worth. Nor can we, along Christian lines, only half suppose that on this moment everything rests and still discover the life of which such a conception is the seed. Nor can we fiddle with mechanical gadgets or read a syndicated newspaper column on science and then expect to experience anything but a variant of our previous mythology expressed in a pseudo-scientific lingo.

It is the special fate of modern man that he has a "choice" of spiritual visions. The paradox is that although each requires complete commitment for complete validity, we can today generate a context in which we see that no one of them is the sole vision. Thus we must learn to be naïve but undogmatic. That is, we must take the vision as it comes and trust ourselves to it, naïvely, as reality. Yet we must retain an openness to experience such that the dark shadows deep within one vision are the mute, stubborn messengers waiting to lead us to a new light and a new vision.

At first one lives with one vision for years before there is readiness for another. After the accumulation of experience and of acquaintance with more than one of these ways of seeing, the movement from one organizing view to another can come more rapidly. This shifting of visions is not then any the less a matter of genuine and deep commitment. It is not a sampling or tasting, not an eclecticism. For one calls upon a vision with a life, one's own, behind it. One earns a vision by living it, not merely thinking about it. Eventually, however, when several such lives have been lived, one can shift from life to life more often and more easily, from vision to vision more freely.

Here a Buddhist image helps. We are told that there are degrees of enlightenment and, further, that with the higher forms of enlightenment, the enlightened one can move from realm to realm, from world to world, from dharma to dharma, with ease; yet he is at home in each. The Buddha uses doctrine; he is not a slave to it. Doctrine is the ferry, and the enlightened one knows there are many ferries which travel to the farther shore. But when he is ferrying, he is skillful, wholehearted, and at one with his craft.

We know also that, even in Buddhist terms, the very Buddhas and Bodhisattvas have their special or favorite powers and realms. We must not ignore the fact that in this last analysis, commitment to a specific orientation outweighs catholicity of imagery. One may be a sensitive and seasoned traveler, at ease in many places, but one must have a home. Still, we can be intimate with those we visit, and while we may be only travelers and guests in some domains, there are our hosts who are truly at home. Home is always home for someone; but there is no Absolute Home in general. And reality is a favored base of operations, a favored place from which to greet the world, not an Absolute Place in general. With all its discovery of relativism, the West has been fundamentally absolutist and therefore parochial: we claim to tolerate other visions than the logical and technological; we explain them, praise them, enjoy them; and, gently, skillfully, appreciatively, do we not, too often, betray them?

NOTES

(See List of Bibliographical Abbreviations, p. 343.)

1. Moore, G. F., *Metempsychosis*, Harvard University Press, Cambridge, 1914, p. 67.
2. Evans-Wentz, W. Y., *The Tibetan Book of the Dead*, Oxford University Press, New York, 1927, p. 179.
3. *Saddharma-smrtyupasthana Sutra*, Chap. XXXIV, in *Buddhist Texts*, Conze, E., Philosophical Library, New York, 1954, p. 283.

4. Evans-Wentz, W. Y., *op. cit.*, p. 162.
5. *Loc. cit.*
6. *Brihadaranyaka Upanishad*, IV, iv, 5, in *The Upani-shads*, Prabhavananda & Manchester, F., Mentor, New York, 1957, p. 109.
7. Percheron, M., *Buddha and Buddhism*, Harper & Bros., New York, 1957, p. 66. (Anguttara-Nikaya)
8. *Brihadaranyaka Upanishad*, IV, iv, 2. (Mentor, p. 108.)
9. *Saddharmapundarika*, V, 70, in *Buddhist Texts*, p. 125.
10. *Ibid.*, V, 71, p. 125.
11. Lao-tse, *Tao Te Ching*, II, in *The Way and Its Power*, Waley, A., The Macmillan Co., New York, 1934, p. 143.
12. Siwek, Paul, S. J., *La Réincarnation des Esprits*, Des-clée, De Brovwer et Cie., Paris, 1942, II, 2.
13. McTaggart, J. Mc. E., *Some Dogmas of Religion*, Edward Arnold, London, 1906, pp. 127–139.
14. Moore, G. F., *op. cit.*, p. 69.
15. Freud, S., "Moral Responsibility for Dreams," in *CP*, V, p. 156.
16. ———, "Psychoanalysis," in *CP*, V, p. 128.
17. Liebenthal, W., "The Immortality of the Soul in Chinese Thought," *Monumenta Nipponica* 8:327–397 (1952).
18. McTaggart, J. Mc. E., *op. cit.*, Chap. IV.
19. Freud, S., "Thoughts for the Times on War and Death," in *CPW*, XIV, p. 295.
20. Kubie, L. S., "The Neurosis Wears a Mask," in *Moments of Personal Discovery*, MacIver, R. M., ed., Harper & Bros., New York, 1952, p. 34.
21. Wittels, F., "Unconscious Phantoms in Neurosis," *Psychoanalytic Quarterly* 8:141–163 (1939).
22. Fenichel, O., *The Psychoanalytic Theory of Neurosis*, W. W. Norton & Co., 1945, p. 222.
23. Freud, S., *Group Psych.*, in *CPW*, XVIII, pp. 105–110.
24. Wexler, M., "The Structural Problem in Schizophrenia: The Role of the Internal Object," in *Psychotherapy with Schizophrenia*, Brody, E. B., and Redlich, F. C.,

eds., International Universities Press, New York, 1952, pp. 196–197.

25. Rapaport, D., *Organization and Pathology of Thought,* Columbia University Press, New York, 1951, p. 725.

26. *Ibid.,* p. 73.

27. Sullivan, H. S., "Psychiatry: Introduction to the Study of Interpersonal Relations," in *A Study of Interpersonal Relations,* Mullahy, P., ed., Grove Press, New York, 1949, pp. 98–121.

28. Woolf, V., *Mrs. Dalloway,* Harcourt, Brace & Co., New York, 1949, pp. 231–232.

29. Freud, S., "Thoughts for the Times on War and Death," *op. cit.,* p. 291.

30. Lewis, W., *Time and Western Man,* Beacon Press, Boston, 1957, pp. 192–193.

31. Poulet, G., *Studies in Human Time,* Johns Hopkins Press, Baltimore, 1956, p. 353.

32. *Ibid.,* p. 296.

33. Coomaraswamy, A. K., "Eastern Religions and Western Thought," *The Review of Religion* 6 (1942), p. 137.

34. Baudelaire, C., *Les Paradis Artificiels,* in *Œuvres,* Librairie Gallimard, Paris, 1954, p. 456.

35. Freud, S., *Gen. Intro.,* p. 195.

36. Aeschylus, *The Furies,* Morshead, E. D. A., trans., in *Harvard Classics,* Vol. VIII, p. 119.

37. *Brihadaranyaka Upanishad,* IV, iii, 7–10, in *The Principal Upanishads,* Radhakrishnan, S., George Allen & Unwin, London, 1953, pp. 256–258.

38. *Ibid.,* p. 253.

39. *Ibid.,* IV, iv, 6, pp. 272–273.

40. Bergson, H., *The World of Dreams,* Philosophical Library, New York, 1958.

41. Devereux, G., *Reality and Dream,* International Universities Press, New York, 1951.

42. *Ibid.,* p. 82.

43. *Ibid.,* p. 83.

44. *Ibid.,* p. 90.

45. *Ibid.*, p. 86.
46. Freud, S., "Moral Responsibility for Dreams," *op. cit.*, p. 156.
47. Devereux, G., *op. cit.*, p. 93.
48. Freud, S., *op. cit.*
49. Devereux, G., *op. cit.*, p. 89.
50. Erikson, E. H., "The Nature of Clinical Evidence," *Daedalus* 87:69–70 (1958).
51. Quinn, P. F., *The French Face of Edgar Allan Poe*, Southern Illinois University Press, 1957, p. 154.
52. Raglan, F. R., *Death and Rebirth*, Watts & Co., London, 1945.
53. Boss, M., *The Analysis of Dreams*, Rider & Co., London, 1957, p. 85.
54. *Ibid.*, p. 122.
55. Schachtel, E., "On Memory and Childhood Amnesia," in *A Study of Interpersonal Relations*, p. 36.
56. Greenacre, P., *Trauma, Growth and Personality*, W. W. Norton & Co., 1952, p. 190.
57. *Loc. cit.*
58. *Loc. cit.*
59. Rapaport, D., *op. cit.*, p. 720.
60. Schachtel, E., *op. cit.*, p. 37.
61. Ferenczi, S., "Transitory Symptom Constructions During the Analysis," in *Sex in Psychoanalysis*, Basic Books, New York, 1950, pp. 204–206.
62. Hutchinson, E. D., "The Nature of Insight," in *A Study of Interpersonal Relations*, p. 441.
63. *Ibid.*, p. 445.
64. Meyerhoff, H., *Time in Literature*, University of California Press, Berkeley, 1955, p. 55.
65. Goldberger, L., and Holt, R. R., "Experimental Interference with Reality Contact (Perceptual Isolation): Method and Group Results," *Journal of Nervous & Mental Disease* 127:110 (1958).
66. *Ibid.*, p. 111.
67. Freud, S., *Psychopathology*, pp. 265–269.

68. Schilder, P., "Studies Concerning the Psychology and Symptomatology of General Paresis," in Rapaport, D., *op. cit.*, p. 573.

69. Freud, S., "Recollection, Repetition and Working Through," in *CP*, II, p. 368.

70. ———, "From the History of an Infantile Neurosis," in *CP*, III, pp. 523–524.

71. Poulet, G., *op. cit.*, p. 314.

72. *Ibid.*, p. 317.

73. *Brihadaranyaka Upanishad*, III, vii, 23, Nikhilananda, trans., *The Upanishads*, Harper & Bros., New York, 1956.

74. *Ibid.*, IV, iii, 14.

75. Radhakrishnan, S., *The Principal Upanishads*, p. 74.

76. Poulet, G., *op. cit.*, p. 268.

77. Boss, M., *op. cit.*, p. 112.

78. Freud, S., *Gen. Intro.*, p. 200.

79. ———, "The Poet and Daydreaming," in *CP*, IV, p. 177.

80. Schilder, P., "The Psychopathology of Time," *Journal of Nervous and Mental Disease* 83 (1936), p. 541.

81. Freud, S., *Moses*, p. 162.

82. ———, "The 'Uncanny,'" in *CP*, IV, p. 403.

83. Pound, E., Pisan Canto XCI, in *Selected Poems of Ezra Pound*, New Directions, New York, 1957, p. 180.

84. Keats, J., *Ode on a Grecian Urn*.

85. Meerloo, J., *The Two Faces of Man*, International Universities Press, New York, 1954, p. 45.

86. This important point was first brought to my attention in the relevant context in discussion with Henry Seidenberg, M.D. It is also made by Meerloo in a purely psychoanalytic context.

87. Freud, S., *Dreams*, p. 331.

88. ———, "Dreams and Telepathy," in *CP*, IV, p. 421.

89. Brenman, M., "Dreams and Hypnosis," *Psychoanalytic Quarterly* 18 (1949), p. 457.

90. Sterba, R., "Dreams and Acting Out," *Psychoanalytic Quarterly* 15:175 (1946).

91. Szasz, T. S., "The Classification of 'Mental Illness,'" *The Psychiatric Quarterly* 33:1–25 (1959).

92. Stevenson, I., "Comments on the Psychological Effects of Mescaline and Allied Drugs," *Journal of Nervous and Mental Disease* 125:438–442 (1957).

93. Tillich, P., "Existential Analyses and Religious Symbols," in *Four Existentialist Theologians,* Herberg, W., ed., Doubleday, New York, 1958, p. 290.

94. Freud, S., "Thoughts for the Times on War and Death," in *CPW,* XIV, p. 295.

95. Hume, D., "Essay in Immortality," in *Philosophical Works of David Hume,* Vol. IV, Little, Brown & Co., Boston, 1854, p. 553.

96. McTaggart, J. Mc. E., *op. cit.,* pp. 119–120.

97. Dodd, E. R., *The Greeks and the Irrational,* Beacon Press, Boston, 1957, pp. 151–152.

98. *Brihadaranyaka Upanishad,* IV, iv, 3–4.

99. See, for example, *Brihadaranyaka Upanishad,* IV, iv, 6, particularly the Nikhilananda or Prabhavananda translations, and *Mandukya Upanishad,* 3–5 and 10.

100. *Majjhima-Nikaya Sutta 63,* Warren, H. C., trans., quoted in Griffin, N. E. & Hunt, L., *The Farther Shore,* Houghton Mifflin Co., Boston, 1934, p. 33.

101. Evans-Wentz, W. Y., *op. cit.,* p. 167.

102. *Ibid.,* p. 181.

103. Goddard, D., ed., *A Buddhist Bible,* E. P. Dutton & Co., 1938, p. 529.

104. Chuang-tse, Book II.

105. Rhys Davids, T. W., *Lectures on the Origin and Growth of Religion,* Williams & Norgate, London, 1891, pp. 91–94.

106. Moore, G. F., *op. cit.,* pp. 71–72.

107. Radhakrishnan, S., *Indian Philosophy,* The Macmillan Co., New York, 1929, I, p. 128.

108. *Ibid.,* p. 51.

109. *Matt.* 5:27–28, Moffatt translation.

110. Dhammapada, Chap. I in *The Wisdom of China and*

India, Lin Yutang, Modern Library, New York, 1942, p. 327.

111. Granet, M., *La Pensée Chinoise,* La Renaissance du Livre, Paris, 1934, p. 23. (Author's translation.)
112. *Ibid.,* p. 24.
113. *Ibid.,* p. 31.
114. Weakland, J. H., "The Organization of Action in Chinese Culture," *Psychiatry 13:*361–370 (1950).
115. Granet, M., *op. cit.,* p. 22.
116. Percheron, M., *op. cit.,* p. 183.
117. Abegg, L., *The Mind of East Asia,* Thames & Hudson, London, 1952, p. 310.
118. Raglan, F. R., *The Hero,* Vintage Books, New York, 1956, p. 3.
119. Roberts, D. E., *Psychotherapy and a Christian View of Man,* Charles Scribner's Sons, New York, 1950, p. 87.
120. Firth, R., "Elements of Social Organization," in *Reader in Comparative Religion,* Lessa, W. A., and Vogt, E. Z., eds., Row, Peterson & Co., Evanston, 1958, p. 128.
121. Chuang-tse, Book II. (Author's translation.)
122. Whitehead, A. N., *Science and the Modern World,* New American Library, New York, 1948, p. 56.
123. *Loc. cit.*
124. Lewis, W., *op. cit.,* pp. 199–200.
125. Eliot, T. S., "The Family Reunion," in *The Complete Poems and Plays,* Harcourt, Brace & Co., New York, 1952, p. 276.

CHAPTER 6

THE MID-PHASES (2):

Art, Therapy, the External World

THE EMERGENCE FROM THE WORLD OF "BONDAGE TO UNCON-scious infantile selves," of "karmic illusion," coincides with a new relationship to real persons. The real other person, instead of being a mere occasion for the evocation of inner-fantasy oriented responses, becomes the real object of concern. Instead of being an "it," serving as an instrument of fantasy gratifications, the other person becomes a potential "Thou."

This process is the natural concomitant of release from the various "Me's," the binding ideas of self, and the liberation of the generative "I." The "Thou" and the "I" are integral to each other. The gesture toward the real Other can only be taken as there is an "I," a person free to be open to the reality which comes. In psychoanalytic language: Infantile inner conflict is complemented by infantile interpersonal relationships; we must emerge from both concurrently. It is only our discussion that must present the matter in two parts.

The guiding questions in the present chapter are several. What is the nature of this new orientation to other persons? What is its psychological character? How is this related to spiritual texts treating of human relations? What can we learn by consideration of material from such special human situations as psychotherapy and the esthetic experience?

Time and again in the literature of both East and West, we meet the ideal person as one who offers love and sympathy and selfless devotion while remaining in some sense "disinterested," "detached," "uninvolved," "ruthless." Compassionate objectivity, humanhearted but disinterested understanding: the paradox in these phrases is evident. This paradoxical notion of compassionate objectivity will be the principal subject of our inquiry here. We shall move into new areas and more deeply into familiar ones. But first we must elaborate and sharpen the data which will occupy us. And we can do this by considering this relationship or attitude in three different contexts: religion, psychotherapy, and art.

Constant at its core, though appearing in varying guises, we find in many cultures the ideal of the enlightened-agonist: he who insistently guides us through the ordeal which liberates, who joins in it though he is above it, who is disinterestedly our burden and our ally.

Socrates, Jesus, Gautama Buddha—each represents a human being of unwavering and selfless dedication to individuals in their struggle for spiritual transformation. Each represents the penetrating power of understanding; each, in his relation with men, grasps the Other's human condition in the very act of dialogue with him; each responds *to* the person, not *with* a theory. They have a mediating role: they are midwife, son, or guide rather than primary source of Being, and they emphasize this. Each is dedicated to man's salvation; martyrdom is not sought but is accepted if necessary. The enlightened-agonist moves dramatically among humanity while remaining himself unmoved, autonomous, detached. All persons are treated with equally compassionate objectivity, and there is no special involvement with any. Each of these enlightened-agonists undergoes no sentimental suffering in leaving human beings to their fate when the occasion calls for it. We say that, in the last analysis, each is moved by the Divine, and this is to say that in some sense their impersonality is radical. Yet it is also to say that their acceptance of the other person as a person rather than as an object is profound.

God, said Eckhart, "is love." [1] Yet Eckhart said with even more emphasis that God is "immovably disinterested." [2] Lao-tse tells us that the divinely enlightened-agonist

is all the time in the most perfect way helping men. . . . [3]

He rears them, but does not lay claim to them, controls them but does not lean upon them. . . . [4, 5]

The Sage is . . . ruthless; To him the people are but as straw dogs. [6] [The latter, in ancient Chinese custom, being treated with duly reverent ceremony on ritual occasions, but cast into the fire after the ceremony is over.]

Although cast in less mythic proportions, a relationship reminiscent of this is found described in the literature of psychoanalysis. We turn to descriptions of the ideal psychoanalyst.

A sample canvass of the relevant comments at first seems to reveal a wide range in the descriptions of the ideal attitude of the psychoanalyst.

. . . he [the analyst] remains neutral, aloof, a spectator and is never a co-actor. [7]

Moving gradually toward the "warmer" pole, we find a series of phrases in the literature such as "benevolent neutrality," [8] "benevolent curiosity," [9] "compassionate neutrality," [10] and "benevolent friendliness." [11] We read of "identi-fication" [12] but of a "detached" kind. Gitelson says:

The qualified analyst brings to each patient situation . . . attitudes comprising intellectual curiosity, capacity for empathy, and the wish to be helpful.[13]

Berman summarizes the "typical" paradox in the literature.

The answer could simply be that the analyst is always both the cool detached surgeon-like operator on the patient's psychic tissues, and the warm, human, friendly, helpful physician. I think that such an answer is essentially correct.[14]

That these are not necessarily incompatible descriptions but are varying emphases on a stance which fuses them all is evident in Greenson's excellent summary.

Freud described the analyst's behavior as resembling that of a mirror. By that he meant that the analyst should not distort. . . . The analyst should be able to be human without overreacting. . . . The analyst works in the more intimate personal way with his patient, yet he must always preserve a certain distance. . . . This distance must be a respectful rather than a disdainful one. His closeness must resemble the closeness of the physician who examines the sick body of his patient. He must be able to be intimate and personal without being "familiar" . . . preserving his anonymity and yet remaining an understanding human being.[15]

What is the nature and meaning of this neutral dedication, this nonfamiliar intimacy? It clearly contains a kind of understanding, of concrete, intimate grasp of the human condition of the person before one. It also contains an affective-conative dimension, an acceptance or openness, and, indeed, deep commitment. And it involves a characteristic and perhaps even more obscure aspect of "nonentanglement" in the affairs of the other. The similarities to the stance of the enlightened-agonist are apparent.

In the case of the esthetic experience, the same paradoxical complex of traits—understanding, openness, dedication, objectivity, and detachment—are also notable. The work of art is at once a unique and profound object of our comprehension and dedication; we must be open to it in the living act of intercourse with it. Yet, at the same time, there is about the experience an "isolation," a "detached," "objective" quality, a "psychic distance" which is vital to the experience. The intimate consciousness of the object as unique, the respect for it and its integrity, the sense of its having an independent, autonomous life—all this is as central to the ideal generic relationship of person to art object as it is to that of enlightened-agonist to his flock and therapist to patient.

This threefold juxtaposition—the enlightened-agonist's understanding, the psychoanalytic therapeutic attitude, and the esthetic transaction—define more precisely the subject matter of inquiry in this chapter. We shall begin with a study of the matter from the standpoint of psychoanalysis and of the psychoanalyst's therapeutic stance.

The first essential, then, is to sketch the ideal form of inner structure of the analyst's understanding response to the patient. In this way we will be able to specify an ideal toward which, ideally, the patient is himself moving.

II

FACED WITH ANOTHER PERSON IN THE THERAPEUTIC SITUATION, the psychoanalyst attempts to grasp what life means to this person. How? Of course he uses his technical, theoretical information and his personal and professional experience. But these are background. He brings all his knowledge and talents to bear in the actual course of therapy by means of "empathy." It is the intuitively empathic perception which is the medium of psychoanalytic therapy, and therapeutic intervention is therefore an art, a procedure requiring "creative inventiveness." [16] This is true however much—as in the case of any sound artist—the way may have been prepared by rigorous objective study of theory and of materials and by many years of training in techniques.

The immediate task, then, is to discuss that specific form of empathy which characterizes the psychoanalyst's relation to his patient. This therapeutic understanding I analyze in terms of two major schemes: (a) identification, introjection and other psychoanalytic variations on "putting oneself in the other's shoes," and (b) the synthetic functions of the ego, which most specifically aim at "that state towards which all the ego's endeavors are bending, a reconciliation of its manifold allegiances." [17] Our task here is to go behind these labels and consider at some length their meaning and their bearing upon therapy, art, and human understanding. We shall have to consider these conceptions in some detail.

How and in which sense does the analyst "identify" with the patient? What *is* identification? Although the term is a central one in psychoanalytic psychology, its meaning, particularly in connection with empathy, presents a problem which, Freud said, "we are far from having exhausted." [18, 19] In most general terms and very roughly, one becomes in some sense like another person when one identifies with that person. Identification may involve modeling one's general behavior on that of another person, or it may consist only in modeling oneself after some selected complex of traits of another person. Or, instead of doing as the other fellow does, it may involve "putting oneself in the other person's shoes" in order imaginatively, vicariously, to enjoy the quality of his life.

The preceding accounts of identification are still impressionistic. In order to introduce more precise and systematic theoretical conceptions necessary to the discussion, we shall have to recall briefly a few postulates of psychoanalytic theory. In psychoanalytic psychology, one distinguishes between the real object and the psychic representation of that object within the psychic system of the perceiver. This distinction is vital. Psychic representations ("ideas") are cathected either as object-representations or as self-representations. These psychic representations are more or less accurately coordinated to the real objects. They are our ideas of these objects.[20]

A discovery which Freud exploited fully was the fact that a psychic representation may remain constant in nature while its function in the psychic economy may vary. For example, an idea functioning as object-representation shifts its function, in introjection, and becomes a self-representation. In projection, a self-representation (or part thereof) begins to function as object-representation. This functional shift is conceptualized in instinctual terms as a shift between object-cathexis and narcissistic cathexis. Another variant of this process is what Freud called displacement.

Jacobson is not alone [21] in having pointed out that there is a widespread tendency to ignore these theoretical points. She stresses that

> the terms introjection and projection refer to *endopsychic* processes. . . .[22] [Italics added]
>
> Strictly speaking, we may apply the term projection whenever something belonging to the self is ascribed to an object; i.e., whenever *endopsychic object images* assume the traits of the self or self-images, respectively. . . . The object images on which the self has been projected thus commonly but need not always be attached to real external objects.[23] [Italics added]

Identification proper is a state of psychic organization resulting from a series of rather complex introjective-projective processes.[24] It may be thought of as a rather enduring and central psychic reorganization resulting from such processes,[25] the culminating phases being dominated by intro-jection.

The variations possible in this threefold relation—self-representation, object representation, and real object—are numerous and require discussion. How do we get our ideas of others and of our self? What sorts of distortions enter?

The content of an object-representation may have its origins in realistic perception of the object. On the other hand, this content, although functioning as object-representation, may be—and probably always is to some degree—constructed out of the prior experience and fantasies of the subject. To this extent there is projection or displacement: qualities belonging respectively to the self or to other object-representations are, without realistic grounds, fused with the new object-representation. Another variable involves the completeness or incompleteness with which the real object is reflected in the mental object-representation. Highly specific aspects of a real object may be selected for representation and the rest ignored: a specific character pattern, a single trait, a value held, a skill—indeed, any part or aspect of the object or of its functioning may be singled out for representation and will then, mentally, "stand for" the object. In the extreme cases where the object-representation is so inadequately representative, or so loosely coordinated to the doings of the object, or so replete with projected and displaced fantasy as to make the correspondence between the two grossly inadequate, we have psychosis. The common resort to stereotyped perception of others in standard situations—butcher, maid, policeman, doctor—is an adaptive version of this highly selective object-representation.

Let us consider in a schematic way some illustrations of the processes in question. I will sometimes use "image" as the equivalent of "representation." A man may coordinate key elements of his mother-image (an endopsychic object-representation) to a real, "external" object, for example, a woman of about his own age. This displacement then may be a basis for a romantic attachment, the cathexes of the mother-image now being discharged on the *new* real *object* (but via the *same* object-*representation*). The wife, as we say, represents the mother; though we would express it more exactly if we said that the wife is represented, in the husband's mind, by an image which is to a significant extent that of the mother. Early, painfully frustrated, aggressive feelings toward his mother may have been ejected from his childhood self-images and included in the object-representation of his mother (projection). Thus the image of his wife is a displaced mother-image which, in turn, is constituted in part of projections of infantile self-images. With marriage, he may, by systematic attempts to coordinate his object-representations of his wife with his wife's actual behavior, gradually adjust the content of the endopsychic image which represents his wife. This will depend on the broadness and firmness of the general base of realistic perception and freedom from inner conflict that he has achieved.

Let us suppose, however, that the husband is unable substantially to correct his perception (and, concurrently, his attitudes and behavior). There is marital misunderstanding, friction, and the marriage breaks up. But he is still unable to give up the cathexis of the mother-image. He retains it by coordinating it to a new real object, a new wife, again perceived in terms of the same mother-image. Instead of displacing the mother-image onto a new wife, he may incorporate the image into his own self-image (introjection). This process may in some cases be integrated and rationalized so that, without undue sex-role conflict, the key features of the mother-image are now integrated with his own self-image. If this is accomplished, an identification has been accomplished. If he cannot either find a new real object, incorporate the mother-image successfully, or give up the cathexis of it, then it may be perceived as operative but uncoordinated either to self or any other real object: it may function as a "disembodied" hallucinatory figure.

This example, highly oversimplified as it is, is offered as illustrative of the main lines of the theoretical account just preceding it. We shall be more specific when necessary in the following. But before we go further, a brief parenthetical comment is necessary in order to avoid raising unnecessary questions.

We have used here the notion of the "correspondence" of a mental representation—an "idea" in more or less Lockian terms—to an "external" object. This is implicitly based in a theory of knowledge which is deeply rooted in Western thinking, the so-called correspondence theory of knowledge, mental ideas being supposed somehow to "correspond" to "external" objects. The virtues and inadequacies of this notion have been examined intensively for several centuries. In using these notions here, however, I do not think we need make a commitment to any specific theory of knowledge. The notion of an "idea" which "corresponds" to an "external" object is in certain contexts a usable notion, and the present context is such a one. The history of philosophy and science gives clear warning, however, that our approximations to the truth in this Cartesian-Lockian form will in other contexts inevitably be subjected to more refined epistemological analyses of familiar kinds. Indeed, I have tried to set out on that road in the first chapter of this book. Nevertheless, it is fundamental to the approach in Part II of this book that we must work out of the psychoanalytic material as base, that we go where its genius forces us and not where we would lead it because of extra-analytic considerations.

With the preceding parenthetical proviso, we can return to the elaboration of the psychoanalytic notions. Let us turn, specifically, to the second group of concepts mentioned earlier: the synthetic and related functions of the ego. We shall then be in a position to pinpoint the notion of empathy and its relation to the "disinterested compassion" which is at the core of our inquiry.

A younger sister gives up her pretension to being popular and beautiful; she devotes herself happily to promoting her attractive, older sister's popularity. Here there is a kind of identification. Yet clearly she does not model herself in her behavior after the older sister, nor does she consciously think of herself as being like her sister. Indeed, in many ways she is just what her sister is not. Nevertheless, what she *"feels,"* at times, is presumably very much like what her sister feels. She experiences triumph when her sister triumphs, thrills of romance when her sister is courted, dejection and bitterness when her sister has been spurned. She does not duplicate the motor aspects of her sister's life, nor does she decisively initiate, though she may influence, her sister's actions. Her sister's interpretation and evaluation of events are decisive, never hers. There is duplication in only one area, the area of consummatory experiencing, of enjoying and suffering the felt quality of the experience which ensues from the career of the sister. This consummatory aspect of her sister's experience is actually experienced by her, and it has become part of her. Here, then, we have the incorporation of a *part* of an object-representation into the self-representation. The shift from object-cathexis to narcissistic cathexis includes only that part of the content of the sister-image which represents consummatory experience. Or, to put the same point in another framework: she lives the unconscious fantasy of being the older sister, but only insofar as the latter's consummatory experience goes. Her actual behavior and interpretation of the situation are not distorted by this fantasy, and, indeed, the fantasy itself takes its direction (synthesis and execution) from the older sister's actual actions. Such a partial ("passive") identification may be the price of fear of open competition with her sister. In its way, it is a remarkably adaptive compromise. But it is no surprise that such a specialized and symbiotic integration is likely to lead to tensions and conflicts of its own peculiar kind. Short of psychosis, the younger sister's own tendencies toward autonomy are bound to produce conflict. This, then, is a not uncommon kind of neurotic identification based on introjection of the experience-aspect of the object-representation.

A young man works very hard in the same kind of business as his father. Unfortunately, the son finds that he cannot take pleasure in the work as his father did; in fact, whenever there has been the possibility of any successful culmination of his hard work, the situation has turned out disastrously. From the standpoint of the processes we are here concerned with, the son has identified with his father but only so far as *deciding* and *doing* goes. To *experience* (bring to consummation) the fruit of his labors is too anxiety-evoking. The experiencing aspects of the father-image remain object-cathected. Self-cathexis here immediately evokes guilt and fear. Only the synthetic and executive aspects of the father-image can be introjected without guilt and fear. We need not consider the specific reasons why such a response to Oedipal conflict was adopted. We are only interested here in the fact that it can and does happen.

The examples offered so far have represented pathological adaptions. But identification processes are not always pathological. As we know, the normal infant personality is built up in large part through identifications. In this discussion, however, we are concerned primarily with identification processes in adults, and we shall restrict ourselves accordingly.

A mother sees her child take his first steps. After the first surprise, she smiles and encourages him. Obviously she is enjoying the baby's walking and the baby's pleasure. She is "just as excited as he is!" How is this possible? The mother has identified herself with the infant in the following specific sense: she cathects narcissistically only the infant's experiencing ego. In this way she perceives him as a creature of independent *will* and independent *action;* yet his *feelings* are echoed in her. Thus she shares intimately his pleasures and sadnesses, but she does not "dominate" him. Such a way of handling the new independence of the child is a mature and realistic solution: it provides a profound basis for a unity of interest and affection, and at the same time it allows the child freedom to exert its own initiative and live its own life. The mother, after all, has no realistic need to imitate the child's behavior, but she extends her life in a profound way by sharing its joys. On the other hand, the child does indeed have to learn to behave as the adult does, and therefore the child normally incorporates synthetic, executive, *and* experiencing aspects of the object-representation into his self-image. Let us contrast this with a pathological variation.

Another mother [26] is unable to give up a part of her self-image and re-establish it as an object-representation. Her infant, psychologically a part of her, remains merely an extension of her will and her action as well as her feelings. She has a fine relationship with the infant until he starts to walk and becomes more independent. Then she is irritated and leaves him in part-time care. "Oh, he'll like spinach; I like it," she had once said to an interviewer. The inescapable signs of his autonomy are anxiety-evoking.

The specific psychotherapeutic form of identification toward which the previous discussion and illustrations have been pointed is empathy. With this brief exploration of the intrapsychic character of introjective and identification processes, we are now prepared to turn directly to empathy. Olden has characterized empathy in rather general terms:

> the capacity of the subject instinctively and intuitively to feel as the object does; and the empathic process

[is] an oscillation between feeling as the object does on the one hand and intellectually observing, judging, and understanding it on the other.[27]

Fliess speaks of empathy as a

"transient trial identification" with the patient as the subject of particular strivings, emotions, conflicts, reaction formations. . . .[28]

Such characterizations of empathy are helpful but imprecise.

Of the three central questions in connection with empathy which we must discuss, only the first has received any extensive discussion. (1) *How* are introjection and projection involved in empathy? (2) *What* is it that is introjected and projected? (3) What role does this process play in the psychological economy of the empathizer?

In connection with (1) most writers have stressed introjection but have not described the precise process. Knight is an informative exception. He holds that the therapist

projects his own unconscious responses on to the patient in response to the special stimulation of the patient's material. . . .[29] [Italics added]

Knight is getting at an important point, but he, too, fails to make clear what are for us vital issues which must be distinguished.

The empathic process is not primarily projection, and in any case it is a threefold process, not a unitary one. We can best see this by contrasting projection and empathy in loose terms. Projection consists, in its results, of seeing the other person as having properties belonging to you. Empathic "putting oneself into the other person's shoes" consists, in its results, of imagining oneself as having the properties of and being in the environment of the other. How is this latter result brought about?

The comprehensive object-representation (i.e., the image of the other person-in-his-situation) shifts temporarily to functioning as if it were an element of the self, as self-representation. I perceive John as a part of my self rather than as an alien object. I extend the psychic boundaries of my self. Thus this first phase of the process is one of introjection.

Having introjected the John-image, I now respond *as subject* to the circumstances as they impinge upon my self (i.e., upon the John-image as an element now included in my self-representation). This arouses affects, desires, intentions—in short, the whole inner life *as experienced by me as the subject* rather than as inferred with respect to an object. This second phase of the procedure establishes an amplified John-image, an image including an "inner life" as well as the more "externally" perceivable qualities.

After this second phase of inner experiencing, of thoughtful fantasy, I complete the three-stage empathic process by re-projecting the John-image: that is, the image of John-in-his-situation now once again shifts to functioning psychically as object-representation. Thus I may now properly speak of perceiving empathically John's feelings rather than of merely *inferring* how he feels or, in the mid-stage of the process, of perceiving "my own" feelings. These three theoretical stages correspond to distinctly different, phenomenologically identifiable modes of perception.

When Knight stresses projection in connection with empathy, it seems clear to me that he is concerned with the fact that, in the second stage of the process, the John-image is amplified with emotions and feelings coming *from "me,"* and he is also referring to the fact that this amplified image is then re-projected and coordinated with the real object, John. What Knight slurs over is for us crucial: that there is a first phase of introjecting the image, that this leads to living the experience of the other as subject, and that one lives it, nevertheless, under the conditions which hold for the *other* person, not oneself. Thus, in an important sense, the feelings ascribed to John, though they come *from me* are not *mine;* they are the feelings I have when experiencing the world through John's eyes. This is a realistic, novel, even creative extension of one's own subjective experience; it is not perceiving other persons as copies of oneself in any directly projective way. I believe Knight's formulation points toward this view but fails to provide the systematic basis for asserting it.

Let us compare this empathic process with the normal process of building up an object-representation of John in the first place. This image is built up in part out of the materials of sense perception and in part of empathic perception. Thus, at any stage of getting to "know" John, I grasp those sense-qualities and those previously empathized inner qualities (if any) which are available to current perception. I introject this current object-representation: the qualities are now perceived as "mine." I then see how I respond as the subject of the experience of a person having such qualities as I have been able to perceive. Note again that this is not free fantasy. It is controlled by the qualities already perceived to belong to the other person, that is, by the content of the former object-representation in whatever stage of elaboration it already existed. Then I re-project the new, amplified image and it again functions as object-representation. The next time I perceive the person and am in doubt as to his inner state, I repeat the process, thus adding a new increment of content. The more realistic an object-representation, the more it is built up out of a continuing series of these object perceptions, introjections, thoughtful fantasies, and re-projections.

Neurotic and psychotic perceptions omit and rigidify some phase of the process and engage in projection and introjection in the pathological defensive forms in which these two "mechanisms" were first discovered. To project, without having first introjected and fantasied on the basis of controlled attention to the introjected content, is pathological. This is ascribing one's own inner life to the other person instead of discovering a new form of inner life by "seeing the world through the other's eyes." To introject without reprojecting may also be pathological; it is, however, appropriate in mourning and in certain phases of the healthy maturation process, especially the early years when identification is vital to the building of a personality.

These distinctions made with regard to our first question, the "how" of projection and introjection in empathy, are vital for our main inquiry. For they reveal that the crucial stage of empathy involves our being the other person in both a psychological and an existential sense (as subject, not as object). The psychological distinctions thus point toward profound spiritual ones.

When we turn to the second question (2), the question as to *what* is introjected, we find that Knight, though more precise and explicit than Olden or Fliess, still fails to crystallize the theoretical relationships involved. Knight states explicitly that, although in empathy one lives the other's experience and has feelings appropriate to the situation, one's ideals and behavior are not affected at the time.[30] Loosely speaking, we "feel as" the other person does, but we neither act as he does nor do we confuse ourselves with him. How can this point be made in theoretical terminology? We have already covered this ground, in substance, and it is only necessary to state the point briefly.

We have followed Hartmann's injunction [31] to pay more attention to functional segments within the ego. Specifically, the point is that it is not the synthetic or executive functions of the ego which are introjected by the therapist. This split between judging and experiencing in the therapist's object-representation of the patient corresponds to a split in the ego of the real object, the patient, during therapy. As Fenichel says in connection with the psychic state of the patient who is offered an interpretation:

> . . . particularly necessary, preceding the interpretation, is "isolation" from the critical ego. This isolation corresponds to a cleavage of the ego into an experiencing and a judging portion. . . .[32]

In empathy one sees and experiences as the other does. In everyday life, we probably also introject the synthetic functions, but not the executive functions. That is, we may "go along" with the person in his judgment, but we do not copy his actions. However, it is crucial for therapy that the therapist does not introject the synthetic functions. He wants to be the subject of the patient's experience, to "live" his experience, but he does not want to duplicate within himself the basic judgments and interpretations which the patient forms about that experience. At this point the new and transformative element enters the therapeutic picture. And this brings us to the third question (3), the role of the introjected material in the psychic economy of the therapist.

The psychoanalyst brings to bear *his own* synthetic powers and the "emotionally 'open' system of communication between the various aspects of his character and personality."[33] The psychoanalyst thus achieves deeper insight about the meaning of the experience than does the patient himself. This insight is *dynamic insight*, not description, technical diagnosis, or intellectual comprehension of someone else's inner dynamics. The therapist introjects the experience of a person struggling to achieve integration, *integrity*. He responds not to individual elements of the contents of that experience but to the total pattern of tensions set up by their coexistence in one person, and he responds to the potentialities for achieving an inner equilibrium and autonomy. In empathy he responds to these as the subject of them, not as objects.

In this respect, Olden's comment about the "intellectual process of observing, judging, and understanding" in contrast to "feeling as the object does" is decisively mistaken. It is not a contrast between intellect and feeling but a contrast between the ego's experiencing and synthetic functions. Each of the latter includes *both* affective and intellective aspects.

If this living through of the patient's experience is to be reliable, the analyst's introjection of the experience of the patient must be accurate. Caution is essential. The sense that one is "in tune" with the patient *may* be a mark of empathy.

> But one must be cautious as to what is the subjective reality represented by such "liking" and "resonance." Narcissistic identification and narcissistic infatuation may also produce "resonance" feelings.[34]

The main basis for optimism is the supposition that the analyst, because of his personal analysis, has consciously experienced and synthesized in an individual yet realistic manner the tensions arising out of his own secret, unconscious lives. The patient has conflicts involving much the same elements as the analyst's but somewhat differently patterned. But the patient has blind spots; his neurosis is, among other things, the evidence of the partial failure of the synthetic powers of his ego.

Thus the psychoanalyst uses the Confucian sage's chief art; he "knows others by their analogy to himself."[35] Of course, as we have noted, the psychoanalyst's activities in the public world, and his formal and clinical studies, have an important place in establishing his powers. These studies provide the tradition, intellectual discipline, wide technical knowledge and clinical experience which justify his claim to be a professional in therapy. But, in a peculiarly profound way, it is his personal psychoanalysis which enables him to approximate in greater or lesser degree the Taoist sage:

> Without leaving his door
> He knows everything under heaven.
> Without looking out of his window
> He knows all the ways of heaven.[36]

We have not yet completely answered our third question about the way the introjected material functions in the therapist's psychic economy. We know that even though he experiences what the patient does, the therapist does so with a difference, and he does not—normally—confuse his own experience with the patient's. His introjections of the patient's experiencing ego must be of a very special kind. Fliess calls them "transient." But this is not enough. They are indeed temporary, but this description needs to be fitted into systematic theory if it is not to remain an *ad hoc* conception at the heart of our analysis of empathy.

What we are noticing when we speak of the temporary quality of empathy is connected with the fact that it fits precisely into the category of mental operation which Freud called thinking. Here Freud refers not to logic or conceptual juggling, but to thought as reflection, as deliberation. In this process, we have, according to Freud,

> essentially an experimental kind of acting, accompanied by displacement of relatively small quantities of cathexis together with less expenditure (discharge) of them. For this purpose the conversion of freely displaceable cathexes into "bound" cathexes was necessary, and this was brought about by the whole cathectic process.[37]

The binding of cathexes and the raising of the level of the cathectic process is, of course, the maintaining of the entire process as what he called secondary-process rather than primary-process.

Thus it would not be correct—or at least it would not be clear—to refer to the analyst's empathy as a vicarious experience. The latter phrase often is used to refer to a level of cathexis and discharge which is intense and "real," one which involves full cathexes and substantial instinctual gratification. The mother who delights in her child's walking, the adolescent absorbed in a romantic novel—these are having vicarious experiences. If one wishes to speak so, these may be called "empathic"; usage here is loose. Empathic experience in therapy, however, involves small, secondary-process, "experimental" cathexes.

It is partly in terms of this secondary-process, experimental aspect of the therapist's empathy that we account for the phenomenological quality of detachment, disinterest, uninvolvement. For, although the patient's experience is lived through by the therapist, this is done with bound energies, small in quantity and as a relatively autonomous process.

It is now possible to state in summary the psychological conditions characteristic of the ideal understanding of the psychoanalytic therapist. Psychotherapeutic understanding (empathy) (1) begins with a highly special introjection, i.e., with cathectic and structural shifts such that the experiencing aspect (but not the executive and synthetizing aspects) of his object-representation of the patient becomes self-representation; (2) the introjection is controlled and transient, involving only experimental cathexes in the service of the analyst's ego; (3) its immediate and characteristic aim (and its second stage) is to subject the experience to the analyst's own synthetizing powers in order that he may, as subject, grapple with it as a task of active, dynamic integration rather than one of theoretical description and analysis; (4) this amplified image is then re-projected, once again becoming an object-representation. This object-representation then becomes the basis for tentative interpretations and for cues to ways of further observing the patient. It properly serves as a plan of action rather than a definitive perception.

The usual problems mentioned under the heading of countertransference are now easily and systematically formulated. It is easy to see that there are a variety of ways in which this delicately balanced operation, psychotherapeutic empathy, may get out of kilter. The perception of the patient's behavior, speech, and manner may be distorted by the therapist, either through ignorance about background features of the patient's life and culture, or through projection or displacement by the analyst due to pathological defense on his part. With an inaccurate object-representation, he will of course introject erroneous material as the basis of his attempts at empathic understanding. When elements of the patient's experience and behavior are similar to elements of inadequately resolved conflicts in the analyst, the introjection may escape secondary-process control.

> The absorption of the patient's problems into the self, which is necessary to a degree, may lead to a fusion of those problems with the same unmastered ones in the analyst.[38]

This fusion of "experimental" cathexes with similar unbound cathexes dissolves the ego boundaries essential to therapeutic detachment; it evokes full-fledged defensive and impulsive maneuvers by the therapist.

While countertransference has been defined in a large variety of ways,[39] it seems to me that a distinction along the lines which Fliess makes[40] is particularly relevant. Where the conflict aroused in the therapist is such that the patient as a real object is coordinated with the analyst's conflict-involved *object*-representation, then countertransference exists. This is because the analyst has fused an object-representation of some significant figure in his past life with his object-representation of the patient. This is, like all transference, a displacement. Where, however, the process proceeds via introjection rather than displacement, where the representations of infantile elements in the patient are fused with infantile elements in the therapist's own self-image, then we may speak of counteridentification.

Countertransference is a failure to empathize. Counteridentification, on the other hand, is a pathological and arrested form of the empathic process. In the former case, the therapist does not really perceive the patient's problem, though he may think he does. In the latter case, the therapist does actually perceive some aspects of the problems but is prevented from seeing the whole because these very problems fuse with and mobilize his own similar problems.

Counteridentification thus involves a realistic perception of the patient (to a special degree). That is to say, the patient, by virtue of his real qualities, is a provocation to the therapist's unresolved conflict. Hence the patient must either be given up or the therapist's inner conflict resolved. Countertransference, however, involves only a specific displacement. If the displacement onto this specific patient can be corrected, the countertransference is removed without necessarily resolving the therapist's neurotic conflict as a whole. This supports Fliess's contention that counteridentification is, other things being equal, the more serious problem of the two.

The discussion of countertransference and counteridentification leads us to consider the personal development of the psychoanalyst. When formulated in simple and ideal terms, it is clear that the psychoanalyst's personal analysis follows a path such as we have been outlining in the course of this book. It parallels the enlightened-agonist's illumination which consists in the discovery and acknowledgment of his many secret, past selves, the consequent liberation from the wheel of karmic illusion and striving, and the ability and courage to accept others, to be open and to understand objectively while remaining "unattached," unclinging.

We must no more smile at the extent to which the real-life psychoanalyst falls from this high ideal than we smile at the all-too-human beings who have struggled, in other spiritual traditions, along the path of inner knowledge and spiritual freedom. The perfect psychoanalyst is as much a mythic image as is the Buddha or Confucius or the Christ. What appears disappointingly human and fragile, when measured by the infantile wish for a perfect parent, shines forth an achievement to the humbled will and the mind which apprehends the darkness even of our light. Indeed, the very failings of the psychoanalyst become the medium by which his own self-integrity is advanced. For he does not merely perform a service or experience empathically another person's way of life.

A counter-transference reaction, if the analyst is "open" enough to analyse it, can be an integrative experience along the road of interminable analysis. For such reactions seem to be defences against what the analyst discovers of himself in and through the patient. If this is a part of the analyst's deepest realization, both he and his patient are protected. . . . The real emotional acceptance of the patient by the analyst consists in his acceptance of his own unconscious community with the patient.[41]

. . . the conscious feeling of understanding which follows the therapist's contact with the patient stems from the therapist's unconscious perception of a similarity of personal problems.[42]

The analyst's personal analysis, like anyone else's is "interminable."

We are now in a position to elaborate the implications of our theoretical discussion as it bears upon the general topic of human and esthetic understanding.

III

THE ANALYST ACHIEVES A PARADOXICAL FEAT. HE LIVES
through the very same life as the patient and at the very
same time as the patient. As Ella Sharpe has said,

> Perhaps what makes me most glad that I chose to be a
> psycho-analyst, is the rich variety of every type of hu-
> man experience that has become part of me, which
> never would have been mine either to experience or
> understand in a single mortal life, but for my work.[43]

In thus establishing within himself a living reflection of
the patient's experience, the psychoanalyst is "passive," like
a "mirror."

> The Sage [says Lao-tse] has no unvarying self;
> So he makes the people's self his self.[44]

He has achieved a new innocence, like that of the mythic
child-image.

> Except ye be converted, and become as little children,
> ye shall not enter into the kingdom of heaven.
> Whosoever therefore shall humble himself as this little
> child, the same is greatest in the kingdom of heaven.[45]

The enlightened-agonist and the psychoanalyst make
themselves, in the sense of Jesus' saying, the "servant of
all" and "last of all." [46] And the paradoxical result is the
same, for they are then "first." They lead.

> . . . the Sage
> Puts himself in the background;
> But is always to the fore.[47]

This is not only because the analyst, like the "child," is more
open, but also because he brings to bear a broader and
deeper understanding, greater skill in perceiving the immi-

nent possibilities of synthesis and their consequences. The psychoanalyst is, psychologically, a powerful "auxiliary" ego (and superego) of the patient's. This is to say that he is a wiser, more objective, more liberated, and a voluntary sharer of the spiritual burden of the patient. Like the bodhisattvas and enlightened ones of many cultures, he has not only gone through the ordeal himself, but he returns and voluntarily goes through it again, though in many different forms. And, although his sharing is genuine, yet it is not identical with that of the patient's, for the latter is still in bondage, while the enlightened-agonist is free.

Being free, the enlightened-agonist can accept the other. That is, he dares to take the other's experience as his own. Acceptance is not a matter of "approval" or "pity." The analyst seeks, just as does the patient, to find meaning in terms of this present and actual experience, as it comes, without challenge or rejection. This is acceptance: the simple readiness to share the experience and problem with the other, to work out its meaning with him. Acceptance heals for many reasons; man is a social being and any form of sharing reduces the burden. But in the case of the enlightened-agonist, there is not only sharing but also greater understanding and control than in the one helped.

The term "passion" originally referred to *pass*ive suffering rather than acting-upon. Thus we may say the patient has passions; the therapist is com-passionate. The therapist prehends, and thus enables the patient to com-prehend. Daya, compassion, is one of the three ancient and cardinal Hindu virtues enunciated in the Brihadaranyaka Upanishad. Radhakrishnan says,

> *Daya* or compassion . . . is love in action, fellowship in suffering. It is feeling as one's own the circumstances and aspirations to self-perfection which we find in others.[48]

This accepting, compassionate aspect of the relationship has its opposite face: detachment, uninvolvement. At the same time that he introjects the patient's experience, the psychoanalyst maintains and can evoke at will his own autonomy, his own perception of and response to the realities.

But the psychoanalyst's detachment is much more than this. The therapist systematically interprets transference. In doing this, he is working to disentangle, to detach himself from the attempts of the patient to "use" him as a figure in a private fantasy life. This "disentangling" appears at times as cold, objective, even ruthless. But it is not merely the defense of the therapist's integrity, his refusal to be "used"— although it is that, and hence expresses his respect for his own personality. Ideally, however, the therapist is secure in this respect and his refusal to be used is not a mere rejection. It is the kind of "rejection" of the patient's gesture which both illuminates the gesture and shows acceptance of the person. It is, that is to say, an insightful interpretation. This means that the therapist does not confront gesture with countergesture, blow with blow, riposte with defense. Instead he confronts the patient's gesture with a description of—and a demonstration of concern for—the pattern of struggle for personal integrity out of which the patient's gesture arose.

If the therapist were to respond directly to the angry remark, the fearful tone, or the seductive compliment, he would in effect be taking the gesture as having meaning for him in his personal life. But this is contrary to the realities, for these gestures are addressed to fantasy-persons; they are quite "inappropriate" as directed to a physician. Furthermore, the patient does not even personally know the analyst in his status as a private person. (Exceptions to this latter point are peripheral to the main issues here involved.) Although a direct response to the gesture is what we tend to call "taking the gesture personally," it is at the same time a denial of the real person opposite him. It betrays the patient and it puts the analyst "first" at the very point where he should "serve" and be "last." In addition, it focuses on that which is social, stereotyped, and duplicable—the gesture—instead of focusing on what is unique, the person who, in his struggle for individual integrity, makes the gesture. A response to the gesture, as such, is thus not personal but strictly impersonal from the standpoint of the patient. Furthermore, a response to the gesture per se is a serious technical mistake, for it is to accept as legitimate the patient's stereotyped, neurotic, "solution" of his inner conflicts. It fails to turn him toward an examination of the conflict which needs a new solution.

Not to respond directly to the gesture is often described as being "impersonal." Yet it in truth can be profoundly personal. Accompanied by proper interpretive hints, it not only turns the patient's gaze to the pattern of conflict, it illuminates it. And it is this *pattern* of conflict and potential integrity which lies at the heart of person-ality. The isolated and easily duplicable gestures are nonpersonal. There are, of course, times when a gesture is genuinely directed toward the therapist as a real person. There is no transference here and therapy becomes in this respect inappropriate. When such gestures predominate, the therapeutic relationship is at an end.

It is true that we deny another person's status as a responsible agent when we respond to his motives and not to his gesture to us. The response *ad hominem* can be frustrating and subversive. It can say, "I do not accept you as agent, though I understand you as object. You say such and such to me, but I refuse to take your statement at face value, for I know your motives." This is "handling" a person rather than genuinely responding to him as a person. It is the subversive way of the manipulator of men, however innocuous or goodwilled he may claim to be.

But this is not what the psychoanalyst does. In his case, it is true, there is no response to the face value of the gesture, but this is because it is not really directed toward him; he merely represents an inner fantasy figure of the patient's. If he were to respond, this would be countertransference, "an accidental casting of the analyst in an intrusive part in the psychoanalyst's drama."[49] Thus he does not reject the patient as autonomous agent; he "ruthlessly" (systematically and unsentimentally) but tactfully exposes to the patient that the latter has not acted autonomously, is already self-subverted. However, as has already been noted, it happens at times that gestures are made toward the therapist as a real person. When this is so, to ignore the face value of the gesture and to analyze the motives is a subversive intrusion on the patient's autonomy. Such mistakes occur,[50] though patients tend often to overemphasize this possibility for purposes of neurotic rationalization. But when such mistakes really do happen, they are mistakes, not therapy.

As a concomitant of the therapist's attitude, the patient is led toward giving up his use of others as puppets in his own fantasy lives; he is forced to respect the autonomy and reality of the Other. And at the same time, and as a result, the patient comes to see himself as separate, autonomous, capable of shaping and forming himself and his existence.

Thus the detachment here involved is not a rejection of personal relationships. It is a detachment from the psychic clichés which keep us in alienation. This detachment is the essential ground out of which relationships among genuinely autonomous individuals can arise. Indeed, it is not only the ground out of which genuine personal *relationships* arise; it is the ground out of which the *person himself* emerges. Buber says:

To be aware of a man, therefore . . . means to perceive the dynamic center which stamps his every utterance, action and attitude with the recognizable stamp of uniqueness. Such an awareness is impossible, however, if and so long as the other is the separated object of my contemplations or even observation.[51]

. . . in order that he may coherently further the liberation and actualization of that unity in a new accord of the person with the world, the psychotherapist, like the educator, must stand again and again not merely at his own pole in the bipolar relation, but also with the strength of *present realization* at the other pole, and *experience* the effect of his own action. But again, the specific "healing" relation would come to an end the moment the patient thought of, and succeeded in, practicing "inclusion" and experiencing the event from the doctor's pole as well. Healing, like educating, is only possible to the one who lives over against the other, and yet is detached.[52] [Italics added]

For reasons such as those just discussed, the therapist, like the sages, responds differently to similar gestures; he often says one thing to one man, another thing to another. Or he may even appear to contradict himself with the same person. For he does not, as therapist, offer general theories intended to be true independent of persons and context. On the contrary, he speaks to the "human condition" of this person in his uniqueness, in the here and now. The therapist's words may have general meaning but his *point* in using them is to clarify the individual constellation of dramatic forces *operative* now in the patient and (empathically) in the therapist. It is only for the transmission of technique and theory to other professionals that the patient becomes a specimen of schematized defenses, impulses, ideas, and affects. We shall return to deal more fully with this point in the following chapter.

There is still another important aspect to the therapist's and the enlightened-agonist's detachment, their objectivity and "ruthlessness." The psychoanalyst's primary interest is not in passively experiencing what the patient does; he is interested primarily in "solving a problem." He encounters painful disunity and meaninglessness, and is concerned with the task of finding meaning and unity. Thus he is objective, moved by a kind of "objective curiosity." As we have seen, he does not respond to the patient's hate, love, disgust, shame, guilt in themselves and as isolated responses. Nor is he merely enjoying "voyeuristic" gratification, though sublimated voyeuristic impulses may be involved. He responds to specific maneuvers of the patient's in the context of a total configuration, of the mind's task of achieving a dynamic equilibrium, of a man's attempts to "pull himself together," to achieve salvation. This is a profound concern for the individual's own fate, not a passionate need for gestures from the individual to him. It is *disinterested* love and understanding; that is, it is love and understanding without personal goals getting in the way. One becomes disinterested by putting aside one's personal goals and "surrendering" oneself to the meaning of the Other's fate. Thus disinterested *dedication* is a characteristic of the enlightened-agonist and the psychoanalyst.

These considerations should make clear that the desire to cure on the part of the psychoanalyst, like the would-be altruist's desire to "help" or to "do good," is ineffective,[53] even dangerous.[54] The desire to cure is a specific personal desire of the psychoanalyst's. It is external to the patient and his fundamental concerns. The psychoanalyst's conception of cure is a medical conception. In its proper medical connotation, it cannot be found in the ordinary patient's experience as introjected by the analyst. (The patient who happens to be genuinely acquainted with the medical concept is only an apparent exception. Intellectualizations along medical lines, insofar as they function in neurosis, turn out to be rationalizations of quite other psychic content.) Since the problem of psychic integration is set in terms of the patient's experience as empathically experienced by the analyst, the attempt to introduce or impose a medical conception is a distortion of empathy. It leads, however subtly, to imposing the analyst's personal and institutional goals or fantasies upon the situation. The situation is even worse if the desire to cure is itself a disguise for neurotic aims.

Of course, a genuinely insightful resolution of the patient's conflicts will in fact be classifiable as a medical cure. And, of course, the institutional goal of medical psychoanalysis is cure, and rightly so. But in therapy itself the therapist must be aim-less;[55] he must live through and help integrate the current experience offered by the patient. What the patient offers is fear of social groups, or quarrels with his wife; he does not come with the motive of "strengthening his ego" or of "resolving infantile conflict." External medical formulae, systematically used, have their place before therapy and in critical reflection after a therapeutic session; they can be vital aids toward correcting and deepening empathy and toward developing interpretive strategies. But, in the therapeutic act itself, the organizing factor is the patient's currently presented pattern of conflict, empathically experienced *in the patient's own terms* but with the synthetic powers of the analyst's ego brought to bear.

We can summarize certain aspects of our discussion in terms of a simple schema. If we think of a bipolar range of relationships to a person, then someone who is a casual acquaintance of that person stands at one pole. The acquaintance responds almost entirely to the standardized meaning, the face value of the person's gestures in situations as socially defined. Good friends and intimates fall somewhere in the middle of the range: they respond to the face value of the gesture, but they also are more or less keenly responsive to the "personal meaning" of the gesture. That is, they grasp something of its role as an expression of a total pattern of personal integration. Finally, near the other pole from the casual acquaintance is the psychoanalyst. He responds preponderantly to the psychic integration problem; he responds to the gesture only as an element within the pattern. For all the storm and fury visited upon him, he is, as Greenson suggests, not a friend but a doctor; for all his detachment, he is not an acquaintance but an intimate. I have called him an enlightened-agonist. Socrates would have called him a midwife. He participates in the agony and in the contest of the spirit, helps to bring victory out of defeat, a new birth out of a death. Yet, enlightened, he is somehow above the contest, an unaffected helper.

IV

THE PHENOMENOLOGICAL SIMILARITIES BETWEEN THE THERApeutic and the esthetic transaction are interesting and illuminating. They suggest important psychological processes in common—along with important differentia.

Barbara Low wrote:

> To take the introjected material and bring to bear upon it law, order, and unity, is the method whereby unconscious urges are satisfied: to project it again in new form gratifies sublimated desires. This is the work of the artist and scientist, and so must it be the work of the analyst.[56]

The differentiating psychological characteristics of art and therapy are blurred in Low's statement and hardly hinted at in Ella Sharpe's comment that

> . . . there must be a fundamental pleasure in listening for one who chooses this vocation (psychoanalysis), not essentially different from the pleasure of those who enjoy music, in spite of the fact that the patients' communications are stories of discord.[57]

The coexistence of passionate concern and detached objectivity is nowhere more sharply apparent than in esthetic appreciation. Granted the excitement, fascination, participation, and dedication of the person involved in the esthetic transaction, these are always bounded and controlled in characteristic ways. For the esthetic experience, too, is selfless: the esthetic object controls. As does the therapist, the esthetic spectator surrenders himself to the object and becomes the *medium* within which the object works and realizes itself.

If there is anything which distinguishes the esthetic from the practical, political, moral, or other dimensions of life, it is precisely that it is consummatory rather than instrumental, contemplative rather than active. And yet we know that, just as with the psychotherapist, there is a sense in which the esthetic "spectator's" mind and spirit must be creatively active. It is by a kind of empathy that one surrenders to and then actively participates in the independent life of the work of art.

What can we mean by "independent" in this esthetic context? In art, as in human understanding, it is the esthetic form—dynamic form—which governs. The interest in the elements of a work in isolation from their pattern of integration is no more adequate for esthetic understanding than is sexual curiosity adequate for psychotherapeutic understanding. The direct interest in the elements must be there, but in "sublimated" form.

In art as in human understanding, what counts are the forces inherent in the individual plastic, literary, representational, or symbolic elements as they work in relation to each other. It is the work's unity, its synthesis, which defines its boundaries and shows how the elements function. Without a sense of the coherent pattern, we have no criteria of esthetic relevance, criteria of adequacy of execution.

As in therapy, there is no way of decisively grasping this

esthetic unity of a work of art by means of intellectual or descriptive analysis. Theoretical, critical, and other technical conceptual formulations may be helpful clues to the spectator and useful devices for the artisan, but they never govern. They are used in the service of the esthetic "conception." Much as we may wish we had more helpful terminology to express the point, we cannot deny that, in some sense of the words, it is essential to get at the "inner life" of the art work in order to see its point, its meaning, its *integrity* as a work. Without this "grasp" from within," we perceive at most isolated elements which may be pleasant or unpleasant, isolated propositions which are true or untrue, important or trivial, and we see what we take to be evidences of acts performed skillfully or unskillfully. But none of these go to the heart of the matter.

The inner, independent life of the work is a phenomenal datum. Its existence cannot be legitimately questioned, though the explanation of the phenomenon or the analysis of our language may be obscure. From a psychological standpoint, the vast amount of work done with the Rohrschach inkblots demonstrates as well as anything that the most amorphous of physical entities can be approached in such a way as to perceive it to resonate with all the vital psychic forces of human experience. Beres [58] has elaborated on the specific role of "imagination" in art and in therapy, and what we are concerned with here is closely related to what is often called creative imagination.

True, with the Rohrschach inkblot, we project almost all the content and the dynamic structure. But this reveals two important truths. (1) It shows how natural and immediate is the human susceptibility to respond in dynamic terms when responding to things, *any* things. (2) It emphasizes that the work of art is distinguished precisely by virtue of its objective content and structure and by the fact that it is these objective properties which govern the content and pattern of the dynamic forces experienced.

Wood, paint, words—these, in the perceptual transaction, generate dramatic tensions, the kinds of psychic tensions with which the ego can and does deal. The aim, as in therapy, is to integrate the felt forces by arranging the materials. In art, the materials shaped have an existence autonomous from that of the personal life of the shaper; in therapy, it is the self and the personal life which is shaped. Both art and therapy are experiments in dramatic integration.[59]

The psychoanalytic theory of art, like that of dreams, must be reconstructed in the light of developments since Freud's early formulations. The main relevant shift in emphasis is the shift from concern with the id to concern with the ego. We do not reject the earlier formulations, but we supplement them. In the case of dreams, Freud's early statements were from the perspective of the id: The dream is really a wish-fulfillment fantasy which, being unacceptable to the censor, is "disguised." [60]

Today we recognize that the function Freud referred to as "disguising" is a characteristic function of the ego. The word "disguise" suggests something secondary, less real, less portentous as compared to that which is disguised. Today we recognize the fundamental nature of ego activity, its close relation to what we call character, its work of reorganizing, restructuring the various competing demands upon the self so as to make them mutually compatible. Correct as the early version was, it is now misleading. It needs to be coupled with a formulation in terms of ego psychology. And what is true of the dream is true of art.

Psychoanalytic discussions of art since Freud have commonly centered around the role of unconscious contents in art. They follow the lines of Freud's early and famous formulations [61] in terms of disguised and "sweetened" unconscious fantasies, of sexual symbols and of pre-Oedipal and

Oedipal conflicts common to artist and audience. But such id contents, while fundamental in experience, are ubiquitous; shared fantasies are common. Yet art remains a relatively rare achievement. Once again we must turn, for the distinctive element, to the ego. Once more we must recognize that id contents, defensive mechanisms, cultural contents and traditions, and physical elements—all are important but in themselves are nonpersonal, nonesthetic. It is the style and pattern in which these are integrated which generates the unique: the esthetic object or the human self.

This stress on the dynamic form, the integration of dramatic forces, has been foreshadowed in the arguments of Herbert Read in his memorial lecture on psychoanalysis and esthetics.[62] Read here sees the psychoanalytic view of art in the older terms of id, superego, and the mechanism of identification. Ignoring the relevance of the synthetic function of the ego, he argues that the psychoanalytic view is inadequate because *form* and not identification is basic in art. In order to introduce the notion of form he finds it necessary to introduce concepts of Gestalt psychology, particularly the concept of "closure." His efforts demonstrate neatly that if there were no concept of the synthetic, integrating function of the ego, we would have to invent it.

Read quotes Susanne Langer approvingly when she writes that "the first task of the artist is always to establish the primary illusion, to close the total form and set it apart from reality." [63] This, too, is but another way of pointing to that dynamic equilibrium, what Freud called the ego's "reconciliation of loyalties," which sets the esthetic transaction off as an internally integrated unity, an autonomous and dynamic center of meaning.

It is this integrity, this integration of forces, which is that ineffable entity which we call the "meaning" of a work of art—or of a life. We have heard much of positivistic notions that "the meaning of life" is a phrase without meaning, of the esthetic doctrine that "a poem should not mean, but be." [64] These positions are misleading. The inner integrity of the work or of the person's life is what constitutes, in the relevant sense, *the* meaning. The positivist of the 1930's, because of his preoccupation with verification procedures in science, was concerned with meaning as an external relation between signs and their referents; thus he often failed to see that spiritual meaning or significance has to do with internal relationships of the whole, with relationships which establish integrity, not reference. The artist and critic also dominated by this referential analysis of meaning could only establish the primacy of the autonomy of a work over its referential functions by arguing that one must not ask what a work of art means. The religionist who is dominated by the same referential notion of meaning must suppose that, if life has a meaning, then that meaning must be a reference to some entity external to life. In art and religion this same notion of referential meaning can lead logically to two opposite extremes: the attempt at systematic exclusion of all reference in contemporary art in order to be "pure," and the systematic insistence upon a Being entirely external to man in religion. But the kind of meaning thus eschewed or sought is not the kind which ought to be in question here.

The use of "meaning" in the sense of internal unity is too ancient and honorable to be ruled out of order. Job saw finally that the divine meaning of life is to be found in the numinous and indwelling quality of life lived and accepted in all its mysterious and untamable variety, not in supposed references to superlife Entities, Doings, or Compacts nor with an eye to the earthly rewards and punishments visited upon us from such a superhuman world. Job learned that the meaning of life is not something outside life upon which to lean, not something outside life to which life points.

We spoke earlier of the undesirability of the therapist's being dominated by the desire to cure. This has its exact parallel in the case of the artist: he is frustrated the more he directs his attention to "creating a successful work of art." The reasons are similar in each case. The category "successful work of art" comes from a different context than that of the act of artistic creation; it comes from the institutional domains of art history, or, perhaps, of systematic art criticism. Of course what the successful artist creates is, by definition, a successful work of art. But in order to create, he must not be immersed in the analysis of abstract categories of this kind; he must be struggling with the particular and peculiar problems posed by this piece of wood, its texture, grain, shape, color, and how these generate forces which point to and act upon particular moods, impulses, objects, events, and meanings. When the idea "this is a work of art" dominates the would-be creative act, it is like the idea "this is love" dominating the would-be loving gesture: In both cases the gesture is adulterated and deflected, rendered impotent, and the outcome is sentimentalized. At most, such self-consciousness may be used as an ironic or satirical device. These are only apparent exceptions which we cannot discuss here.

Creativity grows out of a loving, discriminating, and respectful cooperation with things and persons, with their qualities and powers, and with their potentialities for cooperating while yet retaining their individuality. Sentimentality and portentousness arise out of the *using* of things and persons in the service of a fixed idea of one's own, whether it be "to cure," "to create," "to love," or "to save."

For the artist and the enlightened-agonist

Things operate; they are not rejected by him.
They come to birth; they are not possessed by him.
They become effective; they are not used or leaned on by him.[65]

Gitelson says that for the psychoanalyst

empathic compassion . . . is distinguishable from sympathetic identification, and helpfulness . . . is distinguishable from omnipotence or masochism.[66]

From the preceding discussions it follows that, for artist and art contemplator, the personal life is an essential ground of esthetic experience. But the work of art is no more a "symbolic" embodiment or reflection of the artist's life than of the contemplator's. The strictly personal aspect of a work of art is only one aspect, and it is in some ways esthetically the least important. The unity and integrity of the work of art is as much an outgrowth of the physical properties of the materials, the traditional styles and ideas embedded in the work, the objective powers of the skills and tools used, and the other kinds of cultural meanings as it is a product of the artist's or contemplator's personal biography. What makes the art work *new, alive, significant* is not that it reflects aspects of the artist's biography—for it does; nor that it reflects the culture—for it does; nor that it embodies an esthetic tradition or style—for it does. Not only every successful work of art, but every failure does this, too. What is significant is that these are integrated in a new way.

The significance of the fact that art is *creation* and that what is created is an *autonomous* entity has in this context received insufficient attention. It is true that for the artist the act of creation must include psychological openness to his "secret lives." And these must be integrated. But in the case of art, the integration and awareness are not achieved solely by examining and shaping the self. They are achieved in an "indirect" way, in and through shaping and integrating the materials of the work of art. The integration created is not one of the self but of a *separate*, autonomous entity which includes many other elements besides the personal.

This helps account for the fact that we expect that the artist will be open to experience, but not that he will himself be a Sage. I do not mean here to suggest the cliché of the artist as an eccentric who "feels" but is intellectually disorganized and psychologically pathological. I am simply redescribing and emphasizing the familiar fact that by "sage" or enlightened-agonist we mean one whose personal life shows integration, whereas by "artist" we mean a person whose artifacts show integration. Further it is well recognized that there is no necessary connection between these two.

We should expect the artist to experience a complex sensation of gratification, relief, and of distance when he succeeds. The successful integration produces the satisfaction and relief characteristic of creative consummation. And, because the integrity produced *is* an integrity, unique, and as such sharply distinct from the pattern of his personal life, the creator becomes curiously detached from his past creations. He has literally "got it out of his system." He is not himself free, but he has given his creation its own kind of freedom, and he is free *of* it. The artist's past creations are of interest to him only as clues and pointers for *current* creative work (or as marks of status and other values extrinsic to the creative act).

Thus the artist resolves his inner tensions by systematically objectifying them and giving them an objective life of their own; the enlightened-agonist, therapist, and patient resolve their inner tensions by creating a new life for themselves.

The excitement and true danger in the life of the therapist, artist, and enlightened-agonist lie in their humanly falling short of the ideal, as they do. Then, to avert complete subversion, the defensive forces are brought into action. The goal becomes that of protecting the old clichés; the best means are usually the invasion and domination of the Other. Thus the so-called "personal" element enters. But in truth it is just what is *not* personal; it is the loss of control of self, the abandonment of the other person, the betrayal of the esthetic work. It is the resort to the impersonal, the stereotyped, the "safe." The therapist plays God; the artist becomes a hack.

A specific form of esthetic failure parallels the typical initial misstep in psychoanalytic therapy. The dynamic synthesis, if it is grasped at all, is often grasped "intellectually" rather than by empathy. Or else individual elements or esthetic gestures are responded to in isolation. We pity, or love; we sensually or emotionally revel in the materials which are used to build the art work. Without the orientation and equilibrium provided by the esthetic unity, the experimental, controlled character of the cathexes of the individual elements break down. This is to say that what those in the arts call "psychic distance" has been lost. The love, hate, suffering, and pity we feel does not have that "objectivity," that detachment from the personal biography that they have in the genuinely esthetic response. We *feel* real pity instead of discovering by direct experience what pity can *mean*, what its nature and quality are when grasped as a functioning element in a unified whole.

The response to a gesture or an element in terms of one's personal life is associated with "subjectivity" in art. Gitelson has been quoted earlier as decrying the analyst's allowing himself to be cast "in an intrusive part in the psychoanalytic drama." T. S. Eliot makes essentially the same point in connection with the staged drama.

> When a character *in* a play makes a direct appeal to us, we are either the victims of our own sentiment, or we are in the presence of a vicious rhetoric. . . .[67]
> It is essential that we should preserve our position as spectators, and observe always from the outside though with complete understanding.[68]

We should note Eliot's phrases suggesting disinterestedness —"from the outside," "spectators"—and then balance these with another statement of his:

> Poetry . . . has its own function [which is] not intellectual but emotional.[69]

The preceding discussions of the esthetic transaction apply both to art creator and art contemplator. The differentiating psychological conditions are not relevant to those discussions. It is enough to note that the creator must constantly step back and play the role of audience. (Even in the original creative act, God stepped back at each stage and "saw that it was good.") And the audience, in turn, must in some secondary but important sense be creative. But we must now add a few last words with regard to the esthetic and the therapeutic attitudes. And here what is said will show at least one crucial distinction between artist and audience, as well as showing how artist and therapist are alike.

Let us consider first, briefly, a distinctive aspect of the phenomenology of the esthetic experience. I refer to the paradoxical juxtaposition of (1) the suspense generated by the freedom and unpredictability of esthetic development, e.g., the free will of the characters in a drama, and (2) the sense of inevitability, of the fatedness and "rightness" of what is presented. This paradoxical perception of freedom and inevitability is present in all art but is perhaps conceptually most explicit in tragic drama.

What can we make psychologically of this remarkable esthetic quality?

In the play or story, we empathically experience the dramatic character's problems, and we try to resolve them along with him in *his* style. Thus our empathy is of the everyday rather than the therapeutic kind: we interpret and judge as well as experience in *his* way. In so doing, we experience existentially the problems the dramatic character faces, and thus we have the inner experience of his freedom of choice. No matter what else goes on within us at the time, it does not change the fact that we are having the experience, as subject, of freely choosing.

But something else of importance is going on at the time, and it is quite in contrast to the experience of free choice. As onlookers, we are aware of the entire relevant context of the protagonist's actions. For we also introject—not the artist's personal ego—but what might be called the "esthetic ego," the esthetic form of the whole work. The artist has created for us an imaginative total world with a luminous structure of dramatic forces in tension. The spectator is as if he were an ideal therapist: he responds to the total pattern of contending forces with an intuitive and comprehensive awareness like that of the ideal analyst's. The protagonist of the drama responds to those forces also but with an ego which is systematically blind to the forces that count. For the tragic hero will not see, because of his very nature as originally given, exactly what it is necessary for him to see. And the neurotic *will* not see, by his very nature as neurotic, exactly what he needs to see.

There is a formal parallel here between psychological repression and what might be called "esthetic repression." [70] The hero cannot be told the truth early in the game; it will be an irony, for he will not see its point though he may accept it verbally or in the wrong sense. Likewise, the neurotic patient cannot be told what he is repressing; he must come to it as the culmination of a dramatic self-exploration naturally consummated in the "discovery," the insight. The protagonist and the patient do not see. We observers (audience and therapist) may very well see. But this insight cannot be "given." It may be explicitly formulated and confirmed by a mediator or by the playwright's Chorus, but only after it has been earned is it genuinely received.

The crucial difference between therapy and art is that in art the audience must remain as if hypnotized; there is nothing we can do, nothing to be done to help the protagonist earn his knowledge. The artist has already arranged things perfectly: he has created the precise forces which do in fact progress in perfect, dynamic equilibrium to culminate in an ideal synthesis and resolution of conflict. But in therapeutic situations, just as in the act of artistic creation, there is no prearranged adequate synthesis of the contending forces. The patient must create such a synthesis, and the onlooker, the therapist, can in fact interfere and help at crucial moments.

Thus in the appreciation of art there is a kind of passivity which does not exist in therapy. And yet, in other ways we are in suspense and vitally active. Our activity comes not merely from participating empathically in the existential and free acts of the dramatic characters; it also comes from the precondition of this empathy. There must be an active, critical effort before we can achieve accurate empathy; we must constantly check the sentimental projection of our own personal feelings and attitudes toward the situation into the character.

With one part of ourself, then, we perceive directly, like gods, the inevitability of the tragic hero's doom. With another part of ourself, we live through the inward experience of his free choice. Hence we *know,* deep in our bowels, that he *can* do otherwise at the crucial moment, and yet, just as inwardly and profoundly, we *know* he can*not.* It is from this that there arises the hypnotic, fascinated suspense which occurs repeatedly in spite of our knowing "how it will all end."

This freedom and this inevitability are not theoretical, scientific concepts. They are existential.

Thus the artist presents us with independent and objective spiritual tasks, tasks involving materials connected with our personal spiritual tasks. He enables us to live, in an existential but controlled and "experimental" way, through the entire process of the movement toward integrity. He thus provides us with objective embodiments of the ideal toward which the personal spiritual life moves. In this way he teaches spiritual truths. But he does not preach: he does not tell us how to shape our own personal life.

V

THE THERAPIST SEES, IDEALLY, WHAT IS AT ONCE UNIVERSAL and unique in all men. He sees each person who comes before him as a person struggling to achieve integrity out of the universal materials of man's experience. In this respect, he sees all men—himself included—as brothers. And he sees the uniqueness of the particular patterns, the tasks and solutions, the kinds of integrity achieved or aborted. In this he sees the unique dignity of each human soul. The psychoanalyst, grasping the oneness and the separateness of all men, loves others as himself. It is not a question of having a passionate attachment to them; it is, rather, that his central love for himself is as a person, an integrity; and it is through this specific kind of concern and love, and in terms of it, that he has come to know others. In opening himself to the "I," he has opened himself to the "Thou." In this respect the ideal psychoanalyst is the enlightened-agonist of mythic history.

The artist achieves a comparable condition. But the range of his perception of brotherhood is not limited to other men; it is that of imagined men, of physical objects, of moving human bodies, of sounds and sights. In all of these he sees the potentialities for the achievement of dramatic integrity, of a unique and objective life which can be shared by artist and audience, a life which has a dignity and value of its own.

Compassionately comprehending, disinterestedly fascinated, we participate in the Divine. Finite, willfully blind, using rather than accepting the Other because we use rather than accept ourselves, we are human, all too human.

NOTES

(See List of Bibliographical Abbreviations, p. 343.)

1. Blakney, R. B., trans., *Meister Eckhart,* Harper & Bros., New York, 1957, p. 244.
2. *Ibid.,* p. 85.
3. Lao-tse, *Tao Te Ching,* in *The Way and Its Power,* Waley, A., The Macmillan Co., New York, 1956, XXVII.
4. *Ibid.,* II.
5. *Ibid.,* X.
6. *Ibid.,* V.
7. McAlpine, I., "The Development of the Transference," *Psychoanalytic Quarterly 19* (1950), p. 535.
8. Feldman, H., "From Self-Analysis to Transference Character Traits," *Psychoanalysis & Psychoanalytic Review 47* (1960), p. 63.
9. Sharpe, E. F., *Collected Papers on Psychoanalysis,* Hogarth Press, London, 1950, p. 12.
10. Greenson, R. R., "The Classic Psychoanalytic Approach," in *American Handbook of Psychiatry,* Arieti, S., ed., Basic Books, New York, 1959, p. 1415.
11. Gill, M., "Psychoanalysis and Exploratory Psychotherapy," *JAP 2* (1954), p. 776.
12. Little, M., "Counter-transference and the Patient's Response to It," *IJP 32* (1951), p. 35.
13. Gitelson, M., "The Emotional Position of the Analyst in the Psychoanalytic Situation," *IJP 33* (1952), p. 4.
14. Berman, L., "Countertransferences and Attitudes of the Analyst in the Therapeutic Process," *Psychiatry 12* (1949), p. 160.
15. Greenson, R. R., *op. cit.,* pp. 1408–1409.
16. Kris, E., "Ego Psychology and Interpretation in Psycho-

analytic Therapy," *Psychoanalytic Quarterly* 20:15–30 (1951).

17. Freud, S., "Neurosis and Psychosis," in *CP*, II, p. 253.

18. ———, *Group Psych.*, p. 108.

19. For a good review of the literature on the concept of identification, see Axelrad, S., and Maury, L. M., "Identification as a Mechanism of Adaptation," in *Psychoanalysis and Culture*, Wilbur, G. E., and Muensterberger, W., eds., International Universities Press, New York, 1951, pp. 168–184.

20. For a systematic analysis of these problems, see the theoretical essays of Rapaport, D. in (a) Rapaport, D., *The Organization and Pathology of Thought*, Columbia University Press, New York, 1951, and (b) Knight, R. P., ed., *Psychoanalytic Psychiatry and Psychology*, International Universities Press, New York, 1954.

21. See also, for example, Beres, D., "Psychoanalytic Psychology of Imagination," *JAP* 8:252–269 (1960).

22. Jacobson, E., "Contribution to the Metapsychology of Psychotic Identifications," *JAP 2* (1954), pp. 248–249.

23. *Loc. cit.*

24. See, for example, Knight, R. P., "Introjection, Projection, and Identification," *Psychoanalytic Quarterly 9* (1940), p. 335.

25. Cf. Axelrad, S., and Maury, L. M., *op. cit.*

26. Coleman, R. W., Kris, E., and Provence, S., "The Study of Variations of Early Parental Attitudes: A Preliminary Report," in *The Psychoanalytic Study of the Child*, Vol. VIII, International Universities Press, New York, 1953, p. 33.

27. Olden, C., "On Adult Empathy with Children," in *The Psychoanalytic Study of the Child*, Vol. VIII, pp. 112–113.

28. Fliess, R., "Countertransference and Counteridentification," *JAP 1* (1953), p. 280.

29. Knight, R. P., "Introjection, Projection, and Identification," *op. cit.*, p. 339.

30. *Ibid.*

31. Hartmann, H., "Technical Implications of Ego Psychology," *Psychoanalytic Quarterly* 20:31–43, 1951.
32. Fenichel, O., *Problems of Psychoanalytic Technique*, Brunswick, D., trans., The Psychoanalytic Quarterly, Inc., Albany, N.Y., 1941, p. 73.
33. Gitelson, M., *op. cit.*, p. 4.
34. *Ibid.*, p. 5.
35. Confucius, *Analects*, Book VI, Chap. XXVIII, Par. 3. (Author's translation.)
36. Lao-tse, *Tao Te Ching*, XLVII, *op. cit.*
37. Freud, S., "Formulations on the Two Principles of Mental Functioning," in *CPW*, XII, p. 221.
38. Sharpe, E., *op. cit.*, p. 118.
39. Cf. Orr, D. W., "Transference and Countertransference: A Historical Survey," *JAP* 2:621–670 (1954).
40. Fliess, R., *op. cit.*, p. 284.
41. Gitelson, M., *op. cit.*, p. 7.
42. Mann, J., Menzer, D., and Standish, C., "Psychotherapy of Psychoses," *Psychiatry* 13 (1950), p. 19.
43. Sharpe, E., *op. cit.*, p. 19.
44. Lao-tse, *Tao Te Ching*, XLIX. (Author's translation.)
45. *Matt.* 18:3–4.
46. *Mark* 9:35.
47. Lao-tse, *Tao Te Ching*, VII, p. 150. (Waley translation.)
48. *The Principal Upanishads*, Radhakrishnan, S., ed., George Allen & Unwin, London, 1953, p. 291.
49. Gitelson, M., *op. cit.*, p. 7.
50. Cf. Greenson, R. R., *op. cit.*, p. 1408.
51. Buber, M., "Elements of the Interhuman," *Psychiatry 20* (1957), p. 109.
52. ———, *I and Thou*, Charles Scribner's Sons, New York, 1958, 2nd ed., p. 133.
53. Sharpe, E., *op. cit.*, p. 116.
54. Freud, S., "Recommendations for Physicians on the Psychoanalytic Method of Treatment," in *CP*, II, p. 327.
55. *Loc. cit.*
56. Low, B., "The Psychological Compensations of the Analyst," *IJP 16* (1935), p. 7.

57. Sharpe, E., *op. cit.*, pp. 120–121.
58. Beres, D., "Psychoanalytic Psychology of Imagination," *op. cit.*
59. Cf. *ibid.;* Rosen, Victor H., "Some Aspects of the Role of Imagination in the Analytic Process," *JAP* 8:229–251 (1960); Kris, E., *Psychoanalytic Explorations in Art,* International Universities Press, New York, 1952.
60. Freud, S., *Dreams,* in *CPW,* III, IV.
61. Cf. Freud, S., "The Relation of the Poet to Day-Dreaming," in *CP,* IV, pp. 173–183.
62. Read, H., "Psychoanalysis and the Problem of Aesthetic Value," *IJP* 32:73–82 (1951).
63. Langer, S., "The Primary Illusions and the Great Orders of Art," *Hudson Review, 3* (1950–51), p. 230.
64. MacLeish, A., "Ars Poetica," in *Collected Poems,* Houghton Mifflin, Boston, 1952, p. 41.
65. Lao-tse, *Tao Te Ching,* II. (Author's translation.)
66. Gitelson, M., *op. cit.*, p. 4.
67. Eliot, T. S., *Selected Essays,* Harcourt, Brace & Co., New York, 1932, p. 28.
68. *Loc. cit.*
69. *Ibid.*, p. 118.
70. This point emerged in the course of discussions with Professor Fred Hagen.

CHAPTER 7

THE CONSUMMATORY PHASE:

Mystic Selflessness

I

THE ACCEPTANCE OF GUILT AND THE ASSUMPTION OF RESPONsibility lead to a new mode of spiritual existence. We have seen that this involves a reorganization of psychic structure and function, a transformation of the Self and of the relationships with the world. In practice, only a limited area of life and of the psyche are thus transformed. There are always unexplored areas remaining into which one could, at least in principle, extend the arena of insight, responsibility, and transformation. Moreover, the phaselike retrogression and progression of the "working-through" process is a lengthy and yet a necessary labor if the areas already opened up are to be made secure and if they are to be cultivated so that the new roots grow deep. Psychoanalysis, as Freud said, is terminated in practice but is interminable in principle.[1] And so it is with all spiritual knowledge and transformation.

Nevertheless, the temporal processes of working through and of reaching to new areas of insight are not our main concern in this book. We shall do as is so often done: we shall treat the process as if it were a wholesale, once-for-all affair. This simplification is not an ideal but a practical necessity. We know it can be a misleading practice. It tempts us to indulge in fantasies; we are bemused by the myths of "The Completely Analyzed Patient," "The Free Man," "The Enlightened One."

This danger we must accept if we are to concentrate upon another task which is not necessarily more important but which happens to be ours. For these studies are not primarily aimed at the details of technique of self-transformation nor at the practical questions of time-order and scope of inquiry connected with a particular insightful self-transformation. The objective here is to consider self-transformation in the abstract, to consider of what, in general, insightful self-transformation consists, and to consider what are the principal stages and categories in terms of which it must, in the last analysis, be analyzed.

It is in this sense that we may speak of the consummatory phase of self-transformation. For the liberation which is achieved and the new modes of action which accompany it involve a new sense of one's existence and of reality. The fact is that we here enter a phase of experience which must be viewed in the context of mysticism. As in the case of the discussion of karma, I must at once warn the reader that by "mysticism" I do not mean mystification, superstition, or theological paradox meant to be worshiped though not understood. The temptation is ever present to read into the word "mysticism" meanings derived from our Western tradition, a tradition which is, basically, though not completely, antimystical. As in prior chapters, I find it illuminating to begin by viewing the problematic phenomena, in this case those of mysticism, in conjunction with a review of certain aspects of psychoanalysis. Not only does each throw light on the other, but the illumination thus generated casts its glow over yet other, neighboring areas of the life of the spirit.

The theme of this chapter is that the psychoanalytic way

to insight runs parallel to the mystic's way of self-liberation. Of course it would be absurd to argue that the two "ways" are identical. Indeed, in the greater part of the literature on the subject, it is the *differentiating* characteristics which have usually been stressed. This stress is partly due to the fact that early psychoanalytic studies in all fields of study were largely id-oriented and clinic-oriented. This familiar "classical" treatment of the matters at hand can, I trust, be safely left until the latter portions of the chapter. By then, the differences between psychoanalytic insight and mystical experience will not have disappeared but will have re-appeared, and in a new light. Our main energies and our first steps, however, must be directed to developing the picture in terms of the more recent psychoanalytic conceptions usually classified under the heading "ego psychology." This perspective tends to reveal the hitherto underempha-sized similarities, the profound parallels between the two "ways." The balance is thereby redressed, and the old, fa-miliar facts then have a new "feel." In the course of devel-oping the chapter's theme, we shall not only help "reani-mate" the language of mysticism, but we shall clarify and extend the contemporary psychoanalytic concepts of regres-sion, pathology, creativity, sublimation, infantilism, and fantasy.

II

BY WAY OF SETTING THE STAGE, LET US REVIEW AT ONCE, although quite briefly, the apparently extreme opposition between the ideal mystic state and the ideal therapeutic goal of the psychoanalyst. Since we often think of the two as contrasting, I shall try to set the problem in the form of the sharpest possible contrast.

In the great mystical classics of Christianity, Hinduism, Buddhism, and Taoism, it is characteristically said that the mystic insight results ideally in egolessness, selflessness, absence of desire and of striving, passivity instead of control, cessation of logic, thought, and discrimination, and a life beyond morality, beyond sensation, and perception. The psychoanalyst, however, aims (ideally) at using insight to strengthen the ego, and to develop a self—a self with a rich variety of goals and the substantial ability to gratify desires, with reasonable self-control and mastery of the environment, and with the ability to perceive realistically, discriminate clearly, and act with a sense of the appropriate values.

The way of psychoanalytic therapy aims at minimal disruption of everyday life. The mystic way notoriously involves unusual practices and symptoms, for example, trances, ecstasies, visions, asceticism, and stigmata.

I wish to present now, in an informal and preliminary way, some data which suggest the hypotheses I shall subsequently develop. Essentially I propose to set side by side some introspective reports of a psychoanalytic patient and some mystic sayings. In this way we can begin to probe the degree of contrast and of similarity in terms of the primary data rather than in terms of a generalized "summary" of mysticism and of psychoanalytic goals such as the preceding.

Strange to say, in the literature of psychoanalysis it is difficult to find a sensitive and extensive account, in nontechnical language, of the "feeling" of one's "subjective" experience *after* successful analysis. I present here a few extracts from a nontechnical, informal, and introspective report in which a woman compares her postanalytic with her preanalytic experience.

No detailed account of the interviewee's analysis or life history is given since the interview material is not intended to function as evidence for the thesis of this paper. The interview material, obtained by the writer, is illustrative. It is presumed that, with a slight effort at empathy, the naturalness and appropriateness of Katherine's language will be apparent to those with psychoanalytic experience.

Katherine is a woman in her early thirties who has worked through some important neurotic conflicts in psychoanalytic psychotherapy. It is essential to note that while Katherine, a housewife, is an intelligent college graduate and a woman of culture, she is not a "professional intellectual" nor is she particularly interested in psychoanalytic theory. She has nothing but the most casual acquaintance with mysticism. Insofar as she has any conception of the life and literature of mysticism, she conceives of it as obscurantist, pathological, and alien to her life and her intellectual loyalties.

Katherine is asked, specifically, to consider her relationship with Alice, a friend around whom strong conflicts formerly raged and with respect to whom an important segment of her analysis was concerned. The interviewer requests that technical, psychological terms be avoided. She is not to worry about being systematic, "scientific," or logical. She is to try as best she can to "get across" the "feel" of life by talking about herself, her desires, her feelings, her judgments, and so on. As a starter, she is asked what are her present desires in connection with Alice.

Katherine reflects a moment and then says, "Well, I don't have any desires now. I used to want Alice to be shown up in her true colors, to have people see how wrong she was. Now I just don't think about it. I just act. I get along."

Katherine's spontaneous and informal comments are challenged by me. Surely she cannot mean *exactly* what she says. Surely if she has social relations with Alice, there must be thinking going on; the existence of at least some ordinary desires is implied in saying that they ate, talked, and generally coordinated their activities during social visits. And, finally, does Katherine mean to imply that she gets along now because she lets herself be stepped on at will, ignoring the rights and wrongs of Alice's behavior toward her? I expressed my assumption that the relationship is not one of total passivity and self-abnegation on Katherine's part.

"Well, of course," replies Katherine, "I still may think that what she's doing is wrong at times, but it doesn't matter much. That is, well, I would defend myself if she did anything wrong to me . . . but, well, I wouldn't *dwell* on its being wrong. I'm just not involved. It doesn't matter *in the same way.*"

Katherine was impressed by the peculiar nature of the comments she had made, examining them, as it were, in reflective retrospect. She volunteers: "It's funny, but if anyone ever looked at what I've said, they'd get the impression of a very strange and quiet person without real emotion, someone who didn't care about anything. That's not a good picture of me at all. It's true, it takes a lot more effort to get angry now, and yet I explode all the time. The difference is that I used to get angry all the time and never exploded. Now, when I'm angry, I explode and yell, but somehow I'm not really even worked up about it." (In her observable behavior, Katherine is neither affectless nor meek. She is, if anything, a person who tends to hold strong opinions, can act and speak forcefully, and, when she violates the "mean" at all, tends toward the pole of intense participation, warmth and empathy rather than withdrawal, coldness or tranquility.)

At one point in the interview, Katherine is asked about her attitude toward being praised, something which used to mean a great deal in her life. She replies: "I used to get a lot of satisfaction out of it. Now I don't get any." Upon being challenged, she adds that what she has said may be misleading. "I did get satisfaction, for example, out of being praised for making that dress a while ago, but that was because I *had* done it very well. But the praise was just *that,* period! All the competition's sort of left, too. I'm calmer; I don't try so hard."

It is of interest to add here another comment of Katherine's when asked whether she was angry when, as she said, she "exploded." Her answer was: "No! . . . well . . . yes, that is . . . I'm angry at the thing and not in general. It's hard to explain."

Under the conditions set by the interviewer, Katherine spontaneously—and without ever having spoken this way before—finds herself forced to use locutions which she realizes are unusual, contradictory, inadequate, and in constant need of corrections which are in turn bound to be inadequate. It is clear that she is trying to put something into language which the language is not equipped to communicate in any routine, news-reporting fashion.

Nevertheless, she does not feel that language fails her entirely. One senses that *to her* the words communicate in some sense. There is, in fact, a kind of "logic" or "order" in her exposition which I shall eventually make explicit.

I shall, for convenience, introduce here the notion of "the language of self." By "the language of self," I mean our everyday language insofar as it expresses experience in terms of the self as an acting and suffering *person* rather than a physical, physiological, psychological, or social process. "I think, I feel, I want, I believe, I see, I hear, I ought"— these, when used in the context of personal action, enjoyment, or commitment rather than that of scientific description or philosophical speculation, are the stuff of the "language of self."

Katherine's comments are paradoxical. She tends to begin her account by denying self-activities such as desiring, thinking, judging, emotion: then she proceeds to acknowledge the existence of these very self-activities: and finally she suggests that everything is meant in a different sense, making the whole affair difficult or impossible to express.

Nevertheless, she continues in fact to express herself in this language.

In Katherine's remarks—as I shall show next—there is a precise, detailed, and systematic parallelism to the language of the mystic. (When this was pointed out to Katherine subsequently, she was surprised, annoyed, and interested.)

III

I HAVE SPOKEN SO FAR OF "MYSTICISM," BUT IT IS TIME NOW to state more precisely what I have in mind. While I particularly wish to stress that the present analysis is relevant to important Jewish and Christian, as well as to Hindu, Buddhist, and Taoist traditions usually labeled "mystical," I shall, as a practical matter, limit myself largely to the latter group. Occasional references to Western mystics, and in particular to Meister Eckhart, will be provided when they can be fit easily into the context. The specific strain of mysticism selected from this vast Eastern literature is one which, as mysticisms go, is especially congenial to the Western mind. In the special form known as Zen, it has become an object of relatively wide interest in the West during the past two decades. This study will by no means restrict itself to Zen, however.

It is, as was recalled earlier, well-known that the Eastern mystic cultivates "desirelessness." Could we interview a hypothetical "composite" mystic of this type, he would tell us that the enlightened ones are without desire, beyond good and evil, uninvolved, neither thinking nor discriminating, without ego, utterly serene. (Recall Katherine: "I don't have any desires"; "I just don't think about it"; ". . . what she's doing is wrong at times, but it doesn't matter much"; "I'm just not involved"; "somehow, I'm not really even worked up about it.")

Suppose, however, that we challenge our hypothetical mystic with a series of further questions. The "answers" which follow are, of course, culled and quoted from a variety of mystical writings as indicated previously. (Material in single quotes consists of exact passages from the mystical texts.)

"When you speak of 'enlightenment' in this fashion, you are speaking of some sort of trance state, no doubt?" we ask. The mystic's denial is clear and sharp. In analogy to Katherine who denied that her words betokened pathological behavior, we are warned by our composite mystic against those who seek Buddha by "going off by themselves in solitude." [2] "All of this is ignorance," we are told. "Those who sit quietly and try to keep their minds blank are 'foolish people,' 'heretics.' " [3] "Zen [that is, mystic enlightenment] is your 'ordinary mind.' " [4]

We are reminded that even the great Christian mystics, St. Theresa and St. John of the Cross, warn the one who treads the mystic path against being seduced by the raptures and delights of trances and visions.[5]

"But in this case," we argue, "in spite of what you said earlier about desirelessness, you must in truth experience desire?"

"Of course," replies the mystic, apparently contradicting his earlier statements. " 'Even a wise man acts according to the tendencies of his own nature.' [6] 'If you have the wisdom of Prajna, you can practice Zen in the world of desires.' [7] 'Desire flows into the mind of the seer but he is never disturbed.' " [8]

We continue trying to catch the mystic in further contradictions: "If you are not speaking of trance states of one kind or another, then you must have not only desires but sensations and perceptions; you must think; you must make judgments of better and worse, and you must have feelings and emotions after all."

"What you say is true," says the mystic. " 'Ignorant ones . . . imagine that Nirvana consists in the future annihilation of the senses and the sense-minds. This is not so with the genuinely enlightened,' [9] '[nor does the enlightened one try to] get rid of notions of good and evil.' [10] And as for thinking—'It is a great mistake to suppress all thinking.' " [11]

"As for emotions," continues our mystic, "you must recall the famous Zen master who yelled vociferously when dying; [12] recall also the other Zen master whose laugh was heard over several counties." [13] "[The enlightened one] 'is found in company with wine-bibbers and butchers.' " [14]

At this point we throw up our hands and accuse the mystic of flagrant self-contradiction. All his talk of egolessness, desirelessness, serenity, and such is now completely denied, it seems. To this, he replies: " 'I am trying to describe to you something that intrinsically is ineffable, in order to help you get rid of fallacious views. If you do not interpret my words too literally, you may perhaps know a wee bit of Nirvana.' " [15]

Should we ask at this point how we can ever be informed of the ineffable, the mystic either remains silent or proceeds to talk in much the same manner as before—or, if he is a Zen master, perhaps he gives us a blow with his stick.

It is understandable that Leuba, the renowned student of the psychology of mysticism, could say of this kind of talk that it is "obviously nonsense!" [16] Yet, on the other hand, we are not surprised to find logical nonsense in poetry or "falsehoods" in novels. Careful examination of our own everyday speech convinces us of the remarkable communicative power of nonlogical, nonscientific modes of speech. The intellectually fascinating model of scientific language—an esoteric language, after all—blinds us to the ubiquity and efficiency of nonlogical modes of speech in everyday life. To interpret the mystic as scientist or theoretician of any sort is a blunder comparable to pointing out the contradictory statements within a poem.

As a first hypothesis, I suggest that the mystic is trying

to distinguish between two important but different kinds of experience, both naturally expressed by the same introspective self-language. He wants us to achieve one kind of experience and to guide us away from another mode of experience which, as it happens, is expressed by the same sort of language. Later I shall pursue the question as to the nature of this difference in modes of experience.

With this hypothesis, we can take a step toward making sense of the mystic's paradoxes: since the only language we have for both modes of experience is the one language, the language of self, it inevitably appears that the mystic constantly contradicts himself. Furthermore, the only means he has of hoping to make the distinctions clear is to use the language with a keen sense of context, a careful sensitivity to both his own and the other's experience at the moment. Hence he must sense as quickly as the swordsman the play of the shifting modes of experience within changing contexts, and he must, as quickly, shift his way of talking until the listener is somehow able to perceive the pattern underneath the superficial nonsense of his talk. There is something here partly analogous to and partly identical with Freud's technique. As Freud found that the transference could be the chief instrument of therapy rather than the ultimate obstacle, so the mystic finds that the troublesome paradox inherent in his plight, when its use is carefully selective and timed, is a powerful device for enlightenment.

"My words have an ancestry, my deeds have a lord; and it is precisely because men do not understand this that they are unable to understand me," says the mystic sage, Laotse.[17] This is understood to mean that his words are neither "savage" nor "wild"; they are related to a "definite system of thought." But their utter simplicity is not perceived because their "ancestry" is unseen; therefore they are "murky."

We must understand that "system" does not mean "logical system." The Chinese word "lord" with its anthropomorphic connotation of a pattern of *purposes* is closer to the fact than the impersonal English word "system." The mystic's words are "skillful means" to the practical purpose of evoking enlightenment. They are not elements in a theoretical system.

The mystic's words are like an analyst's therapeutic interventions: they are designed to be effective in producing specific change, not to embody universal truths. The "pattern" underlying the mystic's words is, in short, pragmatic, not logical.

The mystic, then, uses the one language of self in paradoxical ways in order to distinguish two overlapping modes of subjective experience and in order to shift the balance in favor of one mode as against the other.

In the following section, I shall propose some psychoanalytic hypotheses as to the conditions under which a person might be expected to communicate the nature of his subjective experience in language identical or analogous to that of the mystic.

IV

I PROPOSE NOW TO INQUIRE WHETHER THERE IS A SIGNIFICANT relationship between any psychoanalytic usage of the term "self" and the usage of "self" and related terms in mysticism. Ultimately, however, I am concerned with developing a psychoanalytic understanding of the mystic's notion of self regardless of whether the latter includes anything which can be called self in the psychoanalytic sense.

In psychoanalysis, the term "self" has no unambiguous systematic use. It occurs usually as part of hyphenated compounds used in varying contexts and with differing connotations. In his early views, Freud[18] used the term "self" in connection with such notions as the "self-preservative instincts." These early notions, later substantially modified, involved no specifically psychoanalytic conceptions of the self. Freud was using the word to connote loosely the total person in his status as an individual rather than as a member of the species.

The term "self" has been used by Freud,[19] however, in close connection with the term "ego." In the early days of Freud's inquiries, he often used "ego" interchangeably with "self." Later "ego" came to have a specific and much narrower meaning. It is this shift in the meaning of "ego" that has at times confused discussions of the self. "Ego," in its later and still current use in psychoanalysis, is a theoretical term referring to a hypothesized (metapsychological) structure. This structure consists of a set of dispositions, specifically the dispositions to perceptual, thinking, evaluative, integrative, and executive behavior of the person.

The ego is therefore not only to be distinguished from id, superego, and environmental reality, it is to be distinguished from the introspectable "contents of the mind." Like id and superego, it is a theoretical entity, not a datum of perception. The effects of its action, however, *may* be conscious.

It is clear from the previous that the ego is neither the total psychic self nor is it the "self" of introspection. It is therefore not the self of the mystic, according to the hypotheses already proposed. I might add that it is not the self in any of the usual moral senses of the term, either. Hence moral or mystic "egolessness" is not equivalent to "egolessness" in any psychoanalytic sense. The use of "ego" in introspectively oriented discussions about moral or spiritual questions is exceedingly common and leads to frequent confusion when it occurs in close connection with psychoanalytic ideas. *It is essential to see that the psychoanalytic "ego" is not to be identified with the "ego" or "self" of mysticism or introspective analyses.*

To psychoanalysts, the mystic's stress on loss of self and "unity of all with all" is likely to suggest that there is a psychotic-like confusion of "inner" and "outer," a loss of the self-object distinction as in hallucination and paranoid delusions.[20] The decisive evidence for the inadequacy of this view arises from observation of the behavior of great mystics and of those ordinary persons such as Katherine who speak in a quasi-mystic way. For, far from showing a confusion between self and environment, they act with unusual effectiveness and with a clear sense of the social realities. They often show great practical organizing ability and a particularly keen sensitivity to the real relationships between their own attitudes and desires and those of the persons they deal with.

Let it be recalled here, and with emphasis, that the trance states and visionary states so commonly identified with the culminating mystic enlightenment are in truth only frequent forerunners. Insofar as enlightenment is achieved, visions and trances, if they were present at all, are given up, and active life within the world is resumed or simply continued. As varied a group of the classic commentators on mysticism as Underhill,[21] Leuba,[22] and Bergson[23] agree on these questions. *Thus the self which is lost in mystic enlightenment is not the self essential to the practical carrying on of one's ordinary daily activities.*

Another use of self in psychoanalysis is found in the notion of "self-representation," a term which—"analogous to the term object representations—refers to our mental concept of the self; that is, to the unconscious and preconscious images of our body self and of our own personality."[24] The self-representation is thus not supposed to be introspectable. This being so, the self-representations are not the self of the mystic. The mystic is concerned with his introspectable, subjective experience, not with hypothesized processes.

I should like to urge an additional and important reason, however, why self-representations are not the object of our search. It is important to remember that the mystic does not claim that he is *in every sense* unaware of himself. Just as he admits to perceiving, thinking, and desiring in *some* sense of those terms, so he must admit to being aware of himself even when he is "self-less." The mystic, in the advanced stages of his development, lives in the world, among "wine-bibbers and butchers," and acts effectively in his relationships with others. This implies that he takes into account his body, his social situation, his personal qualities, powers, and purposes. It is in just these respects that the self-representations play an essential role, for they are the psychic perceptions of the person and his powers and purposes. Hence they cannot be the self which the enlightened mystic has *lost*, and it is this latter "self" that I am directly concerned with.

Another use of the word "self"—a use which *is* relevant to the mystic's use—is in such combination as "self-criticism," "self-esteem," "aggression against the self," "self-consciousness." These concepts are used with varying degrees of precision. Some of this family of "self-" terms are at times used to refer to metapsychological nonintrospectable processes. Thus "aggression against the self" is used to mean a cathexis of the ego by the superego with aggressive drive-energy. Such a hypothetical "process" is quite distinct from, although at times "causally" related to, the subjective experience of "hating oneself," or the overt behavior describable as self-mutilation or suicide.

Insofar as the groups of concepts just mentioned do refer to nonintrospected processes, they are not included in the mystic concept of self. But they become much closer in meaning when they are used to describe subjective (introspectable) experiences of the sort expressed by such phrases as: "I could kick myself"; "I guess I'm not much good"; "I'm so embarrassed"; "I guess I showed them I'm pretty good after all." In such situations, the "self" in the mystic sense is very definitely there; "its" presence is in some sense weighty, at the center of experience—too much so.

It is difficult to find plain and more succinct language, other than the quoted typical phrases, to describe this subjective experience. The term which best covers this whole family of experiences is "self-conscious." This, of course, is not at all the same as being conscious of one's total person. Nor is this "self-consciousness" simply a consciousness of specific self-representations. The self-representations function in some degree in all voluntary behavior, but not all voluntary behavior includes "self-conscious" feelings. "Self-consciousness," in this colloquial sense, is very much a part of what the mystic means by the sense of self from which we need liberation. Before proceeding to an examination of the metapsychological conditions associated with "self-consciousness," I wish to discuss another important kind of subjective experience which is also directly associated with that "self" with which the mystic is concerned.

Federn [25] has developed the concept of "ego-feeling" in connection, particularly, with the phenomena of estrangement and depersonalization. This concept has not been readily accepted. Among other things, it confuses concepts appropriate to subjective experience ("feeling") with metapsychological concepts ("ego"). Nevertheless, Federn's data and his concerns are important and illuminating in the context of the present inquiry in spite of the conceptual confusion.

Federn describes estrangement and depersonalization as experiences involving an absence of "ego-feeling." The language confusion is unfortunate here, for what he calls an "absence of ego-feeling" is in truth not an absence of a feeling but a *positive feeling*—the feeling that something is absent. In these experiences, the sufferer clearly experiences his activities and feelings, and he knows in a kind of intellectual or "external" way that they are his—but what occupies his attention is the uncomfortable feeling that something is missing. Somehow he feels that *he* is not really doing and feeling these things, and the feeling is distressing, often acutely so. The patient breaks out in despair to say: "Language has no words to describe my state, but it is as I say." Federn tells us that "[the patient] use similes and symbolic language because they find that the usual expressions are unsatisfactory." [26]

An ego-process (hence a nonintrospectable process) is certainly involved in this matter. But the subjective effect (the introspectable phenomenon) produced by that process is not an *absence of feeling* but a peculiar and distressing *feeling* of absence. On the other hand, Federn's language requires us to say that when we are perceiving normally, there is present an appropriate kind of "ego-feeling." This phrasing obscures the point that what, according to Federn, is the presence of "ego-feeling" is, subjectively, not a feeling at all but an *absence* of certain peculiar feelings. Federn himself makes this last point very effectively (but without seeing its implications for his terminology) when he says, "Normally, there is no more awareness of the ego than of the air one breathes." [27] One could hardly put the matter more incisively! Of course we must add that there is never any awareness of the *ego* as such, but one need here only substitute the word "self" for "ego." Then it is evident that Federn has pointed to a fundamental feature of our normal subjective experience.

The introspective "sense of self" occurs in the context of the *disruption* of "normal" ego activity. We do not normally have the *feeling* that our actions and decisions are or are not ours; we simply act or decide. The normal introspective self-"feelings" are like the feeling of the air we breathe. *Normally* we neither feel that the air exists nor that it has ceased to exist. Only when there is trouble do we become aware of the air. At such times we may have a sensation of "absence," of something missing; or it may be that we have a sensation of something present but noxious or troublesome. So, with our introspective sense of self: sometimes, as in self-consciousness, it "weighs" upon us; at other times, as in estrangement, it seems positively absent. Both are "abnormal" situations. Both give rise to a subjective concern with self.[28]

The theoretical question which requires immediate consideration is that of the meaning of "abnormal" in this context. Such an inquiry will lead to a formulation of the metapsychological conditions of the concern with self. And this formulation, in turn, will confirm itself by leading to additional important phenomena of mysticism which we have not yet dealt with in this section of the chapter.

The relevant ambiguity in the phrase "abnormal functioning of the ego" is avoided, I believe, if we formulate the matter in terms of the concept of anxiety. Of course anxiety itself is, in a very important sense, a perfectly "normal" ego phenomenon. However, the crucial condition for that "normal" subjective unconcern with self which is like our normal unawareness of the air we breathe is the *absence* of significant amounts of anxiety.

In terms of anxiety, the fundamental question implicitly raised by our concept "abnormal functioning of the ego" is as follows: Is the psychological context one of defensive functioning of the ego stimulated by anxiety, the latter, in turn, generated out of intrapsychic conflict? Or is the psychological context one of anxiety-free, autonomous ego functions, that is, functions activated by sublimated (neutralized) instinctual energy operating within a conflict-free portion of the ego? In the latter case we have the sense of "normal ego functioning" which is relevant to the present inquiry. (Where the ego function is anxiety-motivated, the ego may very well be functioning adaptively and in that sense "normally." I am not concerned here to legislate in general about the use of the word "normal.")

The matter may be put briefly and suggestively, if not too precisely, as follows: the introspected, self-conscious "I" is not in fact a perception of one's own total person; it is some particular part, affect, idea, or action of the person as perceived by the person in a context where the dynamically dominant affect is some form of anxiety. These experiences are often expressed in the language of self: "I feel," "I am so worthless," "I desire," "I believe," "I love," "I am hated by," "I must have," and so on. "Consciousness of self" is not an awareness of some self-identical entity; it is, rather, *any consciousness colored by intrapsychic conflict and anxiety.*

This fundamental relationship between the sense of self and anxiety was clearly stated by Freud. According to him, prototypical anxiety is generated by the earliest separation-situations.[29] It is out of these painful (quasi-anxiety-filled) separation-situations that he supposed both anxiety proper and the distinction between "self" and "other" to arise. The earliest separation-situation was a prototype of intrapsychic conflict, for the mother was included in the primal "self."

Where, on the other hand, the ego-functions are anxiety-free, we have that "self-forgetfulness"[30] so characteristic of autonomous ego functions using neutralized instinctual energy. "Self-forgetfulness," let it be noted again, is not the failure to take oneself and one's functions into account; on the contrary, this latter is most efficiently done in the context of subjective self-forgetfulness, of "*un*self-consciousness."

What relationship does the "language of self" have to anxiety? The language of self, in its ordinary use, expresses without distinction either of two profoundly different forms of subjective experience, the anxiety-generated *or* the anxiety-free. The subtler aspects of the linguistic manner or style may differ, but the words and the grammar are the same.

We should not be surprised that, partly as a result of the ambiguity of the language of self, many persons fail in one degree or another to distinguish these two different forms of subjective experience. This is true even though the difference, once perceived, is profound. Certain anxiety symptoms (for example, "nervousness," faintness) are easy to distinguish. But most often the anxiety-motivation of behavior is masked, the behavior frequently being rationalized. Thus the man who has always worked compulsively at his job is likely to be unable to distinguish his behavior from that of industrious and enthusiastic but anxiety-free work. The attempts of others to use language to suggest to him the subtle but profound difference in the "feel" of the two experiences will most likely be met by him either with incomprehension or defensive scorn or both. When he asks them to describe in "plain" language how *they* approach their work, victory is his—for they have to use the very same language-forms he does. If someone says that anxiety-free work has a kind of absorbed and devoted character, the compulsive replies that those are just the words that describe his work! And he is right.

It is for such reasons, among others, that the mystic renounces the attempt to communicate by means of generalized, theoretical discourse. This renunciation is closely related to the psychoanalyst's recognition that general and theoretical discussion of neurotic (anxiety-dominated) behavior fails to help the neurotic. If I may be permitted a crude but suggestive analogy: the mystic is always interested in therapy, not theory, and, therefore, to him the attempt to introduce psychological or other rational theory is resistance, defense, an evasion of the heart of the matter. The general statements about the self which have one meaning for the therapist or mystic are easily misinterpreted in quite another meaning by the neurotic and the unenlightened. The language of self is fatally ambiguous.

From the standpoint of his own personal achievement rather than communication with others or helping them, the central task of the mystic is that of achieving an unusually strong ego within an unusually well-integrated personality. This implies maximal ego-autonomy and neutralization of drives, and it implies minimal conflict, anxiety, and defense. If, for the moment, we consider the self to be the same as character in Reich's [31] sense—the relatively enduring defensive "armor"—then the mystic aims at minimal defensive-armor and hence the "death" of such a self. The process of achieving a mature personality with an extreme minimum of defensive character armor ordinarily involves major (and stormy) personality reorganization. The soul-racking death which leads to blissful "rebirth" is the death of the subjectively experienced, anxiety-generated "self" perception; it is the emergence into the freedom of introspective "self-forgetfulness" of the psychically unified self.

V

IT IS NOW APPROPRIATE TO TEST THE METAPSYCHOLOGICAL hypotheses presented up to this point by developing their implications and determining whether they are consistent with a reasonably broad sample of the language and phenomena of mysticism. Such an examination will show, I believe, the validity of these suggestions. It will also reveal the need for important amplifications of the psychological analysis. These amplifications will, in effect, show how the more traditional psychoanalytic interpretations of mysticism are to be integrated with the present one to form a more comprehensive view in which the interrelations of ego and id are exhibited.

We assume, in general, that both Katherine and the mystic are trying to express that introspected difference in the quality of experience correlated with the metapsychological shift from anxiety and defense to sublimation and ego-syntonic experience. On this basis one can see the naturalness of denying any "striving." The very word "compulsion," used by Freud in connection with characteristic symptoms of defense against anxiety, is of a piece with such words as "bondage," "attachment," "striving." This peculiar subjective sense of pressure, of need, of not-to-be-brooked desire is in sharp contrast to the subjective experience associated with anxiety-free cathexes. The latter we naturally express as "freedom," especially freedom of inner initiative ("free will"). We have here an experience which, as Knight points out,[32] needs to be distinguished carefully from the deceptive subjective sense of "freedom" associated with certain other types of psychological conditions. This deceptive sense of "freedom" occurs in the child during flights of fantasy; it is also reported by the person who, unconsciously driven by intense defiance, carries out criminal, libertinist, or other spurious acts of "independence." I call this a deceptive sense of freedom because freedom includes much more than merely subjective feelings. Furthermore, it is possible, though not easy, to distinguish introspectively the genuine subjective experience of freedom from the spurious one.

For the child and the neurotically rebellious person to be able to introspect the distinction between the "mature" and the "immature" subjective sense of freedom requires, as we know, long and arduous self-exploration and self-transformation. Nevertheless, from the theoretician's and the trained observer's standpoint, the distinction can be made relatively easily with the aid of the appropriate psychological distinctions and techniques. "Absence of anxiety, of irrational doubt, and of those inhibitions and restrictions which paralyze both choice and action"[33] are the negative indicators of the mature sense of freedom. The ability to make effective, ego-syntonic choices is among the positive criteria.

For the relatively mature person, minor decisions are made with an unqualified subjective sense of freedom. In connection with weighty decisions in life, there is the more complex feeling that one is free and yet that, in terms of one's integrity, "one can do no other." [34]

This latter point of Knight's, and our own discussion of choice in Chapter 2, show that the subjective experience of one who is psychologically mature is naturally described in terms of the mystic paradox of complete freedom coexisting with utter passivity. As a person of thoroughgoing psychological integrity, it is true that "one can do no other"; but in thus doing, while not consciously concerned with "self," one gives expression to a unified and accepted self, an undivided and effective will. "The truth is that the more ourselves we are, the less self is in us." [35] This is precisely the way "emotionally mature, well-integrated persons" feel their activity to be. [36]

Mature individuals, says Knight, have achieved a harmonious integration of the instinctual drives, the superego standards and restrictions, the ego perceptions and discriminative faculties, and the real possibilities offered by the environment. [37] Thus they are at once perceptive and yet, as was noted earlier, "self-forgetful." "Desire flows into the mind of the seer, but he is never disturbed." [38]

In describing generally those who have failed to achieve such an ideally strong ego and well-integrated personality, Knight's language is sharply reminiscent of the language of the Eastern mystics when they talk about *maya* and *samsara*, the world of birth-and-death in which the unenlightened live. Persons who have failed to achieve such harmonious integration, says Knight, meet with obstacles whose nature they do not understand (ignorance), or they are driven by "intense defiance or greed or hostile impulses." [39] Ignorance, pride, lust, and hatred—here is the universally acknowledged "syndrome" associated by mystics with the disease of self-ishness. The psychoanalytic explanation of neuroses is analogous. Unsublimated libido and aggression (lust, hatred, and greed) result in distorted, fantasy-colored experiences ("ignorance," "illusion"). The general traits of self-ishness and conflictful experience thus being established as parallel, it now is appropriate to consider more specific notions found in mysticism.

"Freedom from striving" and "acceptance," key notions of the mystic, are often misinterpreted to mean systematic refusal to take the initiative, consistent absence of goals of any sort, submissiveness. This the unenlightened read into the words in spite of the evidence before their eyes that those who best exemplify mystic enlightenment are people who obviously do take the initiative, who clearly execute well-organized, purposive behavior, and who have indeed modified the world. The misinterpretation is encouraged by the fact that, not uncommonly, those who are *trying to achieve* enlightenment go through a phase of submissiveness.

In order to obviate this particular misunderstanding the mystic must eventually qualify his remarks. He must confess that he *does* have desires and does not merely "submit." He thus admits that the natural way of expressing the matter is unfortunately ambiguous. His language originally suggests a *loss*, an absence, a "giving up." He now tries to suggest that the aspect of his experience in question involves neither sense of presence nor of loss, neither a sense of striving *nor* of surrender. Hence he says that, in truth, what he speaks of is *beyond* "desire" or "no-desire"; it is beyond "freedom" or "bondage." What he really wishes to express is the fact that feelings of these kinds, one way or another, simply do not exist. He tries, tentatively, to speak of Nothingness [40] or *Sunyata*. Yet to speak of *Nothingness* suggests mere emptiness or absence—a gap. Yet life, in truth, is *full*. Worst of all: in the moment of speaking of experience "beyond desire," he lies, for in order to make the point he must make reference to the category of desire and thus he is no longer "beyond" desire!

If only the audience would *see*—there is only one way of taking his language consistently with the facts. But, of course, the audience does not, *will not,* see. Like the patient in psychoanalytic therapy, the mystic's disciple, too, must be ready for the insight or else the interpretation will meet not merely with blank ignorance but with positive resistance. The context of anxiety is then substituted, and all the words are taken in a foolish, paradoxical, or positively hurtful sense.

The mystic says:

> When striving and gaining are balanced, nothing remains,
> Aimless striving is quite different. . . .[41]

In the same spirit the psychoanalyst says: defensive equilibria consist of pitting one set of inner demands against another, thus warding off dangerous impulses by an inner stalemate. Such equilibria are basically self-defeating; they produce ever higher levels of tensions. Ego-syntonic activity is "quite different"—it is genuinely gratifying. The "aimlessness" of the mystic thus refers always to the absence of *inner* aims, i.e., the aims of repression. The mystic language is a language of subjective experience—it does not have to do in the first instance with "external" aims, obviously an inevitable part of life. The confusion arises because our "external" aims—jobs, love conquests, cars—are so often the rationalizations of inner defensive aims. It is in the latter sense of "aim" that the enlightened are aimless. Thus the mystic may well acknowledge that he enjoys food, friends, kindred, honor, and comfort provided he is not anxiously dependent upon them, unable to cope with their opposites.[42] Thus, in a fundamental sense aimless and open to experience, the enlightened pursue and enjoy whatever concrete aims seem appropriate.

Closely related to the absence of striving, of aimlessness, are the phenomena which the mystic describes as "no-discrimination," "no-perception," "no-sensation," "no-thought." If our hypothesis is correct, we should expect that what he is denying is the compulsive, obsessive, acutely self-conscious focusing of attention upon our feelings and our perceptions, our theoretical distinctions and logical proofs. What the mystic decries is, in terms of the psychological conditions which are associated with it, the neurotic drive to achieve security by fitting all experience into a firm, clear, and neat logical system within which one can then manipulate the elements in an absolutely regularized way.

On the other hand, according to our psychological analysis, we should expect that sensing, perceiving, thinking, discriminating are essential functions within the enlightened life, but that they are used unself-consciously, uncompulsively, and flexibly in accordance with the integrity of the individual and the demands of the real environmental situation. They are *used;* they do not dominate.

> [The enlightened] use their sense organs when occasion requires,
> But the concept of "using" does not arise.[43]

Consistent with our inference is the mystic's statement that enlightened meditation is "[observing] things in the phenomenal world, yet [dwelling] in emptiness." Perception *is* present, but it comes as it will to a mind that is "empty," i.e., without compulsive, stereotyped modes of perceiving and thinking.

One way of putting the matter is in terms of the Buddhist notion of "abiding." It is the (neurotically rigid) abiding with specific thoughts or sensations that is the mark of the unenlightened.

In action Prajna [the wisdom of enlightenment] is everywhere present, yet it "sticks" nowhere. What we have to do is to so purify the mind that the six aspects of consciousness (sight, sound, smell, taste, touch, mentation) in passing through their six sense-gates will neither be defiled by nor attached to their six sense-objects. . . . *To refrain from thinking of anything, in the sense that all mental activity is suppressed, is to be Dharma-ridden; this is an extremely erroneous view.*[44] [Italics added]

To suppose that Nirvana is the "mere stopping of discrimination" is to commit the error typical of the philosopher (who takes everything in its abstract, theoretical sense) as distinguished from the person with genuine mystic insight.[45]

The previous discussion makes it clear—and it is consistent with our psychoanalytic theses—that when we speak of enlightenment, we are not talking of an existence divorced from the "everyday world." On the contrary, it consists of life within this world. Zen, says one of the great Zen masters, "is your everyday mind."[46] "Birth-and-death (i.e., our everyday world) and Nirvana are not separate from one another."[47]

This world is the Buddha-world
Within which enlightenment may be sought.
To seek enlightenment by separating from this world
Is as foolish as to search for a rabbit's horn.[48]

At the same time we confidently infer from the psychological analysis what mystic literature also suggests at times: that so far as the subjective feel of life goes, there is in some sense a "world" of difference between that of enlightenment and that of birth-and-death. How can one distinguish the subtle but profound difference between these "worlds" in terms of a subjective language? This difference may be reported as, for example, action in which one "remains poised in the tranquility of the Atman."[49] It is an "inner light" which does not flicker while the everyday life goes on.[50] It is that engagement in the world of joys and sorrows which Eckhart compares with the door which swings back and forth while the hinge at the center remains fixed and solid.[51] It is the life of the Bodhisattvas who are "joyous in heart but ever grieved over the sight of suffering beings. . . ."[52] It is the "inner stillness" which is the "joy of Brahman, which words cannot express and the mind cannot reach . . . free from fear."[53] It is "the inaction that is in action."[54] It transforms the experienced world with its coming. In the poetic language of Indian mysticism,

> . . . there will be music; not only music made by human lips and played by human hands on various instruments, but there will be music among the grass and shrubs and trees, and in mountains and towns and palaces and hovels; much more will there be music in the hearts of those endowed with sentiency.[55]

In Knight's more prosaic clinical terminology, the free man is one with "feelings of well-being, of self-esteem, of confidence, of inner satisfaction based on successful use of one's energies for achievement that promotes the best interests of one's fellow men as well as one's own."[56] This language is a remarkable parallel to another expressive mystic report which I shall now quote. I trust the reader will tolerate my esthetically inexcusable interpolations.

> Free from the domination of words you will be able to establish yourselves where there will be a "turning about" in the deepest seat of consciousness by means of which you will attain self-realisation of Noble Wisdom and be able to enter into all the Buddha-land and assemblies. There you will be stamped with the stamp of the powers, self-command, the psychic faculties, and

will be endowed with wisdom and the power of the ten inexhaustible vows. . . . There you will shine without effort like the moon, the sun, the magic wishing-jewel, and at every stage will view things as being of perfect oneness with yourself, uncontaminated by any self-consciousness. Seeing that all things are like a dream [i.e., seeing that your life has been lived until now in the neurotic fantasy-world] you will be able to enter into the stage of the Tathagatas and be able to deliver discourses on the Dharma to the world of beings in accordance with their needs [i.e., in the manner of therapeutic interventions or the well-timed advice of the wise layman rather than formal lectures or general theories] and be able to free them from all dualistic notions and false discriminations.[57]

We know that neither Knight nor the writer of the Lankavatara Sutra intend us to understand that the enlightened one is a "self-satisfied," neurotically dedicated "do-gooder." We know that for the one who seeks enlightenment to "hold in his mind any arbitrary conceptions about kindness"[58] would be a gross mistake. "Kindness, after all, is only a word and charity should be spontaneous and self-less."[59] Put negatively and in psychoanalytic terms, doing well by others is not the outcome of a moralistic program of "altruistic" action rationalizing narcissism or other neurotic gratifications. Likewise the *thought* that one has attained "Highest Perfect Wisdom" or that one is on the way there is evidence that one is *mistaken*. One who *is* confident does not have a conscious feeling of confidence; one who is wise does not consciously think to himself that he is wise. Those who have such thoughts or feelings reveal that, perturbed by anxiety and doubts, they have had to react with reassurances to themselves.

The enlightened one is, therefore, not only an unassuming and "ordinary" person (as well as an extraordinary one), he is in many ways "more ordinary" than most people. He is not overly proud, not driven by ambition, not prone to keeping up with the Joneses, not given to disingenuous logical or theoretical disquisitions. He tends to shun words. He suffers, enjoys, knows pain and pleasure, but he is not driven and dominated by these. Sensual without being sensualist, he is also aware of his ills without being hypochondriacal. "He does not call attention to himself." [60]

At the same time there are ways in which he clearly stands apart: "I alone am dark . . . blown adrift . . . intractable and boorish." [61] Such a person does not always quite fit because, while he may often conform, he is not a conformist. He will even at times appear "ruthless." [62] For when the ordinary ways conflict with his own integrity, when realism calls for breaking through sentimentality, when life has shattered the old façades, he acts accordingly. His ruthlessness is kindliness in the same way as the parent's realistic discipline may be kinder than a guilt-motivated "permissiveness."

In the last analysis, then, the mystic way is a "simple" and "obvious" way—for those who will open their eyes. For the mystic experience is not the achievement of any finally fixed state of mind or any universal doctrine at all. It is the liberation from neurotic fixation and dogma of all kinds.

> Right views are called "transcendental,"
> Erroneous views are called "worldly,"
> But when all views, both right and erroneous, are discarded,
> Then the essence of Wisdom manifests itself. [63]

This is the emptiness of a mind which is thoroughly open to the world. As Hui-neng says, it is the "voidness" which can be filled. [64] It is not mere "vacuity" or idealessness. Bergson has spoken in this connection of the "open soul." [65]

Dwelling in such a (psychic) "emptiness," our life is full, but not full of our repetitive fantasies. It is pervaded by an elusive but profound sense of joy. How natural then to express this pervasive "peace" as an aspect of the presence of God. But then God becomes the "atmosphere" of life rather than an object within life. " 'God,' said St. Augustine, 'is the Country of the soul'; 'its Home,' says Ruysbroeck." [66] The mystic God is "nothingness" in the sense that God is not an object of contemplation; He is the realm within which all objects exist. It is Emptiness which, in Christian language, appears as the "poverty of the spirit" which is an ultimate joy. Poverty here is not to be identified with asceticism or moral masochism; it is absence of pretense, absence of anxious dependence or "clinging," "openness" to life. God is perceived as a radical "inner stillness." The psychological condition of this perception is, according to our hypothesis, the growth of personality beyond anxiety and intrapsychic conflict to primarily conflict-free integrity.

One must achieve this unself-consciousness by means of transformed knowledge. *This* ignorance does not come from lack of knowledge but rather it is from knowledge that one may achieve this ignorance. [67]

Eckhart here means to distinguish, on the one hand the naïveté of the unsocialized child, or of the neurotic who *will* not learn, and on the other hand the humility and spontaneity of the person who uses his learned skills and his knowledge as a means of *meeting* life in its novelty instead of insisting that life conform to his stereotyped nursery fantasies.

To achieve this simplicity is, as we know, the most arduous struggle, the most radical and intricate operation which we need to perform in our lives. "The Great Way is right before your eye, but difficult to see." [68]

VI

IT FOLLOWS FROM THE THESIS WE HAVE PRESENTED THAT there are likely to be significant similarities between the ways in which the mystic and the psychoanalytic patient achieve "enlightenment." To review this aspect of the matter briefly will help illuminate and validate our theses. As I have said before, there are, of course, substantial differences between the mystic and psychoanalytic "ways." However, with the exception of the last portions of this chapter, I am concerned with stressing the similarities.

Lao-tse says:

> Yet by seizing on the way that was
> You can ride the things that are new.
> For to know what once there was, in the Beginning,
> This is called the essence of the Way.[69]

The literal meaning of Lao-tse's term translated above as "essence" is "main-thread." One could not put Freud's views better than to say that the main-thread by means of which one masters the present is the thread which leads to the past. We cannot do more than note here that the Chinese reference to the past has a double meaning which parallels Freud's treatment of the psychologically significant past. For Lao-tse refers in his verse both to the archetypal or archaic past and to the past of the individual's personal history.

Freud provides us with detailed classifications of the various typical roots of our present psychic troubles. The mystic, however, usually provides us either with very concrete, personal, and hence idiosyncratic accounts, or else he offers very broad but suggestive generalizations. The mystic's fundamental generalizations are remarkably reminiscent of some of Freud's basic postulates. Hui-neng tells us that

When neither hatred nor love disturb the mind,
Serene and restful is our sleep.[70]

We know from Freud that the image is perfectly apt. Provided one interprets "hatred" and "love" as unsublimated aggressive and libidinal instinctual drives, one hardly needs to change a word to consider the verse as a basic psychological truth. Likewise we could consider the following verse in the Bhagavad-Gita as an almost word for word analysis, according to Freud, of the roots of neurotic self-deception in current unresolved libidinal and aggressive conflicts and the unconscious fantasies connected with them:

When a man lacks lust and hatred,
His renunciation does not waver.
He neither longs for one thing
Nor loathes its opposite:
The chains of his delusion
Are soon cast off.[71]

The total picture that we get of the state of existence of man prior to entering upon the path of Enlightenment is expressed in the great Eastern image of the wheel of birth-and-death. Lust, anger, and ignorance bind man ever more tightly to the wheel of suffering. This is the very model of the self-harassed and self-driven neurotic.

How can we control such behavior? More important yet, how can we break away from the wheel entirely? The Buddhist formula is threefold. At the most primitive level, the rules of morality, if strictly adhered to, help to prevent *actions* leading to bad Karma. As a second step, mental and moral concentrated effort help to *suppress* the *thoughts* and *feelings* which lie behind such actions. But to get to the root, to eradicate the source of such thoughts, feelings, and actions, what is needed is insight. It is, in practice, the proper concurrent use of all three which can lead, step by step, to broader and deeper insight with eventual liberation from the wheel.[72] *Perfect* enlightenment seems to be a mythic ideal in mysticism. The ever-present potential in real life for still further deepening insight is expressed in the concept of the stages of enlightenment.

This picture of successive rebirths in Samsara eventuating ideally in release from Karma and the achievement of Nirvana is a wonderful image which parallels in the essential psychological aspects the process of psychoanalytic therapy. We start with neurotic behavior and experience (Samsara). The neurotic, motivated by unresolved instinctual conflict (lust and anger), unwittingly ignorant, creates his own half fantasy experience (the illusory world of Maya). This world provides temporary gratification at the cost of increasing enslavement to the very anxieties and conflicts which are so painful. Thus the neurotic is ever more tightly bound to the wheel. Social codes, repressions, and suppression can, however, keep the actions and thoughts within some control. But the move toward maturity requires insight. Yet psychoanalytic insight takes place not in a vacuum or all at once: it proceeds (ideally) by limited and partial insights in a setting of substantial social conformity (no acting-out) and continuing suppression and repression (no "wild analysis"; careful timing and dosage in therapeutic interventions). The "complete" analysis is a theoretical ideal ("Buddha-hood"). As for the "medium" within which enlightening communication takes place:

> . . . the way of instruction presented by the Tathagatas is not based on assertions and refutations by means of words and logic. . . .[73]
>
> If I should tell you that I had a system of Dhyana to transmit to others, I would be deceiving you. What I try to do to my disciples, is to liberate them from

their own bondage, by such devices as each case requires. . . .[74]

As circumstances arise, [the enlightened] take appropriate action; they give suitable answers according to the varying temperaments of their questioner.[75]

That is to say, liberation is achieved as a way of life and by means of "pragmatic," not theoretical communication, communication oriented to the immediate context and the particular person. It is not a question of proving or disproving theories. Likewise, the psychoanalytic therapist, *as a therapist,* is not primarily concerned with establishing the truth of some general theory; he is concerned to provide specific interventions which enable the patient to *undergo the experience* with concurrent insight.

When Hui-neng says that "they give suitable answers," he is speaking of responding "therapeutically," not of giving the person directions as to how to live his life. Tai-tz'u Huan-chung, the Zen teacher, said: "I do not know how to make answers; I only know where diseases are." [76] This is analogous to the analyst's task which, according to Freud, is to "unmask the roots," not "to play the part of prophet, saviour, and redeemer to the patient . . . but to give the patient's ego *freedom* to choose one way or the other." [77] (And the parallel to the later teachings of Wittgenstein is evident to those familiar with the latter.)

The manner of the psychoanalyst is, ideally, that of the Bodhisattva: one "who practice[s] compassion but [is not given up to petty kindness . . .] practice[s] indifference but never cease[s] benefitting others." [78] This is a clear description of important aspects of the ideal therapeutic relationship.

The actual occasion of insight (out of which decisions flow spontaneously) involves a peculiar shifting of mental gears, as it were.

Suzuki says: "In our religious life, passivity comes as the culmination of strenuous activity; passivity without this preliminary condition is sheer inanity. . . ." [79]

The activity leading up to enlightenment is imbued with a "spirit of inquiry" requiring that we pursue the advice of the master: "Ask of your self, inquire into your self, pursue your self, investigate within your self. . . ." [80]

At the moment preceding *satori,* the Zen enlightenment, we are like a man at the "edge of a precipice." [81] It is a moment of uneasiness, despair, death. At this point, by "letting go," the disciple is awakened as from a stupor.

The characteristic terms for this moment of enlightenment are "one bursting cry," "the bursting of the bag," "a sudden snapping," "a sudden bursting," and so on.[82] It is difficult to avoid recalling the comparable phrases used to characterize insight experience in Western terminology, phrases such as the "Aha! experience," or, in the simple formula of Greenson's patient, "Bong!" [83]

The sense of passive receptiveness in the ultimate phase of mystic enlightenment appears to occur characteristically in all the mystics.[84]

From the psychoanalytic side, Kris [85] has discussed the relation between insight and passivity at length, and he concludes one such discussion by asserting that

> the maturing of thought, the entry into awareness from preconsciousness to consciousness tend to be experienced as derived from outside, as passively received, not as actively produced. The tendency toward passive reception takes various shapes and forms, appears under the guise of various modalities, but the subjective experience remains one of reception.[86]

Kris holds that in the creative solution of problems as distinguished from mere fantasy gratification, there is a feeling of satisfaction as well as mere relief.

We might amplify slightly as follows. The "letting go" is the cessation of defensive "striving." The joy is associated psychologically with the sudden availability of the energy previously expended in the repressive process, energy which is now freed by the "creative" solution of the problem but would not be by a neurotic "solution." In the neurotic "solution" the diminished anxiety accounts for the sense of relief, but there is no "joy" because the neurotic solution requires the energies of repressive countercathexes.

This combination of felt passivity and heightened joy at the moment of insight is a characteristic mark of mystic enlightenment. This, as a part of the characteristic behavior and affect patterns of the mystic, is important evidence that the mystic enlightenment of which we speak is, psychologically, a creative solution of a problem rather than merely regressive fantasy gratification.

VII

KRIS, IN THE COURSE OF THE DISCUSSION OF INSIGHT AND PASsivity cited above, introduces a number of closely connected issues which are appropriately introduced here in our discussion of mysticism. These issues pertain to the specific fantasy and symbolic content of the mystical experiences. They lead to that major amplification of the psychoanalytic theses with which I shall terminate the present discussion.

In spite of the fact that I am not primarily concerned in this chapter with what I shall call broadly the symbolism of mysticism but rather with mystic "selflessness," it remains the case that symbolism in mysticism is so pervasive as to require some comment. I must at least indicate how what I have said up to this point is consistent with the symbolic aspects of mysticism. For this purpose I propose to confine the discussion to the ubiquitous symbols of "oneness" in mystic writings. This will, in turn, lead us back in a new way to the more traditional, id-oriented formulations of the psychological conditions of mystic experience.

The all-engulfing sense of Oneness, the loss of distinction between self and object, is frequently asserted in both Eastern and Christian mysticism to be of the essence of the experience of enlightenment. This aspect of mystic experience has been commented upon by a number of psychoanalytic writers including Freud himself.

Freud's suggestion [87] was that this "oceanic feeling" of oneness, of ineffable ecstasy, is a concomitant of regression to the primal unity with the mother, a unity in which there were yet no ego boundaries and in which gratification was direct and complete. As Lewin says, the experience is felt as *known*, as more certain than anything, because it is the closest we come to what is primal, immediate, unquestioned experience as distinguished from experience mediated by concepts and the subject-object distinction.[88] It represents the primitive narcissistic trust in sensory experience.[89]

It is, of course, essential to recall that the frequently quoted erotic and often orgastic language of a number of the Christian mystics is not interpreted psychoanalytically as a symptom of "genital" orgasm in the psychological sense. Rather what is meant is that the experience, while intensely *libidinal* and orgastic, is on the earliest infantile oral level, the level of primal unity through incorporation.

There is no doubt that the images and the language of the mystics strongly suggest feelings of total gratification and of omnipotence ("A snap of the fingers, and eight thousand gates of the teaching are established").[90] There is no doubt that, at crucial stages along the mystic way, at least momentary trance or ecstasy states occur. This, according to Lewin,[91] is to be expected if we associate the subjective experience with regression to infantile narcissistic gratification at the mother's breast—for this is a state culminating in ecstasy-sleep.

Although the mother-image pervades religious and mystical literature, Lao-tse's language is most explicit and sharp:

> . . . the Doorway of the Mysterious Female
> Is the base from which Heaven and Earth sprang.
> It is there within us all the while;
> Draw upon it as you will, it never runs dry.[92]
> . . . wherein I most am different from men
> Is that I prize no sustenance that comes not from the
> Mother's breast.[93]

The views of Freud and Lewin as to the psychological conditions of the mystic experience are clearly quite different from those I have developed in the earlier sections of this discussion. I have stressed that the experience of loss of self and of the loss of the sense of subject-object relations is in fact loss of a certain kind of anxiety-generated self-consciousness; it is, as such, creative rather than regressive movement. Specifically, it results from ego-syntonic conflict resolution, drive neutralization (sublimation), and consequent absence of anxiety and defense. Furthermore, the sense of joy and power associated with this mode of experience was interpreted, psychologically, as the characteristic result of realistic problem solutions rather than (regressive) fantasy gratifications. The more typical psychoanalytic interpretations just cited, however, imply that this sense of joy and power is, in contrast to what Kris's thesis seems to imply, a result of deeply regressive fantasy gratification. I wish to show now how these two contrasting interpretations are complementary rather than incompatible. *Indeed it is the very fusion of the two processes which constitutes the characteristic psychological condition of the mystic experience.*

The crux of the problem is touched if we follow Kris's well-known development of the psychoanalytic theory of

creativity in terms of "regression in the service of the ego."
Kris states:

> This relationship between creativity and passivity ex-
> emplifies once more one of the leading theses of this
> presentation: the integrative functions of the ego in-
> clude self-regulated regression and permit a combina-
> tion of the most daring intellectual activity with the
> experience of passive receptiveness.[94]

The implication of such a view is that, in "regression in
the service of the ego," it is the movement toward maturity
rather than the concurrent regression which is psycho-
dynamically primary. The appropriateness of this conception as applied to the regressive aspects of mysticism needs
now to be shown.

We have already seen that the mystic is one who "returns to the Beginning" in order to "ride the present." We
have held that this is analogous to the psychoanalytic exploration of the past as inherent in current self-exploration
and re-creation. The return to the Beginning is in essential
respects an uncovering of infantile history and a reintegra-
tion of the personality on the basis of the insights achieved.
We must expect, then, that in the course of following the
Way, the mystic would become subjectively aware of, and
would more or less frequently act out, many of the fantasies
and feelings associated with the various infantile stages of
development in his own life. This, in turn, means that the
mystic's history would be filled with the language—and frequently the symptomatology—of infantile conflicts. We
would expect, ideally, that he would eventually uncover the
earliest infantile memories, the most archaic fantasies and
feelings. Such a thoroughgoing self-exploration and strip-
ping off of the defensive character "armor" is bound to be a
dramatic and long drawn-out struggle. We should not be
surprised if, frequently, the motivation sufficient to con-

tinue such a painful effort is a threatening sense of personal disintegration on a massive scale as the only alternative to success. Such a struggle, while not inevitable, should be relatively common among mystics.[95]

Thus regressive symptomatology is of the essence of the movement toward maturity. This is precisely the case with psychoanalytic self-exploration. What makes the process in both cases essentially *progressive* when successful rather than *regressive* is the fact that the fundamental context is established by the ego in its movement toward increasing integrity and strength. This may, perhaps, be more evident in psychoanalytic theory which is characterized by the systematic attempt to maintain continuously the "splitting of the ego" into the "observing," realistic ego as well as the regressive ego. The mystic (and the creative artist?) may be supposed at times to take the more radical—and risky—step of a more total ego regression, a more total reliving of the old conflicts in the course of creating new, ego-syntonic solutions.

There is a second way in which regression enters the mystic experience: it is inherent not only in the stages leading to enlightenment but in the "enlightenment" experience itself. In the most advanced stage of mystic experience, it is true, the pathological symptomatology, trances, and visions are finally superseded by highly ego-syntonic behavior. Such mature gratifications produce, as has been noted earlier, a subjective experience which is without anxious self-consciousness, without compulsive intellectualization or defensive striving. But the strength of ego and the radicalness of the self-exploration implicit in achieving such enlightenment justify certain further assumptions. We may suppose that such persons have retained, far more than most, a significant degree of accessibility to infantile fantasies and a tolerance of partial instinct gratification within a context of essentially mature behavior. Infantile fantasy and partial instinct gratification would therefore not dominate current experience and make it *anti*realistic, but they would be less rigidly repressed, more ego-syntonic.

Thus the selflessness of anxiety-free experience would be "deepened" and "colored" by the quite different but now complementary selflessness of the primal fantasy. The sense of joy and power generated by conflict-free functioning would have the ecstatic "overtones" of the fantasies of primal gratification and omnipotence. The core of reality perception would be enlivened and enriched by the peripheral but compatible illusions associated with residual partial instinct gratifications. This process is, in effect, no more than a broadening and deepening of processes we know to be characteristic of our "everyday" life,[96] whether the latter involves doing arithmetic, eating dinner, or experiencing sexual orgasm.

We are now in a position to suggest in general terms the lines along which we should differentiate mystic experiences, one from another and also from other related types of experience.

What I have outlined as a psychological schema of the mystic way is an idealized and oversimplified structure. For example, the experience of enlightenment is not a self-identical, permanent, and total experience. Mystic literature often seems to suggest this just as psychoanalytic literature often seems to suggest the goal of being "finally and completely analyzed." In both cases, whenever the issue is at the focus of attention, it is clear that such suggestions do not do justice to the facts: there are, after all, many varieties of enlightenment and "degrees" of enlightenment; the scope of enlightenment is limited, its persistence under stress variable. Such variation is found as well in psychoanalysis, *mutatis mutandis*.

In psychological language, we can express such differences from individual mystic to individual mystic in terms of such matters as the relative balance of regressive fantasy and realism, the specific content of the fantasies which predominate, the strength of the ego, and the scope of the conflict-free area of the latter. The differing linguistic patterns, philosophic-religious trends, and, more broadly, the cultural traditions which contribute to the total experience provide a basis for differentiating types of mysticism. These differentiating factors are not "frills" on an underlying psychological "reality." Importance depends upon purposes and these are, for many purposes, at least as important or more important than the psychological factors common to the various kinds of mystic experience. Their analysis, involving humanistic, historical, and scientific studies of varied sorts is, of course, in the highest degree complex.

Similar considerations hold with regard to the relation of mysticism and psychoanalysis. The psychoanalytic patient's experience is patently different in many important respects from the mystic's. This is in many ways obvious, in others not; but such a discussion is beyond the scope of this chapter.

A final question remains. Are we suggesting that, while the mystical experience is not identical with the psychoanalytic process, it is still, after all, only a "subjective" experience and therefore not a "genuine" revelation of or union with God?

Extended discussion here of such issues is not appropriate. Nevertheless, at least brief comment is required.

The burden of what I have said is, of course, not that there is no union with God in the mystic's experience; it is rather that I am saying there *is* union with God, "dwelling in" God. To let go of this is to let go of the essence. But to suppose that union with God or dwelling in God is union with a substantial person, or existence in a definite place, is naïve. For the mystic tells us—and it is essential to listen seriously to him—that he is not concerned with a sensual or substantial being, nor is the "place" in which he dwells a physical or quasi-physical place having measurable dimensions.

Let us consider an analogous situation. The experience of "three-dimensional space" in a painting is not an experience of physical three-dimensional space. Nor is it an "illusion," for no one is deceived by it. It is an *obviously* different experience from that of three-dimensional physical space. Still, in certain ways, it is sufficiently reminiscent of the physical space experience so that we borrow physical space *language* in talking of it. We call it "esthetic space"—a phrase which perhaps overemphasizes the (limited) similarity. Esthetic space certainly exists, however, and it is no more a mystery than any other perception. To call it an "illusion" or "subjective" is to attack a straw man—as if the artist had ever said or intended us to think that it was *literally* the same as three-dimensional physical space! If one takes it to be physical space, one *is* deluded, of course. But taken as it is, it is a genuine and distinct phenomenon in nature having for some persons its own intrinsic and special value. Just so, the mystical experience of God is illusion only if it is taken naïvely to be what the mystic constantly insists that it is not: a logically impossible, quasi-physical or mental union with a quasi-substantial being who has quasi-human traits.

There is no way of *verbally* communicating about the experience of esthetic space except by means of the potentially misleading analogies with physical space. Just as this esthetic language of space misleads, so the mystic language of personification misleads and suggests a kind of mysterious anthropomorphism.

Not everyone perceives the drama inherent in the forms of esthetic space. Those who do not may feel comfortable calling art an illusion. Such persons find in esthetic space only that trivial value which consists in supposing that it is the product of ingenious technique intended to deceive, having no intrinsic interest other than as deception. But for some persons the perception of esthetic space is, in and of itself, of momentous significance; it establishes a world of its own. And for some, needless to say, the same is true of the experience of spiritual illumination and the apprehension of the divine.

N O T E S
(See List of Bibliographical Abbreviations, p. 343.)

1. Freud, S., "Analysis Terminable and Interminable," in *CP*, V, pp. 316–357.
2. Goddard, D., *A Buddhist Bible*, E. P. Dutton & Co., New York, 1938, p. 353.
3. *Ibid.*, p. 515.
4. Suzuki, D. T., *Essays in Zen Buddhism* (Second Series), Beacon Press, Boston, 1952, p. 85.
5. Underhill, E., *Mysticism*, Meridian Books, New York, 1957, pp. 279–281.
6. *Bhagavad-Gita*, Prabhavananda & Isherwood, C., trans., New American Library, New York, 1954, p. 48.
7. Senzaki, N., and McCandless, R., *Buddhism and Zen*, Philosophical Library, New York, 1956, p. 69.
8. *Bhagavad-Gita*, p. 43.
9. Goddard, D., *op. cit.*, p. 352.
10. *Ibid.*, p. 324.
11. *Ibid.*, p. 547.
12. Suzuki, D. T., *Essays in Zen Buddhism* (First Series), Harper & Bros., New York, 1949, pp. 252–253 fn.
13. ———, *Essays in Zen Buddhism* (Third Series), Rider & Co., London, 1953, p. 57.
14. ———, *Essays in Zen Buddhism* (First Series), p. 34.
15. Goddard, D., *op. cit.*, p. 546.
16. Leuba, J. H., *The Psychology of Religious Mysticism*, Harcourt, Brace & Co., New York, 1925, p. 43.
17. *Tao Te Ching*, in *The Way and Its Power*, Waley, A., The Macmillan Co., New York, 1956, p. 230.

18. Freud, S., "Instincts and Their Vicissitudes," in *CP*, V.
19. *Ibid.*
20. Nunberg, H., "Theory and Practice of Psychoanalysis," *Nervous and Mental Disease Monograph* 74, New York, 1948, pp. 31ff.
21. Underhill, E., *op. cit.*, Chap. X.
22. Leuba, J. H., *op. cit.*, p. 202.
23. Bergson, H., *The Two Sources of Morality and Religion*, Doubleday Anchor, New York, 1954, pp. 227–228.
24. Jacobson, E., "Contribution to the Metapsychology of Psychotic Identifications," *JAP* 2 (1954), p. 241.
25. Federn, P., *Ego Psychology and the Psychoses*, Basic Books, New York, 1952.
26. *Ibid.*, p. 244.
27. *Ibid.*, p. 242.
28. Szasz, T. S., *Pain and Pleasure*, Basic Books, New York, 1957, Chap. VII.
29. Freud, S., *Inhibitions.*
30. Jacobson, E., "The Self and the Object World," in *The Psychoanalytic Study of the Child*, Vol. IX, International Universities Press, New York, 1954, p. 94.
31. Reich, W., *Character-Analysis*, Orgone Institute Press, New York, 1949, Chap. IV.
32. Knight, R. P., "Determinism, 'Freedom,' and Psychotherapy," in *Psychoanalytic Psychiatry and Psychology*, Knight, R. P., and Friedman, C. R., eds., International University Press, New York, 1954, p. 372.
33. *Loc. cit.*
34. *Loc. cit.*
35. Eckhart, *Writings and Sermons*, Blakney, R. B., trans., Harper & Bros., New York, 1957, p. 17.
36. Knight, R. P., *op. cit.*, p. 372.
37. *Ibid.*, p. 376.
38. *Bhagavad-Gita*, p. 43.
39. Knight, R. P., *op. cit.*, p. 378.
40. Eckhart, *op. cit.*, pp. 227, 232.
41. Senzaki, N., and McCandless, R., *op. cit.*, p. 55.
42. Eckhart, *op. cit.*, p. 25.

43. Goddard, D., *op. cit.*, p. 546.
44. *Ibid.*, p. 519.
45. *Ibid.*, p. 352.
46. Suzuki, D. T., *Essays in Zen Buddhism* (Second Series), p. 276.
47. Goddard, D., *op. cit.*, p. 324.
48. *Ibid.*, p. 521.
49. *Bhagavad-Gita*, p. 52.
50. Eckhart, *op. cit.*, pp. 246–247.
51. *Ibid.*, p. 87.
52. Suzuki, D. T., *Essays in Zen Buddhism* (Third Series), p. 116.
53. *Upanishads*, Prabhavananda and Manchester, F., trans., New American Library, New York, 1957, p. 58.
54. *Bhagavad-Gita*, p. 52.
55. Goddard, D., *op. cit.*, pp. 38–39.
56. Knight, R. P., *op. cit.*, p. 372.
57. Goddard, D., *op. cit.*, pp. 318–319.
58. *Ibid.*, p. 91.
59. *Ibid.*, pp. 521–522.
60. *Tao Te Ching*, p. 143.
61. *Ibid.*, pp. 168–169.
62. *Ibid.*, p. 147
63. Goddard, D., *op. cit.*, pp. 521–522.
64. *Ibid.*, p. 514.
65. Bergson, H., *op. cit.*, p. 38.
66. Underhill, E., *op. cit.*, p. 420.
67. Eckhart, *op. cit.*, p. 107.
68. Suzuki, D. T., *Essays in Zen Buddhism* (Third Series), p. 46.
69. *Tao Te Ching*, p. 159.
70. Goddard, D., *op. cit.*, p. 521.
71. *Bhagavad-Gita*, pp. 56–57.
72. Thittila, M. T. U., "The Fundamental Principles of Theravada Buddhism," in *The Path of the Buddha*, Morgan, K. W., ed., Ronald Press, New York, 1956, pp. 107–108.
73. Goddard, D., *op. cit.*, p. 284.

74. *Ibid.*, p. 549.
75. *Ibid.*, p. 550.
76. Suzuki, D. T., *Essays in Zen Buddhism* (Third Series), p. 55.
77. Freud, S., *Ego & Id*, p. 72.
78. Suzuki, D. T., *Essays in Zen Buddhism* (Third Series), p. 116.
79. ———, *Essays in Zen Buddhism* (Second Series), p. 276.
80. *Ibid.*, p. 127.
81. *Ibid.*, p. 98.
82. *Ibid.*, pp. 117–118.
83. Greenson, R. R., "On Boredom," *JAP* 1:7–21 (1953).
84. Underhill, E., *op. cit.*, p. 412.
85. Kris, E., *Psychoanalytic Explorations in Art*, International Universities Press, New York, 1952.
86. *Ibid.*, p. 318.
87. Freud, S., *Civ. & Disc.*, Chap. I.
88. Lewin, B. D., *The Psychoanalysis of Elation*, W. W. Norton & Co., New York, 1950, p. 149.
89. *Ibid.*, p. 150.
90. Senzaki, N., and McCandless, R., *op. cit.*, p. 61.
91. Lewin, B. D., *op. cit.*, p. 150.
92. *Tao Te Ching*, p. 149.
93. *Ibid.*, p. 169.
94. Kris, E., *op. cit.*, p. 318.
95. Boisen, A. T., *Exploration of the Inner World*, Harper & Bros., New York, 1936.
96. Sperling, O. E., "Illusion, Naïve and Controlled," *Psychoanalytic Quarterly* 20:204–214 (1951).

List of Bibliographical Abbreviations

Freud's Works

CPW   *The Standard Edition of the Complete Works of Sigmund Freud,* James Strachey, general editor, Hogarth Press, London, 1953. (New volumes in this series are still being issued.)

CP   *Collected Papers,* Basic Books, New York, 1958.

Civ. & Disc.   *Civilization and Its Discontents,* translated by Joan Riviere, Hogarth Press, London, 1930.

Dreams   *The Interpretation of Dreams,* in CPW, Vols. IV and V.

Ego & Id   *The Ego and the Id,* translated by Joan Riviere, Hogarth Press, London, 1927.

Gen. Intro.   *A General Introduction to Psychoanalysis,* translated by Joan Riviere, Garden City Publishing Co., New York, 1943.

Group Psych.   *Group Psychology and the Analysis of the Ego,* in CPW, Vol. XVIII.

Inhibitions   *Inhibitions, Symptoms, and Anxiety,* in CPW, Vol. XX.

Moses   *Moses and Monotheism,* translated by K. Jones, Vintage Books, New York, 1955.

New Intro. Lec.   *New Introductory Lectures on Psychoanaly-*

sis, translated by W. J. H. Sprott, W. W. Norton & Co., New York, 1933.

Origins   *The Origins of Psycho-Analysis,* edited by Marie Bonaparte, Anna Freud, and Ernest Kris, translated by Eric Mosbacher and James Strachey, Basic Books, New York, 1954.

Psychopathology   *The Psychopathology of Everyday Life,* in *CPW,* Vol. VI.

Totem   *Totem and Taboo,* in *CPW,* Vol. XIII.

JOURNALS

JAP   *Journal of the American Psychoanalytic Association*
PQ   *Psychoanalytic Quarterly*
IJP   *International Journal of Psychoanalysis*